Revelations of Self

Revelations of Self

American Women in Autobiography

Lois J. Fowler and David H. Fowler
Editors

State University of New York Press

Published by
State University of New York Press, Albany

For information, address State University of New York
Press, State University Plaza, Albany, N.Y., 12246

Library of Congress Cataloging-in-Publication Data

Revelations of self: American women in autobiography / Lois J.
Fowler and David H. Fowler, editors.
    p. cm.
    ISBN 0-7914-0373-4.—ISBN 0-7914-0374-2 (pbk.)
1. American prose literature—Women authors—History and
criticism. 2. Women—United States—Biography—History and
criticism. 3. Autobiography—Women authors. I. Fowler, Lois
Josephs. II. Fowler, David Henry.
PS366.A88R48 1990
810.9'492—dc20
                                      89-22039
                                          CIP

To Our Parents

Contents

Preface

In the nineteenth and early twentieth centuries women in the United States, like those in other parts of the Western world, began to speak for themselves as they had never spoken before. As farming and rural life gave way to commerce, industry, and urban life, and as the rising middle classes spread literacy and democracy, both women and men began to assume new roles in the family and society. One outcome of these changes was the emergence of a group of literate and articulate women from the privacy of their homes into the worlds of work, literature, and social—even political—action. As they savored their new sense of importance, some of these women began to address the public in the self-revealing mode of autobiography. This book offers five of these early autobiographies.

We have abridged each of these autobiographies so as to permit a diverse selection. In allowing writers to speak for themselves and their times with as few interruptions as possible, the editors have generally refrained from commenting on points of view, even when the writers' versions of events clash sharply with our own understanding of the history of those times. We have kept explanatory interpolations to a minimum, and have italicized and placed them in brackets to distinguish them from the original texts. We have revised neither the authors' ordering of material nor their syntax, grammar, and variant spellings. We have, however, silently corrected obvious misspellings and typographical errors, and we have commented in footnotes on factual errors or other matters in texts when we felt that such comments would be especially useful to the reader. The original titles of chapters have been retained, but because some chapters have been deleted, their numbering has frequently been changed.

We offer thanks to those who have helped us in completing this work, especially to Marilyn Albright, Joan Stein, and Dorothea Thompson of the Hunt Library, Carnegie Mellon University, for doing bibliographical searches and obtaining hard-to-get materials; to Mary Ray, Jean Cooksey, and Jennie Severa, for their excellent work in preparing successive versions of the manuscript; to Kristin Pape for preparation of the index; to Peggy Gifford and Megeen Mulholland of the State University of New York Press for their encouragement and help; and to Fred Stocking, critic and friend, for imaginative and penetrating suggestions for improving the content, clarity, and grace of our introductions to the book and to the autobiographies. We are happy to share with them whatever credit the book may deserve, but retain the responsibility for whatever flaws remain.

Introduction

In 1854 there appeared a book entitled *Autobiography of an Actress, or Eight Years on the Stage,* by Anna Cora Mowatt, issued by the well-known Boston firm of Ticknor and Fields. The publishers, highly pleased with their record-breaking sales of Harriet Beecher Stowe's recent *Uncle Tom's Cabin,* had good reason to suppose that their new female author, a popular actress, would bring them more profits. In the preceding dozen years Mrs. Mowatt had openly defied conventions governing woman's place in society, winning the public's favor while retaining the respect of much of the upper-middle-class society to which she belonged. Her first appearances in public had been as a dramatic reader of poetry to audiences containing men as well as women. She had next published plays and novels. One of the plays, *Fashion, or, Life in New York* (1845), had been staged to great applause in New York and Philadelphia. Turning to acting, Mowatt had gone on to popular successes as a leading lady in both the United States and England. Ticknor and Fields were rewarded: *Autobiography of an Actress* sold more that twenty thousand copies in its first year of publication.

These were remarkable achievements. Although prejudice against women speaking before mixed audiences was both traditional and deep, Mrs. Mowatt triumphed in her debut as a reader before an enthusiastic house in Boston. She was very attractive; she performed well—and the time was ripe. As compensation for the defection of some of her friends, who thought such public exposure a disgrace, scores of the liberal-minded, many of them influential in cultural, business, and public life, rallied to her. Their support testified to their acceptance of the idea that talent, when displayed with dignity and moral purpose, ought to be given free play, even in a woman. Some of these supporters applauded her new career even more enthusiastically when they learned that she performed as much for financial gain as for art or fame; with an invalid husband on the verge of bankruptcy, she needed money badly.

For Anna Cora Mowatt to retain her respectability in society through her subsequent career as an actress—an occupation far more suspect than that of literary reader—was even more remarkable. Her previous successes as playwright and novelist were a help. She appeared on the stage as a society matron with literary talent rather than as a girl without money, influence, and reputation, vulnerable to those who ran the theater or patronized it.

If in 1854 one had tried to identify the American woman most likely to offer her life to the public in the form of an autobiography, Anna Cora Mowatt would have seemed a plausible choice. Now a widow, she still needed money. As a well-known person writing about the theater, a familiar source of titillation for the public, she could probably count on financial success. She might also draw inspiration from a memoir by the leading English actress, Frances "Fanny" Kemble Butler, whose *Journal of a Residence in America* (1835) had offered much personal material. And Mowatt had dared so much, so successfully, and had so much to reveal!

Her stated purposes in writing were conventional enough. According to *Autobiography of an Actress*, Mowatt wished to fulfill a promise made to her late husband to describe her experiences of life and her profession. But she also hinted at feminist feelings:

> If one struggling sister in the great human family, listening to the history of my life, gain courage to meet and brave severest trials; if she learn to look upon them as blessings in disguise; if she be strengthened in the performance of "daily duties," however "hardly paid;" if she be inspired with faith in the power imparted to a strong will, whose end is good,—then I am amply rewarded for my labor.

She concluded her book with a ringing defense of the theater and the acting profession, adding still another motive for writing.

Mowatt's life, as she presents it in the autobiography, seems to the casual reader an entertainment, its central image a woman of vivid personality playing out a drama influenced by her breach of social convention. Yet the memoirs reveal deeper and more important

meanings. Some of them are historical. Her rebellion against conformity symbolizes one of the more striking developments of recent
centuries: women in the Western world escaping from their traditional position of legal and social inferiority, which serves as this
volume's main historical theme. The memoirs hold further evidence
valuable for understanding the broader history of her times, including
details of her own importance as a woman who transformed her place
in society by becoming a public person, yielding the privacy, protection, and conventional regard given by society to the wife and mother,
while risking ridicule, failure, and challenge to reputation in her new
role.

Another significance of Mowatt's memoirs is literary. This story
of her life became a modest landmark, partly because it displayed the
unapologetic consciousness of self that was coming to characterize
modern autobiography, but primarily because its author, as a woman,
added a distinctive voice to that style of expression.

This dual significance—historical and literary—distinguishes
each of the five women's autobiographies presented here. Let us first
consider historical significance. What criteria of importance to history
were used in selecting the five works?

WITNESSES, ACTORS, SELF-REVEALERS

To explore the main theme of the transformation of women's
place in society during the last two centuries, we found it important
to seek the testimony of women who witnessed that process, participated in it, and enhanced the new roles they adopted by presenting
their life stories for sale to the public. To allow their memoirs to reflect
the history of a long period, we chose authors whose collective lives
stretched from 1813 to 1966, even though their autobiographies were
published in the shorter span from 1854 to 1938. And to examine in
more depth the interplay between individual lives and the larger
society, we decided to devote attention to a single national setting.
Since women began to venture into public affairs, and then to publish
autobiographies, most strikingly in the United States, we selected
only memoirs that dealt primarily with their lives there.

To produce a rounded picture of American life as seen by the
women autobiographers, we sought diversity in their backgrounds,
choosing three Protestants, a Jew, and a Catholic; four who were
whites and one who was black; three born in the United States and two

in Europe; two who grew up in families of the well-to-do middle class, one in a family headed by an artisan, one in a slave family, and one in a family of poor immigrants.

To add to this diversity, we selected women whose memoirs reveal widely varying experiences: Anna Cora Mowatt, *Autobiography of an Actress* (1854), already introduced; Harriet Jacobs, writing under the pseudonym Linda Brent, *Incidents in the Life of a Slave Girl* (1861); Elizabeth Cady Stanton, feminist organizer and leader, whose *Eighty Years and More* (1898) appeared near the end of her life; Mary Antin, immigrant from Russia, whose *The Promised Land* (1912) dealt with her experiences as a girl; and Margaret Sanger, whose *Margaret Sanger: An Autobiography* (1938) centered on her work as the founder of the movement to promote birth control in the United States.

In addition to illustrating the transformation of women's place in society, these autobiographies illuminate such other important aspects of American history as slavery, immigration, the westward movement, antebellum politics, economic growth, racial relations, the revolutions in transportation, communication, and other technologies, urban growth, and cultural life.

The autobiographies also tell us much about family relations and other aspects of the private side of life. While readers will discover these revelations for themselves in the individual memoirs, we may note that if the private experiences of all five women are considered together, certain significant findings appear. For example, these five writers show that their mothers gave birth to no fewer than forty children who survived infancy, an average of eight each. As for the writers themselves, Elizabeth Cady Stanton gave birth to seven children, but none of the others had more than three. In all, the five had only thirteen children of their own. This comparison reveals a decline in fertility in the nineteenth century even sharper than that of all white women (the only American group for which reliable statistics exist).

The five women autobiographers shared other characteristics. Despite their differences in social origin, nationality, race, and religion, all were literate at times and places when many people could not read and write; all were more articulate than the average person. The kind of woman who published her memoirs either came from—or aspired to join—the middle classes, acquired enough education to write, was usually brought up as a Protestant—often in an Evangelical church—in a town rather than in a rural area, and eventually had her primary residence in a city or suburb.

This volume therefore has inevitable limitations. It does not include memoirs by Native Americans, factory workers, those who spent their lives on farms (perhaps a majority of women in the earlier period), white Southerners, emigrants to the far West, social radicals like those who peopled the Utopian colonies of the time; certain kinds of conservatives, such as typical Roman Catholic or fundamentalist Protestant women; true reactionaries, such as the Mormon women who embraced the patriarchalism of an earlier day; and women capitalists.

Another sort of limitation, inescapable in any autobiography, should be noted here. In reporting the circumstances and details of daily living, the interplay of people and events, and her relationship to the larger social environment, the autobiographer serves as observer and recorder. Either explicitly or implicitly she offers her memoir as an accurate reflection of life. But because each writer is also a person with a distinct personality, interests, and values, she is necessarily an interpreter. Her memoir will therefore inevitably contain distortions or omissions.

Another autobiography, by Jane Grey Swisshelm, a contemporary of Elizabeth Cady Stanton, provides an example of this kind of personal bias. She herself was a pioneer in advocating changes in the law so as to permit married women to hold property of their own, and by writing newspaper editorials she played a part in the successful reform of the Pennsylvania law on the subject. Such action, she said, was the most effective way for women to improve their status in society. However, when Elizabeth Cady Stanton and others adopted a different strategy—that of holding woman's rights meetings in public to debate issues and to pass resolutions demanding change— Swisshelm charged them with ineptitude in conducting their meetings, thereby bringing down upon women reformers an avalanche of ridicule from male editors and writers. But were they so inept? Swisshelm herself was unable or unwilling to cooperate effectively with others in public ventures, and perhaps she resented being displaced by others as the leader in the early movement for woman's rights.

Readers must therefore be alert to a wide variety of influences that may have shaped a writer's perspectives and judgments. What effect, for example, did the writer's relationship with her mother or father, or her parents' relationship with each other, have on her point of view? What conditioned her openness or her reticence on questions of sexual expression? What part did the social background or the relative poverty or wealth of her family play in shaping her education, her friendships, her choice of husband, her ambitions in life? What were her perceptions of religion, racial differences, class relationships, or labor problems? As she grew up did she participate in a network of close relationships and personal communications among women, separate from men, that influenced her attitudes toward being a female in a male world?

WOMEN IN NINETEENTH-CENTURY AMERICA

If women's emergence into public life helped to transform their place in American society, how did that emergence come about? What general circumstances in America helped or hindered women intent on change?

The most obvious precondition for change in the status of women was the development of society in directions that would make it possible. During the first century and a half of settlement of the Atlantic coastal colonies, the emigrants from Britain and Europe were largely concerned with survival and security, economic and political. The colonies prospered; but even after the thirteen along the East coast gained independence from Britain, their new nation was still overwhelmingly agricultural and rural. There were only a few American cities of any size, and their cultural opportunities were rudimentary by the standards of London or Paris. Their middle classes were correspondingly small.

By the middle of the nineteenth century, however, the American population had risen from three million to twenty-three million through natural increase and heavy immigration, and it occupied a continental domain. Cities multiplied and grew rapidly. During the early nineteenth century the nation's economy, stimulated by huge production of grain, fiber, and meat for the market, as well as the widespread development of industries, helped to shape a society which was increasingly urban and middle-class in tone, especially in the Northeast, the business center of the country.

By that time Americans had also created a large internal market for ideas. The population boasted more readers, whether in raw numbers or in proportion to the whole, than any other nation. Educational opportunities increased rapidly, and in the 1840s states began to institute the world's first systems of universal public education. A network of rapid transportation in the form of railroads was spreading westward, while the instantaneous communication of the telegraph had begun to match it; both served to carry ideas as well as to aid commerce. More newspapers and magazines circulated in America than anywhere else, aided by liberal subsidies from the federal government through the national postal system, itself a prime carrier of ideas.

While economic opportunism permeated the air, so did democratic politics. The ideas and practices of democracy continually subverted elitist pretensions, championing the right of the masses— with the obvious exclusion of slaves and often free blacks and Native Americans—to literacy, free speech, and political participation as the partners of economic opportunity.

Since all these circumstances favored the ready expression of energy and ideas by individuals, and since women—especially those of the middle and upper classes—enjoyed almost as much literacy and education as men, it might seem inevitable that large numbers of women would assume new roles. But two forces discouraged rapid change of that kind. One was the force of the tradition of female subservience to male authority, still strong and not easily modified. The second was a new feminine ideal which owed much, ironically, to the thrust of economic change.

As breadwinners in an increasingly industrial and commercial society, many men now absented themselves from the home to toil for long hours at factories and offices. Their wives took on heavy— sometimes almost exclusive—responsibility for caring for homes and families much of the time. Many women thus added to their accustomed duties their husbands' traditional roles as primary supervisors of their children's moral and spiritual instruction. While these changing circumstances were real, they helped to generate in nineteenth-century society, in both Britain and America, a new ideal of femininity. Historians have suggested two descriptive terms which together capture the essence of this ideal, "domestic feminism" and "Cult of True Womanhood." In popular thought, expressed in thousands of sermons, speeches, articles, and books, there emerged a glorified image of women as superhuman home managers and spiritual leaders.

Many wives and mothers found attractive the idealizing of femininity generated by this combined tribute and demand. It enhanced the theoretical importance of women to society, and provided recognition for the duties that they had to perform. But the resulting satisfaction in being female could be enjoyed only by women who, more than ever, remained firmly fixed in the home, avoiding outside distractions. Those female deviants who tried to enter the male-run world of affairs felt the force of the ideal in a negative way, as male critics reprimanded them for their departures from domestic duty.

WRITING FOR THE PUBLIC

Yet if necessity, tradition, and idealized True Womanhood kept most middle-class females in dutiful service at home, it was also true that American society offered venturesome women a respectable mode of courting public attention. This was the occupation (or avocation) of writing for the public. Writing for publication attracted the energies and talents of thousands of American women in the nineteenth century; most of the autobiographers in this anthology first won public attention in that way. The discipline of this work taught a growing number of women to address the public persuasively, and accustomed a rapidly enlarging number of readers of both sexes to listen to what they had to say. Some of the writers were ready to use their pens explicitly for purposes of social reform, and some of these to dramatize their activism through autobiography.

Writing for the public offered a convenient way for a woman to transcend the bounds of home. She could compose poetry, stories, novels, or occasional pieces without leaving home, even submitting work under a pen name to preserve anonymity and privacy, while enjoying vicarious contacts with a wider world. Or she could seek fame, as well as money, by making her identity known to the public, by writing with the authority that came with a literary reputation. There was little male opposition to these women writers; most were thoroughly genteel and celebrated the virtues of True Womanhood, even if they sometimes called attention to large gaps between the pretensions and the practices of the "Lords of Creation," their sarcastic term for the male sex. After all, if a drunken Lord of Creation were endangering home and family, did not the True Woman have the duty of calling him to account?

By the middle of the nineteenth century American women

authors were producing sentimental poetry, children's literature, guides to home management, and some literary criticism. They were also publishing novels, tales for magazines and the new cheap story newspapers, and periodical articles so prolifically as to provoke Nathaniel Hawthorne's much-quoted complaint that a "damned army of scribbling women" was giving him unfair competition for the favor of publishers and critics. To illustrate this successful female intrusion into a field earlier dominated by men, Richard B. Morris' *Encyclopedia of American History* notes that ten of the sixteen best-selling books from 1850 to 1860 were written by women (all were novels), and that the only author during those years to publish two best-sellers was the novelist Mrs. E. D. E. N. Southworth.

Such women authors had become deeply involved in an occupation that was both widely visible and influential. They were competing successfully with males and in many cases earning all or part of their livings from it. The five autobiographers here profited from the establishment of writing as an honorable profession for women, for a very large audience of middle-class people, male and female, like themselves.

WHO WROTE AUTOBIOGRAPHIES?

When we look at the identities of our women autobiographers and the contents of their books, however, we realize that the above considerations—literacy, participation in the world of ideas and communication, successful competition with males for the attention of a sizable middle-class audience—do not fully explain why some women were led to reveal their own lives in print. For them to do so, it appears, they needed to involve themselves in important events beyond literature.

That requirement was nearly as true for men as for women; few persons in that day could conceive of placing before the public a wealth of detail about a private life unless they could also claim participation in happenings of special interest to that public. The political leader, the traveler to distant places, the adventurer, and the military hero could make such claims. But on what important matters could women focus their life stories?

Anna Cora Mowatt, as we have seen, was a well-known actress. Mary Antin was a participant in the great migration from the Old World to the New and a notable example of the swift and successful

Americanization of many non-English-speaking immigrants. The other women we have chosen were deeply engaged in various movements for social reform, which gave them experience in wrestling with controversial public problems and contending or cooperating with prominent male leaders. Their experiences in dealing with important public questions, coupled with their understandable desire to strengthen the arguments on behalf of their reform interests, furnished them with all the justification they needed to open their lives to the public as examples of work well done.

Unlike the theater and the experience of immigration, these reform causes had flowered only recently. Here the growth in the early nineteenth century of the Evangelical movement within Protestantism, then the overwhelmingly dominant branch of religion in the United States, was important. As historians have shown, this religious movement's powerful emphasis on voluntarism in the saving of souls, as well as the widespread influence of the kind of Perfectionism preached by the Presbyterian revivalist Charles G. Finney, tended to arouse enthusiasm for the reform of many failings, social as well as personal. Those who joined reform movements typically defined them as crusades to attain true morality, as logical outgrowths of personal commitments to religion.

For many women the first stage of participation in reformist activities was in missionary or benevolent organizations sponsored by their own churches. Many then enlisted in women's groups that were more broadly based but aimed at specific goals, such as the reform of prostitutes carried on by the many chapters of the American Society for Moral Reform. Many reform groups contained both male and female members, but often women organized—or were obliged to organize—separate chapters.

The list of pre-War reform groups is a long one. Their aims included the promotion of such things as temperance, better conditions for labor, prisoners, and the insane, free public schools, and socialism through Utopian communities. But it was probably the antislavery crusade—in its militant phase beginning in the 1830s—that more than any other movement led women reformers into actions that were politically controversial and often highly unpopular in their own communities, and hence often demanding considerable self-assertion. Agitation for specific legal and other rights for women, which was being organized in the late 1840s, then attracted many of these women, now more accustomed to public activities, into feminist causes.

THE AUTOBIOGRAPHER'S PERSPECTIVE

When a person sits down and writes about what happened in his or her life, an autobiography results. It is as simple as that. Or is it? Unfortunately for those who love simplicity, but fortunately for those who delight in complexity, uncertainty, and ambiguity, autobiographies are far from being transparent, lucid, and accurate stories of lives. Each autobiography is of course unique, as the story of a unique individual. However, because that individual—the ultimate insider— is describing his or her own life does not mean that important parts of the story are necessarily as accurate, complete, and full of insight as a version offered by an outsider.

Consider the case of Elizabeth Cady Stanton, one of the autobiographers presented here. In introducing her *Eighty Years and More*, Mrs. Stanton explained that since her other books had told the story of the woman's movement and her part in it, she would now recount, "the story of my private life as wife of an earnest reformer, as an enthusiastic housekeeper, proud of my skill in every department of domestic economy, and as the mother of seven children." But whatever Mrs. Stanton intended to do when she began writing her story of her "private life," and whatever she thought she had done when she finished it, once she had described her childhood and early married years her autobiography turned into another telling of the story of the woman's rights movement. True, she salted and peppered it with anecdotes drawn from some of her experiences in early motherhood and home management. But an astute critic, Estelle C. Jelinek, has pointed out how, as the book's narrative moved from 1848, when Stanton began to organize the woman's rights movement, to 1885, her husband Henry B. Stanton simply went unmentioned. The same was largely true of her seven children; they were virtually missing in her account of her life between the 1850s and the 1880s. Instead she filled these memoirs with references to Susan B. Anthony, her partner in reform.*

Any explanation of this shift away from Stanton's stated purpose is left to the reader, but that problem leads us to reflect on what autobiographies have come to mean to both their writers and their readers, and on whether these meanings are the same for male and female autobiographers.

*Estelle C. Jelinek, ed. and intro., *Women's Autobiography: Essays in Criticism* (Bloomington, Ind.: Indiana University Press, 1980), pp. 71-92.

THE QUESTION OF SELF-CONSCIOUSNESS

From the ancient world to the modern, autobiographical writing has taken varied forms and has had varied purposes. Julius Caesar wrote of his personal conquests in his *Commentaries*, no doubt with pride but also to strengthen his claims to political power; he provided little information about himself as an individual. Augustine, Bishop of Hippo, composing his *Confessions* in the later Roman Empire, added intimate experiences to the account of his youth and early maturity; his focus on struggles with sin was intended to provide guides toward religious faith for other sinners. The Renaissance artist Benvenuto Cellini, in writing his memoirs, took a long step toward an emphasis on individualism by garnishing his account of his trials and deeds with liberal dashes of self-centeredness and boasts of his accomplishments. Jean Jacques Rousseau's *Confessions*, written in Enlightenment France, created an early model of the intimate autobiography that purports to "tell all." Rousseau's intentness on trying to understand and explain himself as a unique individual constituted a new departure; it anticipated the nineteenth century's growth of self-consciousness in autobiographical writing, with its emphasis on the importance and distinctiveness of the individual in society.

These scattered examples and the historical tendency they suggest, however, reflect the traditional domination of Western society by men and male values. Even the relatively few women who produced autobiographical material—religious confessions, reports of travels, chronicles of events, diaries, journals, letters—took for granted the bounds that men had set for the world and for women. Nevertheless, half-concealed and half-conscious within women's writing about themselves was a good deal of evidence that they perceived and experienced the world in ways different from that of their fathers, brothers, and husbands.

Recent analysts of women's autobiographical writing have argued strongly that while intense awareness of self is a striking characteristic of modern autobiography, that self-awareness has not impelled female authors to glory in the uniqueness of their individuality. Rather, these memoirs reveal how the self-consciousness the writers exhibit is that of being women first and individuals second, an awareness similar to that of members of other groups in positions of minority or inferiority.

Even though the five autobiographies that follow were chosen because each illustrated in some fashion the venturing of a woman into the male-oriented world beyond the home, challenging her in some sense to "be a man," they still allow the reader to test the suggested distinction between female and male self-consciousness. Can one see in them a strong sense of collective identity as women? For example, one might expect to find in Harriet Jacobs's *Incidents in the Life of a Slave Girl* a powerful feeling of identification with other blacks. Does Jacobs's narrative also show a strong sense of identification with other women, whether black or white, as females?

THE MYTH OF THE AUTOBIOGRAPHICAL "SELF"

Of the ambiguities encountered in reading autobiography, perhaps the most challenging is the question of what the "self" is that the writer reveals. The writer usually seems to be presenting what is popularly called an "identity," a psychosocial construct made up of such elements as physical being, intellect and emotion, experience, behavior, and attitudes.

The idea that the individual possesses a single, fully defined "true" self, to be either disclosed or discovered, is a myth. For one thing, we often realize that we have been unaware of aspects of ourselves when they come to our attention. For another, the act of reflection may bring new understanding of one's self, and the hard thinking about one's experience that is a necessary part of autobiography is likely to produce new insights as to what one's self is. If a writer should carry on this process of self-examination longer, or more intensely, or at a different time, or under different circumstances, the perception and presentation of the self might well be affected.

In looking at women as autobiographers, we must remember that the selves they put forward are inevitably shaped, perhaps in ways of which they are unaware, by a circumstance of which they are very much aware: their need to conform to—or to rebel against—a society largely defined by the values of a sex that is not their own. Men do not face that challenge.

Thus in seeking each of these women's selves, we should try to identify the particular self that the writer wishes us to see. At the same time we should delve beneath that surface and ask whether we can detect such tendencies as self-dramatizing, self-pitying, self-glorifying, excessive modesty, or self-defensive rationalizing. We should try to define the basic tone of the autobiography, whether angry, generous, lighthearted, self-righteous, resentful, cold and factual, artfully sincere, sincere with artfulness, proud, exuberant, humble, nostalgic—and so on. And in the end we should ask how our answers to these questions make us respond to the autobiographer and her work.

Anna Cora Mowatt (1819-1870)

ALTHOUGH she was a feminist neither by membership in women's organizations nor through explicit pleas for woman's rights, Anna Cora Mowatt undertook a career that broke dramatically with prescribed roles for nineteenth-century women, especially those of the upper and middle classes. She was born in 1819, ninth of fourteen children of Samuel and Eliza Ogden, both descended from patrician American families. She lived her first six years in southern France, where her father's shipping business had taken him, and went to boarding school on the family's return to New York.

From the first she displayed imagination and talent as amateur actress and playwright, both in her family and at school. When only fifteen she eloped with a young lawyer, James Mowatt, but despite her family's disapproval was soon reconciled with them. She continued to stage amateur productions of her own, and published one play, *Gulzara*, in *The New World*, a magazine suitably genteel for the presentation of a young woman's work. When her husband lost his investments in the business depression of the late 1830s and his sight became impaired through illness, Mowatt turned, with both his and her father's support, to earning an income by giving public readings of poetry. She augmented this income by publishing stories, novels, and plays. Between 1845 and 1854 she won acclaim for the successful staging of her plays and for her appearances as a leading actress in both America and England. Her major work as a playwright, a satire on manners entitled *Fashion*, or, *Life in New York*, was one of the more successful American plays of its time and is virtually the only one of that period still produced today.

For her defiance of convention Mowatt paid a price in the loss of some friends, but compensated for this by acquiring new ones in her own social milieu and in literary and artistic circles. She paid another price in impaired health, suffering severely at times from physical and emotional strain, but found considerable relief in undergoing hypnotism (called mesmerism in that day), and obtained spiritual solace in the Swedenborgian version of Christianity, then growing rapidly in popularity.

James Mowatt died in England in 1851 while she was on tour as an actress there. Without children of their own, the couple had earlier adopted three. By 1854 Mrs. Mowatt was ready to remarry and give up her career in the theater. At this point, at thirty-five, she published her autobiography—fulfilling, she wrote, a promise to her late husband. However, the man she was to marry, William F. Ritchie, an editor of the *Richmond* (Virginia) *Examiner*, was neither wealthy nor highly paid, and since Mowatt was accustomed to both financial independence and spending money happily, she no doubt viewed her experiences as a potential source of more publishing royalties.

Despite her well-publicized years as an actress, Mowatt threw herself actively and successfully into the highly conservative social life of Richmond, taking a leading part in the efforts of the Mount Vernon Association to purchase and restore the home of George Washington as a national shrine. Her marriage to Ritchie, however, fell into increasing difficulties; she suspected him of dallying with a female slave at a friend's plantation, and in the crisis of the Union she did not wish to support the South. Shortly before the outbreak of the Civil War they separated for good. Mowatt spent the next decade in Europe with brief visits to the United States. She tried to return to the stage, for she had little money left, but failed to attract offers. She died in England in 1870.

We are curious to know what sorts of influences her parents exerted on this precocious child, especially in view of her elopement at fifteen with James Mowatt without losing their good will and affection. And was her reported seeking of her father's permission when she went before the public motivated simply by convention, or did she really depend on his approval? What is the "self" that Mowatt creates for readers in the autobiography? Does it remain consistent throughout? Does she ever criticize or laugh at herself? How might you interpret her many illnesses, and her response to mesmeric (hypnotic) treatment in the years she was appearing in public as reader and actress? Was she manipulated by men, or did she manipulate them? In the end, do you feel either that a person has taken you genuinely and honestly into her confidence, or that you have been witnessing the equivalent of a stage performance? Or perhaps both?

Autobiography of an Actress, or Eight Years on the Stage

*Anna Cora Mowatt**

CHAPTER I

MY father, Samuel G. Ogden, of New York, was the son of an Episcopal clergyman. For a number of years my father's name was prominent in the community as that of a successful merchant. . . .

My mother, Eliza Ogden, was the daughter of Francis Lewis, and the granddaughter of that Francis Lewis whose signature is affixed to the Declaration of Independence.

My earliest recollections are of a beautiful old country seat, called La Castagne, and situated two miles from Bordeaux, in France. My parents were residing in Bordeaux at the time of my birth, but removed to La Castagne when I was only a few months old. My father's commercial transactions caused him to pass some ten years abroad. During this period four daughters were born, of whom I was the second.

I have dim but most delightful remembrances of La Castagne, which come to me like half-forgotten dreams. I remember a magnifi-

* From *Autobiography of an Actress, or Eight Years on the Stage*. Boston: Ticknor and Fields, 1854.

cent terrace, where we children used to frolic—a beautiful walk, called "Allée d'Amour," lined with tall trees, whose branches met and formed a bower over the head—a large pond, surrounded with statues, and filled with fishes, which it was our daily delight to feed—a gayly-painted pleasure boat, always floating on the pond—a grotto, called "Calypso's Grotto"—a miniature waterfall, our great wonder and admiration—the whole place a very Eden of fruits and flowers. . . .

The performance of private plays seems to have been the favorite amusement of my elder sisters and brothers. I can only remember one of these occasions—the one on which I made my own *début*. The play represented was Othello, translated into French. My eldest sister enacted Desdemona; my eldest brother Othello; the second sister Emilia; the second brother Cassio, doubling the part with that of the uncle; the third brother Iago, doubling the part with that of the judge. The other brothers and sisters filled the remaining characters. . . .

I was in my seventh year when we embarked from Bordeaux for New York in the ship Brandt. Even at this day I cannot think of that dreadful voyage without a shudder. The terrible crash with which we were early one morning waked from sleep still sounds in my ears. The ship was pitching so violently that we children could scarcely hold ourselves in our berths. One little sister was thrown and bruised against the great dinner table. The water was pouring down the companion way, and threatening to flood the whole cabin. . . .

Soon after our arrival in New York, we were placed at Mrs. Okill's boarding school—and there I appeared for the second time on a mimic stage. It was in a little French play,—I do not even recollect its name,—performed, after a public examination of the scholars, for the amusement of the parents and guardians. My sister Matilda and I were intrusted with important parts, and won many praises.

For a long period I did not entirely recover from the consequences of the sea voyage and its terrible excitements, and my school days were frequently interrupted by fits of illness. I was, however, permitted to read as much as I chose, and availed myself amply of the privilege. I read any thing and every thing that I could find. Of poetry I was never tired, and at ten years old I had read the whole of Shakspeare's plays many times over. My reading was not guided—I was allowed to take any book that I chose, French or English, from my father's library. When I look back upon some of the works which I perused with avidity at that early age, I can hardly believe it possible that a child could have waded through them, or culled out meaning enough to render the subjects interesting. I amused myself by writing also, and *fancied* that

I wrote poetry, because I made the ends of the lines rhyme. Every marriage, or birth, or death, or exciting circumstance that occurred in the family invariably furnished me with a subject. . . .

At school I was too wild, too "ungovernably gay," to gain the highest honors. I learned with great rapidity any thing I fancied; but the good marks I got for my studies were too often counterbalanced by bad marks received for talking, making the other girls laugh, or disobeying rules. I and one of my younger sisters were constantly convicted of being ringleaders in all mischief which had merriment for its end. I was generally at the head, or very near the head, of classes for reading, recitation of poetry, mythology, history, physiology, mental philosophy, &c., but as invariably at the foot of grammar, arithmetic, algebra. The multiplication table I never succeeded in learning. . . .

During a portion of our school-day probation, two sisters and I were placed at boarding school in New Rochelle. There I was really unhappy. I had but one source of consolation and delight—the little garden which I was permitted to plant and call my own. We each were given a bit of ground about four feet square, and allowed to work there a short time every day. These are the only happy hours I can remember amongst the many lonely and miserable ones that made up the year. Nor were these miseries imaginary. We were harshly treated—punished for the slightest infringement of most severe rules—inadequately fed—and deprived of all pleasures but a formal walk every afternoon, a short "intermission" twice each day, (at which we were forbidden to make any noise,) and the much-prized and delightful garden digging. When I was twelve years old, we were summoned home. Our father's house seemed paradise, indeed, from the contrast. We once more became day scholars in good schools, and merry as uncaged linnets.

Our favorite amusement continued to be the enacting of plays and reciting poetical dialogues. I soon became stage manager and director of all these dramatic performances, and was called upon to write fresh scenes, add in new characters, or alter the *dénouements*, according to the fancies of our whimsical little corps. Sometimes we invented the plots of these plays—or selected them from incidents in history,—chose characters, dressed for them, and *improvised* the dialogues and the scenes during performance. . . .

I was fourteen years old when I conceived the project of preparing some grand celebration in honor of our father's birthday. We would enact a standard play—a *real* play. It should be studied and produced with great care. The friends of our elder sisters and our parents should be invited as well as our own. For once, we would act before *grown-up people*, and on a great occasion. The play selected—because it required no scenery, and only such characters as we could readily fill, with the assistance of some school friends—was Voltaire's Alzire, translated into English. All our male characters were represented by young girls, for our brothers had passed the days when they could have been persuaded to wear the sock and buskin amongst juveniles. Our parents would not have allowed us to supply their places with any but those of our own sex. . . .

We had many, a great many, rehearsals, some before our parents and elder sisters, who, after witnessing one of these, consented to invite their friends. When the play concluded, the evening was to end with a ball. The performance was to take place in the back drawing room. To supply the place of scenery, it was hung round with crimson curtains, through which we were to make our entrances and exeunts. The audience were to sit in rows in the front drawing room. We had a drop curtain and a prompter, who stood ready with his book and bell (or rather *her* book and bell, for she was a young lady) to mark the division of the acts by the falling of the curtain. . . .

The play went off with great *éclat*, as the tears of the audience, bestowed as freely as their applause, amply testified. I enacted the part of Alzire, and succeeded in losing my own identity in that of the heroine. My father came behind the scenes when the play was over, and his words of commendation sank deep in my heart. I wondered if I really deserved them, and if other people would say the same. Our stage dresses were quickly laid aside for ball costume, and the evening ended with dancing and great hilarity.

Strange to say, up to this period I had visited a theatre but once, and that only a few weeks before our birthday *fête*. For some years our parents and their children had all attended the church of Dr. E———n, now Bishop E———n. I went to Sunday school with my sisters twice every Sunday—at first as pupil, and then as teacher. I had a species of enthusiastic admiration and reverence for Bishop E———n. I loved to see him enter the Sunday school; I loved to hear him in the pulpit; and was happier all day if he accidentally bestowed upon me a passing word. He disapproved of theatres; he pronounced them the "abodes of sin and wickedness." It never occurred to me to inquire what he *really knew* of theatres; but I trusted implicitly in his *supposed* information. I determined that I never would enter such a dreadful place. My sisters went now and then with our father; but, in spite of my decided passion for plays and for acting, the thought of the imaginary monsters of evil, which I was certainly to behold, kept me away.

Fanny Kemble was then taking her farewell of the stage. Her name was on every body's lips; her praises echoed from all sides. I read critiques upon her acting in the papers, and heard her talked of as a most devoted daughter and truly excellent woman. I could not help longing to see her; but the old objections were strong within me, and I was afraid of being laughed at if I confessed that my interest in the woman made me willing to enter such a place, as I supposed a theatre to be, to see the actress. Her last engagement was drawing to a close. My sisters had witnessed several of her performances, and constantly mentioned them with delight.*

One morning my father overtook us as we were walking to school. He accosted my elder sister with, "I am going to take seats to see Fanny Kemble to night in the Hunchback. Would you like to go?"

She, of course, answered in the affirmative. I looked at my father, longing for him to ask me; but I had too often cried down the theatre with childish violence, and quoted Dr. E———n as authority. I dared not request that my father would take me.

Just as he was leaving us, he said, carelessly, "And so you, Anna, are *never* going?"

I could not resist the temptation, and answered, in a faltering voice, "I *should* like to see Fanny Kemble just *once*."

"O, you have changed your mind? Very well; I will take a seat for you to-night," was his reply. . . .

The curtain ascended, and I was all eyes and ears. Fanny Kemble appeared in the second scene, and I thought I had never beheld any creature so perfectly bewitching. The tones of her voice were richest music, and her dark, flashing eyes seemed to penetrate my very soul. Her "Clifford, why don't you speak to me?" made me start from my seat; and her "Do it!" to Master Walter, electrified me, as indeed it did the whole audience. The play was a reality from beginning to end, and I laughed and wept immoderately. . . .

* Frances Anne "Fanny" Kemble (1809-1893), a third-generation descen-
dant of a noted British theatrical family and one of the best-known
actresses of the day, appeared on American stages between 1832 and 1834
in her first visit to this country.

CHAPTER II

I MUST go back to my thirteenth year, to relate one of the most important incidents of my life, the one which was to govern my whole future existence. My eldest sister Charlotte, with her two little children, passed a summer at Rockaway, for the enjoyment of sea bathing. Among the guests at Rock Hall was James Mowatt, of New York, a young barrister of education and fortune. He was much charmed with my sister, imagining her be a youthful widow. This mistake she never discovered until his admiration was expressed in open terms. When informed that he was addressing a married woman, his chagrin was so great that she laughingly consoled him by saying, "O, I have plenty of young sisters at home, and one of them very much resembles me. Call upon me in New York, and I will make you acquainted with her."

In a few weeks she returned to the city. Mr. Mowatt made no delay in paying his respects. The school, which four of us children attended, was directly opposite our residence. While we were in the midst of our studies one day, a messenger came to say that the eldest of the schoolgirl sisters must come home. She was the one that strikingly resembled our sister Charlotte. I asked the servant if any thing had happened. She replied, "No; that there was only a gentleman in the drawing room, who entreated that my sister might be sent for." I had heard Mr. Mowatt much talked of in the family, and felt a childish curiosity to see him. Without permission, I accompanied my sister home, and watched her while her beautiful hair was recurled, and her schooldress laid aside for a more becoming attire. She was ushered into the drawing room; and I, of course, dared not enter.

After waiting about half an hour, I remembered that I had received no permission to leave school, and, certain visions of black marks rising up before me, I thought it judicious to return. But to go back without having seen this much-talked-of beau—I could not do that. I would enter the drawing room on some pretext. After hesitating a while, I opened the door, ran across the room, threw down my satchel of school books upon the centre table,—as though that must be their proper place,—gave one look towards the sofa, and ran out again.

"Who is that?" I heard the gentleman exclaim.

"Only one of the children from the nursery," answered my eldest sister.

"Do call her back," he urged.

My sister came to the door and called out, as I was flying up stairs, tolerably frightened at what I had done, "Anna, Anna, come back and speak to Mr. Mowatt!"

"*I* don't care for Mr. Mowatt!" was the saucy reply that reached his ears; and away I went.

A servant was sent to summon me, but I refused to comply. I waited until I heard the gentleman take his leave, then hurried down stairs to return to school. Mr. Mowatt was standing at the foot of the street door steps, and placed himself in front of me with extended arms. There was no retreat, and he kept me prisoner for some time. . . .

I answered his many questions with saucy, merry frankness, every now and then imploring to be freed. Finding he would not consent, I watched my opportunity, suddenly slipped beneath his arm, and ran across the street to school. I well remember the expression of his face as I looked back, laughing heartily at the astonishment of my discomfited jailer. . . .

From that moment he conceived the project of educating me to suit his own views—of gaining my affections, and, the instant I was old enough to be considered marriageable, of taking me to his own home—his child-wife. His visits to the family became very frequent. He always inquired for me; but I was generally at school, or studying my lessons, or had gone to bed; and he was constantly frustrated in his desire to see me. But his perseverance comprehended no discouragement. Our school was now changed—we were placed at Madame Chegaray's, to be instructed in the higher branches of education. On our way to school (which was about half a mile distant from our home) we regularly encountered Mr. Mowatt. He would walk beside me, carry my books and slate, and question me about my studies. Sometimes he made them clearer to me; and very soon, under the stimulus of his suggestions, my ambition to become an accomplished scholar was aroused. Now and then I would propose to my sisters, for mischief, to take a different road, that he might miss us; but after a couple of days he discovered the stratagem, and stationed one of his clerks to watch which street we took. He was thus instantly apprised if we were going different ways. . . .

He was present at my performance of Alzire, and was naturally the most enthusiastic where all were enthusiastic. The next morning he determined to offer himself, although I was not yet fifteen. It was Saturday, and there was no school. he called very early, and asked particularly for me. While my sisters were making their toilets, I hastened to the parlor in my morning dress. I was eager to listen to praises of the past night's efforts. But I was not more disappointed than astonished when the gentleman awaiting me commenced a serious conversation, without making the slightest allusion to the play. I only comprehended enough to be alarmed. I did not reply, but, jumping up, called to my sister Charlotte to come down stairs quickly. She did so, inquiring what was the matter. Of course, this was an *unanswerable* question, and the situation of two of the parties concerned must have been particularly ludicrous.

When Mr. Mowatt left, I told her what had passed. She laughed, and said he was making sport of me, because I was such a forward child. But the sport proved earnest, and what I refused to listen to that day was conveyed to me by letter the next. A schoolgirl of fourteen pondering over a love letter—an offer of marriage from a man many years her senior. It was in itself an amusing situation; yet I found it a painful one. I carried the important document to my sister Louisa, and, making her promise secrecy, placed the letter in her hands. She read it without comment.

"Well, and what are you going to do? she inquired, at its conclusion.

"Get you to help me to write an answer, and tell him I am too young to marry any body, and say something about *friendship*, and all that sort of thing—because I *do* like him very much."

She told me I must write the letter myself, and she would correct it—she could do nothing more. I went to the nursery, for, ludicrous as it sounds, I still belonged to the *nursery*—slept there, and there kept my books and writing materials; and to the nursery I took my love letter. I began an answer, and tore it up—and began another, and another; and at last succeeded in writing a page of nonsense, which I thought very good sense. I took it to my sister to read. She pronounced that it would do; and the letter was sent by post.

Its effect, however, was very different from the one anticipated. Mr. Mowatt merely laughed at what he considered girlish shyness. He increased, rather than diminished, the number of his visits, and assumed the bearing of an accepted, instead of a rejected, lover. This went on for some time, and he took frequent opportunities of assuring me that he could never be made to comprehend the meaning of the word "No." It was a safe way to woo a child, and when I was within a few weeks of fifteen, the "No" was forgotten, and a "Yes" had taken its place.

My father's consent was asked. He could find no objection to Mr. Mowatt, and made my extreme youth the only barrier. He replied, that, if we both remained of the same mind until I was seventeen, he would give his sanction to our union. Meantime, Mr. Mowatt might continue his visits, and see me as often as any other gentleman.

I was pained to find that Mr. Mowatt no longer enjoyed his daily visits. . . . More earnestly than ever he entreated me to become his wife without further delay. I proposed that we should again attempt to obtain my father's sanction; but *that* Mr. Mowatt pronounced useless. For a long time I resisted his persuasions; but at last, when he had ceased to entreat me, I was so much grieved by the painfulness of his position, and the sight of his deepening melancholy, that of my own free will I gave him a promise that we should be united within a week.

What was I to do? and who was to aid me? I could not leave my father's house alone. I could not be married without a *bridal wardrobe*. These were huge barriers to be surmounted; but I went resolutely to work, determined to overcome them. I first confided my secret to a young nursery maid in the family, to whom I was much attached. I entreated her to accompany me when I left my home, and she consented. Then I went to my sister Matilda, with whom I was most intimate. After making her solemnly promise that she would not betray me, I told her that I intended to be married privately within a week. She was very much startled and overcome. She used arguments, entreaties, prayers, to dissuade me. She tried to convince me that I would not be forgiven; that I might repent through my whole future life the step that I was so rashly taking. My only answer was "I have promised, and cannot break my word. You have promised, and cannot betray me."

Finding that I was not to be moved, she concluded that the wisest plan was to lend me every assistance in her power. Reluctantly and sadly, against her better judgment, she promised me her services. . . .

At length the 6th of October came—the day on which I had promised to be married. My slender wardrobe was completed—all our arrangements made. The day dawned magnificently—every thing looked propitious. It might well be said of that day, as of the new life which it commenced. . . .

My poor sister, I think, suffered even more than I did; the blame was all to fall on her. She had done her utmost to dissuade me, and now had to assist in depriving herself of a beloved companion; for, being next to each other in age, we were very closely united in affection. I could not thank her at the time, but her unselfishness touched me deeply.

We left the house, and, turning the first corner, she threw the bridal veil over my bonnet, gave me the white gloves, and begged me to try and look composed before I met Mr. Mowatt and his friends. . . .

At St. John's Park we met Mr. Mowatt and his two groomsmen. I took his arm and we walked to the house of the Rev. Mr. V———n, my sister and the gentlemen following.

We were ushered into the drawing room. Mr. V———n entered in his robes. He, of course, did not know which of the sisters was the bride. He took his seat, opened a large register, and asked the names and ages of the parties about to be married. When I replied, giving my name, he looked at me steadily, and with some surprise.

"Your age?" he inquired.

"Fifteen."

He put down his pen, and repeated the question. For a few seconds he seemed doubtful whether he ought to proceed. I was thought to look younger even than my years; and I was dressed in a childlike manner, which probably made me appear younger still.

The law sanctions the marriage of a girl of fifteen, and he could not make any reasonable objection. The names were registered. Mr. V———n rose with the prayer book in his hand. We rose also, and the ceremony was performed in French. At its close he delivered a beautiful address, intended for the bridegroom's edification, rather than for that of the childlike bride; wished us both much happiness, and we took our leave. . . .

The next morning immediately after breakfast, I was to join Mr. Mowatt, and, accompanied by the nursery maid, we were to take the steamboat for Nyack. His sister-in-law was residing there, and to her he purposed taking me.

When breakfast was over, I made some laughing excuse to kiss every one present, controlling, with a strong effort, the agitation which I could not but feel. As I stooped to kiss my father for the second time—I had already been at his bedside, and kissed him before he rose—my courage nearly gave way. In another instant I should have told him all. . . .

"Let us run! let us run!" I said to my sister, for all my courage was melting away, and I could trust myself no longer. And we did run, rapidly and without speaking, until we reached the spot where Mr. Mowatt was waiting for us. There I had to bid adieu to my faithful sister. She must go home and bear all the blame—see all the sorrow occasioned by my act, and know in her own heart that no fault was hers. She had only aided, through sisterly love, a step which she could not prevent. Luckily our parting was hurried. I had only time to thank her, and beg her to deliver my letter to our father, and to write to me immediately.

With a heavy heart she returned home, and broke the news to an elder sister. They went together to my mother, and, after some gentle preparation, told her that I was married and gone. She was at first half stunned by the information, but, quickly recovering, made earnest inquiries concerning me—remembered my delicate health, and expressed many fears that I was not provided with sufficiently warm clothing to protect me against the cold, which was becoming severe. Anger had no place in her heart nor in her words. She was full of tender solicitude, but neither chided my sister for the course she had taken, nor pronounced severely upon my own. . . .

It was different with my father; he was indignant with the whole party, with me, with my sister, and, most of all, with Mr. Mowatt. My letter failed to pacify him. He at first declared that he would *never* forgive me, and it was three days before a letter was received, bringing his pardon. Those days seemed like a "never," indeed, to me. I began to believe that I had offended beyond forgiveness. I was almost heart broken at the idea of losing my father's love, upon which I had drawn too largely. My thoughts, "through all the faultful past, went sorrowing," and I could not bear to dwell upon a future of which he did not form the principal feature. But the pardon came, and an invitation to return home. I begged that our visit in the country might be shortened, and we returned in a week. My father, mother, all, welcomed us with open arms, and without one chiding word. It was the true way to make me conscious of my own shortcomings. I might have nerved myself to meet rebukes, but could not bear unmoved the tenderness I had not deserved. Mr. Mowatt they received less cordially, but still with kindness. . . .

CHAPTER III

[At sixteen Anna Cora Mowatt became the mistress of a country house in Flatbush, later part of Brooklyn, New York, but then thinly settled. With her younger sister May as companion, and with servants, horses, carriages, and gardens, she lived a life "without a wish ungratified." She continued her education under her husband's tutelage, reading voraciously. Within a year of her marriage, however, her mother died. Mowatt began writing (anonymously) for publication,

both "fugitive pieces" for magazines, and a "poetical romance," entitled "Pelayo," issued as a book by Harper and Brothers but dismissed by the critics. When an illness was diagnosed as consumption (tuberculosis), she was advised to take a sea voyage. She accompanied her newly married sister Emma, the latter's husband, and an aunt on a trip to England. The three weeks at sea brought a marked improvement in her condition, and in England she enjoyed an active social life, attending many plays in London. She journeyed to Germany, where her husband joined her, but he was soon stricken with a disease of the eyes that threatened his sight. The Mowatts spent some months in France, where Mrs. Mowatt saw many plays. They returned home, he still ill but she with renewed health and energy.]

. . .From the time of our return to America, Mr. Mowatt was forced to abandon his profession, on account of the affection in his eyes. He could neither use them to read nor to write except for a few minutes at a time. He always had a fondness for speculations in land, stocks, &c., which, in the absence of other employment, grew into a fatal passion. He made great ventures, sometimes reaping large profits, sometimes meeting with heavy losses. Of these speculations I at first knew little or nothing, but I could not help noticing the fitful changes that came over his mental horizon.

At times he suffered from deep depression not natural to his temperament, while at other times he was elated to a degree that equally astonished me. In one of those crises which convulse the whole mercantile world, (I use the language which I heard him use to Mary Howitt), he was utterly ruined. Almost the whole of his fortune was swept away in a few days. At first he concealed from me the serious nature of his losses, and it was long before I divined their extent. But our expenses must be retrenched—our mode of living altered—our country home, to which I was so devotedly attached, must be sold!

This intelligence was communicated to me in the most gentle manner. As soon as I could recover from the first bewildering shock, my earnest question to Mr. Mowatt was, "Is there no possible means of saving this house?"

"None that I can imagine," was his dejected answer.

"How long may we remain here?"

"A month perhaps—certainly not longer."

"And where shall we go?"

"Heaven knows!"

I had never before heard the sound of despair in his tones.

Misfortune sprinkles ashes on the head of the man, but falls like dew upon the heart of the woman, and brings forth germs of strength of which she herself had no conscious possession.

That afternoon I walked alone for a long time in the lovely arbor that had been erected for my pleasure. It was a magnificent day in autumn. The grapes were hanging in luxuriant purple clusters above my head. The setting sun could scarcely penetrate their leafy canopy of darkest, richest green. They seemed to typify abundance, peace, prosperity! Eve's "Must I leave thee, paradise?" found its echo in my innermost heart. I sat down in my favorite summer house, and strange thoughts came into my head. At first they were vague and wild, but out of the chaos gradually grew distinctness and order. I thought of my eldest sister Charlotte. Her gift was for miniature painting. When the rude storms of adversity had shipwrecked her husband, she had braved the opposition of her friends, of the world, and converted what had been a mere accomplishment into the means of support for herself and her children. In the Academy of Drawing at Paris she had been awarded a high prize amid hundreds of native competitors, although her name was unknown. Toiling ever, but ever with a cheerful spirit, she had gone on her pilgrimage rejoicing—overcoming trials with patient endurance, and reaping a priceless reward in the midst of many struggles.

Were there no gracious gifts within my nature? Had I no talents I could use? Had a life made up of delightful associations and poetic enjoyments unfitted me for exertion? No—there was something strong within me that cried out, It had not! What, then, could I do to preserve our home? I had talents for acting—I could go upon the stage; but that thought only entered my mind to be instantly rejected. The idea of becoming a professional actress was revolting.

The elder Vandenhoff had just given a successful course of readings in New York. I had been present on several evenings. His ball was crowded, and his audiences were highly gratified. I could give public readings. I had often read before large assemblages of friends—that required not a little courage. With a high object in view, I should gain enough additional courage to read before strangers. . . .

There were deep shadows upon the faces Mr. Mowatt and my sister May, (who was still the beloved companion of our home,) as we three sat down to the tea table; but I was more than usually merry, and now and then succeeded in calling a smile to the lips of one or the other. Several times Mr. Mowatt looked at me in astonishment. It was for my sake far more than for his own that he lamented his reverses. He feared privations for me—not for himself. He valued his wealth because it had ministered to my comforts, surrounded me with luxuries, and fostered my tastes. His own enjoyments were of a simple nature. I answered his wondering glances with mysterious looks, and waited impatiently until my young sister retired. Then I told him of my musings in the arbor—of my hopes—of my convictions—of—could I but gain his consent—my fixed determination! His surprise was at first too great for him to offer any opposition. I made good use of this vantage ground gained, and overwhelmed him with arguments, until my confident spirit had so thoroughly infused itself into his, that he suggested but one objection—the delicacy of my health. I combated that by declaring, and with truth, that I felt an *inner* strength hitherto unknown. I was sure that strength would sustain me under all emergencies.

Midnight found us still discussing my new project; but before I rose to retire, I had gained his consent. My slumbers were as peaceful that night as at the close of the calmest and happiest of the many happy days that had seen me sink to repose beneath that beloved roof.

Once determined upon my course, I lost no time in carrying my intentions into execution. The very next morning I made selections from my favorite poets,—many of them the same that I had heard Vandenhoff read,—and commenced strengthening my voice by reading aloud for a couple of hours each day in the open air. I allowed myself one fortnight to make all necessary preparations for my new and hazardous career.

I shrank from appearing in New York in the midst of my own extensive circle of relatives and friends. I did not desire the support which they might have yielded through personal sympathy. My powers could only be justly tested among strangers. Boston had been pronounced the most intellectual city of the Union—the American Athens. There is always more leniency towards the efforts of a novice where there is true taste. I would make my first appearance in Boston. A literary friend, to whom Mr. Mowatt confided our intentions, furnished us with valuable letters of introduction. Their influence, while it could not insure my success, would command for me a favorable hearing. . . .

It was a most trying duty to make my intended *début* known to my family. My sister May was, of course, the first in whom I confided. She was of a gentle and timid nature, and shrank in alarm from the proposed public step. She could not discuss it without tears and violent emotion.

The sight of her anguish affected me so much that I had not courage to seek my father and make the necessary communication to him. His opposition, should he oppose my wishes, would inevitably paralyze my strength. I wrote to him, and entreated that he would not dishearten me—not throw a clog upon my efforts by his disapproval. This letter was not to be delivered until the day when we started for Boston.

That day soon came. About an hour before the time when it was necessary for us to leave, I went into my sister's room, and found her greatly agitated. "Come, May, let us bid good by to the dear, old place, and pray that we may soon return and be as happy as ever." . . .

We were standing in the old-fashioned room where our little play had been performed, and talking over the pleasures of that eventful night, when the carriage came to the door. Hurriedly we took our seats. . . .

We left my sister, with the letter she had to deliver, at our father's door; and, without waiting to see any of the family, drove to the boat which started for Boston. . . .

CHAPTER IV

AS I look back, I can scarcely believe it possible that in Boston, where now I am bound by so many close, strong ties of friendship, I had then but one acquaintance—an acquaintance casually formed in the ball rooms of Paris. Mrs. B——s called upon me as soon as my arrival in Boston was published. I had known her merely as a woman of fashion, chasing the butterfly pleasure, even as I was doing, in Parisian salons. But now that I had a more earnest, a higher pursuit,—

"All
Her falser self slipped from her like a robe,"—

and she came to me in her true guise. It was the woman of soul that greeted me, full of tender sympathies and eager interest—lamenting our misfortunes, and ready to act the part of a devoted friend. She encouraged me in my undertaking—enlisted in my behalf the good wishes of her large circle of acquaintances—brought a number of them to introduce to me—and exerted herself to the utmost to insure a crowded audience to my first reading. She herself took one hundred tickets. I was strengthened and cheered by her untiring kindness; her hearty enthusiasm gave me new faith in my own success. . . .

Our letters of introduction brought us into communication with many delightful and some distinguished persons. Their interest in my novel undertaking was easily awakened, and their inspiring influence hemmed me around until I seemed to stand within a magic circle, guarded, as by a charm, from all inharmonious existences. The friendships formed at that period have been among the most enduring and most valued of my life.

We had only spent a couple of days in Boston when all the arrangements for my first appearance were satisfactorily completed. . . .

The day before that one which I was to make my *début* I visited the temple, and with a throbbing heart ascended the rostrum which I was to occupy during the readings. I tried my voice, to learn whether it had compass enough to fill the capacious hall. Mr. Mowatt and an old doorkeeper (who treated me in the most paternal and encouraging manner) were my only auditors. Yet it was with difficulty that I could speak in so singular a situation. The words came gaspingly forth, and I seemed to have lost all variety of intonation. I grew sick at heart. If my courage evaporated before an imaginary audience, how could I hope for presence of mind to carry me through the duties I had imposed upon myself when I stood in the presence of an actual crowd? I made effort after effort to recite, but my voice was choked—I could scarcely utter a word. I sat down upon the steps of the rostrum, overwhelmed with doubts and fears, which rushed like freshets over my heart, and swept away all its bright fabrics. I could not weep,—I was too miserable for tears,—and I could not listen to consolation. . . .

We returned to the hotel. Cards, kind notes, and bouquets were awaiting me. One note was from Judge Story, written in the most encouraging strain; another from the poet Longfellow, apologizing for not calling, on the plea of illness. I was dispiritedly putting them aside when a letter was handed me. It was from my father. I had scarcely courage to break the seal. If his disapprobation were added to my present dejection, my failure was certain. The first words reassured me—my father had pondered well upon the course I proposed to pursue, and he gave my efforts not merely his sanction, but his heartiest approval. He bade me never lose sight of the motive I had in view; and, with its help, my talents (as he was pleased to call them) would enable me to achieve a triumph. He gave me his own blessing, and assured me that, as far as I was actuated by a sense of duty, I should win the blessing of Heaven also.

An indomitable energy and perseverance had characterized all the actions of my father's life. I inherited these traits from him, and with them a faculty for happiness that struck out the slender vein of gold in the drossiest earth of circumstance. As I read his letter, my whole nature was quickened by an influx, as it were, from his strong, never-weary, and ever-buoyant spirit. All my hopes returned, and from that moment my courage never wavered.

The sun shone brightly upon the morning of my *début*. The heavens seemed to smile benignantly upon my undertaking. That nothing might disturb my composure, I refused to receive visitors, and passed the day quietly in my own chamber.

Evening found me calm and strong of heart. I entered the carriage that bore me to the temple, not more agitated to outward appearance than if I had been hastening to a ball.

I had resisted all entreaties to wear any rich attire, and was dressed in simple white muslin, a white rose in my bosom, and another in my hair. I wore no ornaments. . . .

The opening piece I had selected was the introduction for Scott's Lay of the Last Minstrel, and the first words I had to utter were,—

"The way was long, the wind was cold."

I could deliver the line feelingly, indeed, for I was shivering violently, and weary and long seemed the way I had just entered.

At length, in an uncertain voice, I commenced to read. Long before I had half finished the poem, my self-possession returned— a genial warmth displaced the icy chill, my voice grew loud and clear, and I found it easy to divest myself of all consciousness of the audience. I began also to become accustomed to the applause which at first oppressed and frightened me. I went through the various selections in order, and without betraying any further emotion.

When half the entertainment was over, there was an intermission of ten minutes, and I was at liberty to withdraw into the retiring room. There I was greeted by a host of friends, all loud in their congratulations and a note from my faithful ally, Mrs. B———s, told me of the delight of her party, and assured me of my perfect success.

With renewed spirit I reascended the rostrum, and read the concluding poems with as much ease as I should have done to a select party of friends in my own drawing room.

My father's delight and pride, warmly and openly expressed, compensated me for the sufferings inflicted by others—sufferings for which I was wholly unprepared. Some beloved relatives, and some who had been my nearest, dearest friends,—friends from my early childhood, who were associated in my mind with all the sweetest, happiest hours of my life,—now turned from me. They were shocked at my temerity in appearing before the public. They even affected not to believe in Mr. Mowatt's total loss of means. They tacitly proscribed me from the circle of their acquaintance. When we passed in the street, instead of the outstretched hand and loving greeting to which I had ever been accustomed, I met the cold eye and averted face that shunned recognition. . . .

Under the heavy pressure of mental suffering, added to the exhaustion produced by unusual exertions, my health gave way. After fulfilling the course at the Stuyvesant Institute, I became seriously ill, and was forced to make several postponements of the time announced for my reading before the Rutgers Institute for Young Ladies. When I was scarcely convalescent, I read there one night. The hall was filled with an assemblage of lovely-looking young girls, and their evident enjoyment inspired me to read with more energy and feeling than I had done since my nights in Boston. The effort cost me a relapse of some weeks. Again I rallied, and gave a course of four nights' readings at the Society Library. I met with the same success as before, but my strength was overtaxed. The continued coldness of some of my dearest friends preyed upon my mind, and threw me into a state of morbid nervous excitement. I was attacked with fever and hemorrhages of the lungs. For several months I was considered by my physician, Dr. C———g, in a state which rendered recovery very improbable. . . .

CHAPTER V

THE illness which I mentioned in the preceding chapter was of long duration. As a faithful historian, fulfilling a trust, I cannot omit the narration of events which were produced by that illness. But I allude to them with reluctance—a reluctance which has perhaps no reasonable foundation.

Dr. C———g, of New York, was called in to attend me. He considered my state dangerous. On the occasion of his first visit, after numerous inquiries in regard to my symptoms, he turned to Mr. Mowatt, and said, "If she is susceptible to mesmerism, I think she can be relieved more readily than by any medicine that I could administer."*

Mr. Mowatt had not any knowledge of mesmerism, nor had I. We had never seen a mesmeric subject—never heard a case fully described. He strongly objected to my being made the subject of an experiment. An argument ensued which I did not hear. It ended in Dr. C———g's assurance that I might be greatly benefited by mesmeric treatment, but could not be injured. Mr. Mowatt finally assented to the doctor's proposition. I was suffering too much to express an opinion, or even to have one.

When Dr. C———g first proposed to mesmerize me, I was reclining in an arm chair. The doctor now placed himself in front of me. I remember his making what are called "passes" before my eyes. Very soon my head grew slightly dizzy—the room seemed filled with a dim haziness—the objects began to dance and float, and then to disappear. I recollect nothing further.

I was afterwards told that in less than twenty minutes I fell into a very deep sleep, from which I suddenly emerged into a state of somnambulic consciousness. A similar deep sleep, I am assured, always subsequently preceded my state of mesmeric somnambulism. It was the drawbridge separating the waking from the "sleepwalking" state, over which I had inevitably to pass. Even when I had become so sensitive to the mesmeric influence that I could be put by it into the somnambulic state in less than a quarter of a minute, I am told there would be, to outward appearance, an absolute insensibility and suspension of all consciousness for an interval of several seconds, during which, if standing at the time, I would fall to the ground, unless supported. On entering the somnambulic state, thus induced by mesmerism, I am further informed I would be entirely unconscious of the presence of other parties than the magnetizer, until they were *put in communication* with me by him; and that often I was subjected to much pain, and even thrown into convulsive shudderings, by being inconsiderately touched by persons not in communication.

It should be stated that, from childhood, I had been occasionally addicted to natural somnambulism, and had repeatedly been known

*Now generally referred to as hypnotism, the procedure took its name from the Austrian physician Franz Anton Mesmer (1734-1815), who developed and publicized it in Paris. Mesmer was widely regarded as a charlatan, however, in part because he associated hypnotism with both electrical treatments and a good deal of mystery. Yet hypnotism survived to become used by physicians and other practitioners with good reputations.

to walk and talk in my sleep. It is said that persons of this habit are especially susceptible of the mesmeric influence.

In regard to my first mesmeric trance, I must rely solely upon the testimony of others as to what transpired during its continuance. I had, and still have, no conscious recollection whatever in regard to its experiences. I can only repeat what I was told by those whose good faith and accuracy I cannot distrust.

On being awakened from the state of somnambulism, I felt very much relieved and refreshed. The fever from which I had been suffering had nearly left me, and my head, which had ached incessantly for three days, was free from pain. I had slept between two and three hours. . . .

It would seem, from this common and undeniable phenomenon, as if there were an inner consciousness occupying a higher plane than the external, and commanding a more extensive prospect—a consciousness undeveloped in most minds except by *flashes*, and retiring within itself before the external can distinctly realize its presence.

How shall we account for the thick veil of separation, dropped at once by the cessation of somnambulism (whether independent or induced by mesmerism) between the normal and abnormal—the external and internal consciousness? An analogy drawn from intoxication or insanity is not precisely applicable here; for, under somnambulism, one may be as calm and rational, and as completely in possession of all his faculties, as ever in his waking state; nay, those faculties may be considerably quickened and exalted. And yet a wave of the mesmerizer's hand will bring the subject back from the higher to the lower every-day consciousness, where all that he has been saying and doing in his somnambulic state is an utter blank! Another wave of the hand,—or an access of natural somnambulism, entirely independent of mesmerism,—and lo! all the knowledge of the former state is restored, as if a curtain had been lifted. . . .

CHAPTER VI

AUTUMN did not find me sufficiently reestablished in health to resume my public readings, as was proposed. This was a heavy disappointment, but I was well enough for less fatiguing occupation. So little had been saved from the wreck of our fortune that there was strong need for exertion. I wrote a series of lively articles under the *nom de plume* of "Helen Berkley." They were published in various popular magazines, and I was well remunerated. These articles consisted of sketches of celebrated persons with whom I had been brought into communication, and humorous stories, generally founded on fact. The larger portion of them have since appeared in London magazines. Several were translated into German, and reprinted. Under my own name I at that time published nothing but verse.

I had half determined to attempt a tale of some length, and was pondering upon the subject, when a friend informed me that the New World newspaper had offered one hundred dollars for the best original novel in one volume. The title must be the Fortune Hunter and the scene laid in New York. The novel must be completed in a month, or within six weeks at the latest.

"Why do you not try what you can do?" said my friend. "Write a story in your Mrs. Berkley style—you can easily make the title apply. Ten to one your novel will be the one accepted."

Thus encouraged, I lost no time, and that very day made the sketch of a plot, which I submitted to my counsellor and friend. He approved, and I went to work diligently. At the time appointed, the book was completed. It was presented to the New World publishers, and the note for one hundred dollars sent me in return, was the most agreeable evidence of its acceptance. The Fortune Hunter had an extensive sale, and, after my identity with Mrs. Berkley became known, the publishers chose to affix my name to the work. The copyright being theirs, my consent was not even asked.

I was very much amused by an article that appeared in one of the papers accusing me of being an *imitator* of Mrs. Berkley, and more than hinting that the imitation fell far short of the original.

The Fortune Hunter has lately been translated into German.

I continued to write for various magazines—the Columbian, Democratic Review, Ladies' Companion, Godey's, Graham's, &c. I used fictitious names, and sometimes supplied the same number of a magazine with several articles, only one of which was supposed to be my own. I also prepared for the press a number of works, the copyrights of which were purchased by Messrs. Burgess & Stringer. They were principally compilations, with as much or as little original matter as was found necessary—book cement, to make the odd fragments adhere together. The subjects of these books were not of my own choosing—I wrote to order, for profit, and to supply the demands of the public. In this manner were produced Housekeeping made Easy, (the name of Mrs. Ellis was not affixed by me), Book of the Toilette, Cookery for the Sick, Book of Embroidery, Knitting, Netting, and

Crochet, Etiquette for Ladies, Ball-room Etiquette, Etiquette of Matrimony, and similar publications, the very names of which I cannot now remember.

The remark of a seamstress, who was sewing for our opposite neighbors, was repeated to a domestic of mine. "If Mrs. Mowatt is fond of children, and cares any thing about poor people," said the seamstress, "I wish somebody would tell her of the Greys, an English family, who are living in Harlem. They are people that have seen better days; but the father is blind. There are several children,—one of them a sweet little girl, a much finer child than that Esther,—and they are actually starving." . . .

[The "Esther" referred to was a poor girl whom Mrs. Mowatt had taken in, fed, and clothed because, herself childless, she "loved the presence of childhood about the house." Esther's duties were to run errands. When the girl's father took her away, Mrs. Mowatt became interested in bringing another such child into her home. After searching through Harlem, a section of New York then largely rural, she entered a shanty where she had been told the Grey family was living.]

I entered a room where poverty had undisputed reign. The floor was bare—scarcely an article of furniture was to be seen. In the centre of the room stood a small stove; but the fire had quite died out, though it was a piercingly cold day. In front of the stove lay a little boy, half naked and shivering with the cold. Upon a small wooden box sat a baby, strapped by its waist to the back of a chair. Beside them, so close to the stove that his clothes must have burned had there been any fire within, sat their father.

"Can you tell me if Mr. Grey lives here?" I asked, on entering.

The man rose with a kind of dignity that I did not look for in so rude a place, and bowing, answered, "My name is Grey."

He advanced to find me a chair, but with uncertain steps, and one hand extended as though feeling his way. By his movement only could one have divined that he was blind. His eyes were large, of a clear, light blue, and did not seem to me wholly expressionless. He was tall, well made, and handsome, in spite of the traces of suffering upon his countenance. I could not but notice the courtesy of his manner as he bowed on offering me the seat. I entered into conversation with him— his language was not that of an uneducated man. I drew from him his history, though he was evidently inclined to be reserved. He had been cheated by his partner while conducting a prosperous business, either in England or Ireland, I forget which. The partner had absconded, and Mr. Grey, totally ruined, had brought his family to America, in the hope of almost "digging gold in the streets." Shortly after his arrival in New York, his eyes began to trouble him, and soon became so blind that he could barely distinguish light from darkness. His wife had tried to get work; sometimes she obtained a little sewing, sometimes a little washing, but often she could get no employment at all. They had no friend but Mr. G———n, who had known them "in the old country." He had been very kind, but he had a family of his own. Had he not helped them, they must have starved. I inquired for Mr. Grey's wife. She was out, and his little daughter Margaret was also absent. He hoped they would "bring back something to make the *fire burn*— this winter weather was so hard upon the little boys." I looked upon the baby faces turned wonderingly to mine—they were blue with cold.

I could not ask whether his wife was gathering chips for the fire, or whether she was endeavoring to obtain money to purchase fuel; there was something about the bearing of the man that would have made any one guarded in running the risk of wounding his feelings. I told him that, if I liked his little girl, I might take her to live with me; then gave him my address, and expressed a desire that his wife would call the next day with the child. . . .

The next morning brought Mrs. Grey and her little daughter. The former did not impress me so favorably as her husband, but the sweet face of the child, with its large, blue, frightened eyes, won spontaneous interest. She was nine years old, but small for her age, and thin almost to emaciation. Her fair hair fell in disordered masses to her waist. Her features were pinched and sharp, and she had that look of quiet suffering which it is so painful to behold in the countenance of childhood.

The mother joyfully consented to leave little Margaret with me. It was arranged that the family should remove from Harlem to New York to more comfortable apartments. The influence of my friends could readily procure for her work or needful assistance. . . .

[The Mowatts next took a second Grey child, a boy, into their home, and then took in the youngest.]

I used to send Margaret on a weekly visit of inquiry after the youngest child. One day she returned, sobbing so loudly that I heard her before she entered the room where I was sitting. "My little brother! little Willie! poor little Willie!" was all that she could say.

At first I thought the child was dead, and reproached myself for having bestowed so little care upon him. As soon as Margaret could speak, she told me that he had been ill with the measles, and was just recovering; but the people where he was staying said they could be burdened with him no longer. They had arranged to send him that very day to the Orphan Asylum.

The weeping child ended her tale with "Don't let him go! let me bring him here! Only let me bring him here for a little while!"

Her grief was so persuasive that I could not resist her entreaties. An hour after, she came into the room again, staggering under the weight of the little boy in her arms—but this time her face was covered with smiles.

Willie was about two years old, an apple dumpling-shaped, rosy-cheeked little boy, who could just toddle about and prattle in an unintelligible language. I had no intention of keeping him—no fixed intention towards the children at all. They were quiet, manageable, and winning. Mr. Mowatt took a ready interest in them. They grew into his affections as rapidly as into mine. They were my pupils; and if they added much to my cares, they contributed as largely to my joys. Little by little they became an acknowledged part of our small household. At first we anticipated finding some person or persons who would like to adopt the two boys. No such party sprang up, and the idea was tacitly abandoned—or rather, it was gradually forgotten. . . .

CHAPTER VII

"WHY do you not write a play?" said E. S——— to me one morning. "You have more decided talent for the stage than for any thing else. If we can get it accepted by the Park Theatre, and if it should succeed, you have a new and wide field of exertion opened to you—one in which success is very rare, but for which your turn of mind has particularly fitted you."*

"What shall I attempt, comedy or tragedy?"

"Comedy, decidedly; because you can only write what you feel, and you are 'nothing if not critical'—besides, you will have a fresh

*The E. S——— to whom Mowatt refers was the New York writer, critic, and dramatist Epes Sargent, who encouraged her work, helped to further her career, and remained her lifelong friend.

channel for the sarcastic ebullitions with which you so constantly indulge us."

It was true that at that period of my life a vein of sarcasm, developed by the trials through which I had passed, pervaded all my thoughts, and betrayed itself in much that I wrote as well as in conversation. E. S———'s suggestion appeared to me good, and I commenced Fashion. If it is a satire on American *parvenuism*, it was intended to be a good-humored one. No charge can be more untrue than that with which I have been taxed through the press and in private—the accusation of having held up to ridicule well-known personages. . . .

There were no attempts in Fashion at fine writing. I designed the play wholly as an *acting* comedy. A *dramatic*, not a literary, success was what I desired to achieve. Caution suggested my not aiming at both at once.

Fashion was offered to the Park Theatre. In the usual course of events, its fate would have been to gather dust amongst an ever-increasing pile of manuscripts on Mr. Simpson's table—heaps of rejected plays, heaps of plays, the merits of which were never even investigated. It generally takes several months to induce a manager to read a new play—several months more before he consents to its production. Making an exception to prove this rule, Mr. Simpson read Fashion at once. He liked it, and handed the manuscript to his stage manager, Mr. Barry, who also approved, and pronounced that the play would make a hit.

A few days more, and I received official information that Fashion was accepted by the Park Theatre—that it would be produced without delay, and in a style of great magnificence—also, that I would receive an author's benefit on the third night, and a certain per centage of the nightly receipts of the theatre for every performance of the play after it had run a stipulated number of nights. . . .

. . . Fashion was produced. With an anxious heart I took my seat in the same private box from which I had overlooked the gloomy rehearsal on the day previous. What a different aspect every thing wore! The theatre flooded with light, the gay decorations, the finely-painted drop curtain, the boxes filled with beautiful women, the dense crowd in the pit and galleries, the inspiring music,—all seemed the effect of some Scottish *glamour* rather than a reality.

The music ceased. The gentleman who was to personate the *Count* in the comedy appeared before the curtain and delivered a prologue, written by Epes Sargent. It was a capital prologue—one calculated to put an audience in good humor; and thus it took the first gigantic step towards insuring the success of the play.

Fashion was played nightly to full houses for three weeks, and only withdrawn to make room for "stars" who were engaged before its production. . . .

We were accompanied to the theatre by Mr. and Mrs. Mason—the charming Emma Wheatly of Park Theatre memory. Our box was furnished with white satin bills, printed in letters of gold. At the close of the play the actors were all called before the curtain. Then rose shouts for the author. The audience had become aware that she was in the theatre. If I had reflected on the subject, I should have expected this summons; as it was, I chanced to be wholly unprepared, and the unlooked-for demonstration affected me unpleasantly. Our party were seated in the first tier, and exposed to the full gaze of the audience, who now turned themselves *en masse* towards us. The shouts continued, and Mr. Mowatt and Mr. Mason entreated me to rise and courtesy. I could not muster courage, and felt much more inclined to make a cowardly escape. The audience grew more vociferous at the delay.

"There is no use of refusing; you will be obliged to rise," whispered Mrs. Mason.

I saw she was right, and answered, "I will, if you rise also and courtesy with me."

She objected at first, but finding that I would not move, and that the shouts were only redoubled, she amiably consented. We rose together, and were greeted with prolonged cheering. I courtesied several times, she did the same. This ceremony over, we took our departure as rapidly as possible. I little thought that, in less than two months, I should courtesy to an audience from the stage of that very theatre. . . .

I had played plays before I ever entered a theatre. I had written plays from the time that I first witnessed a performance. My love for the drama was genuine, for it was developed at a period when the theatre was an unknown place, and actors a species of mythical creatures. I determined to fulfil the destiny which seemed visibly pointed out by the unerring finger of Providence in all the circumstances, associations, and vicissitudes of my life, in my intellectual tastes and habits, and the sympathies of my emotional nature. I would become an actress.

Mr. Mowatt's appreciation of the drama was, I think, even

greater than my own. My wishes met with a ready response from him. His only fear was, that I had not physical strength to endure the excitement and fatigue of an arduous vocation. This had to be tested.

The consent of one other person was all I required; it was that of my father. I had not courage personally to communicate my intentions. Mr. Mowatt, in a private interview with him, explained the state of his own affairs, the theatrical propositions I had received, and my resolves, should these resolutions meet with his sanction. After they had conversed for some time I could endure the suspense no longer, and entered the room. My father spoke but two words as I silently put my arms about his neck. They were "Brave girl!" . . .

The instant my projected appearance was announced, I had to encounter a flood of remonstrances from relatives and friends—opposition in every variety of form. But tears, entreaties, threats, supplicating letters could only occasion me much suffering—they could not shake my resolution. . . .

CHAPTER VIII

WE made the tour of the United States, and met with an uninterrupted series of successes.

Every night not consumed in travelling was engaged at various theatres for a year in advance. In New York we fulfilled a long engagement at Niblo's, but did not appear again at the Park Theatre until spring. In that first year I acted *two hundred nights.*

When I made my *début* I was only prepared in one part; yet, before the close of the year, I had enacted all the most popular characters in juvenile comedy and tragedy. From this fact some estimate may be formed of the amount of study requisite. Often after a protracted rehearsal in the morning, and an arduous performance at night, I returned home from the theatre wearied out in mind and body; yet I dared not rest. The character to be represented on the succeeding night still required several hours of reflection and application. Sometimes I kept myself awake by bathing my heavy eyes and throbbing temples with iced water as I committed the words to memory. Sometimes I could only battle with the angel who

"Knits up the ravelled sleeve of care"

by rapidly pacing the room while I studied. Now and then I was fairly conquered, and fell asleep over my books.

Strange to say, my health, instead of failing entirely, as was predicted, visibly improved. The deleterious effects of late hours were counteracted by constant exercise, an animating, exhilarating pursuit, and the all-potent *nepenthe* of inner peace. I gained new vigor and elasticity. With the additional burden came the added strength whereby it could be borne.

As may be readily imagined, I was often weary to exhaustion, even during the performance. On one occasion my fatigue very nearly placed me in a predicament as awkward to me as it would have been amusing to the audience. We were fulfilling a long engagement at Niblo's. I was playing Lady Teazle in the School for Scandal. When Lady Teazle, at the announcement of Sir Peter, is concealed behind the screen in Joseph Surface's library, she is compelled to remain a quarter of an hour, or perhaps twenty minutes, in this confinement. I was dreadfully fatigued, and glad of the opportunity to rest. There was no chair. At first I knelt for relief. Becoming tired of that position, I quietly laid myself down, and, regardless of Lady Teazle's ostrich plumes, made a pillow of my arms for my head. I listened to Placide's most humorous personation of Sir Peter for a while; but gradually his voice grew more and more indistinct, melting into a soothing murmur, and then was heard no more. I fell into a profound sleep. When Charles Surface is announced, Sir Peter is hurried by Joseph into the closet. Lady Teazle (according to Sheridan) peeps from behind the screen, and intimates to Joseph the propriety of locking Sir Peter in, and proposes her own escape. At the sound of Charles Surfaces's step, she steals behind the screen again. The cue was given, but no Lady Teazle made her appearance. She was slumbering in happy unconsciousness that theatres were ever instituted.

Mr. Jones, the prompter, supposing that I had forgotten my part, ran to one of the wings from which he could obtain a view behind the screen. To his mingled diversion and consternation, he beheld Lady Teazle placidly sleeping upon the floor. Of course, he could not reach her. I have often heard him relate the frantic manner in which he shouted, in an imploring stage whisper, "Mrs. Mowatt wake up! For goodness' sake, wake up! Charles Surface is just going to pull the screen down! Wake up! You'll be caught by the audience asleep! Wake up! Good gracious, do wake up!"

I have some confused recollection of hearing the words "wake up! wake up!" As I opened my heavy eyes, they fell upon Mr. Jones, making the most violent gesticulations, waving about his prompt book, and almost dancing in the excitement of his alarm. The hand of Charles Surface was already on the screen. I sprang to my feet, hardly remembering where I was, and had barely time to smooth down my train when the screen fell. A moment sooner, and how would the slumbering Lady Teazle, suddenly awakened, have contrived to impress the audience with the sense of her deep contrition for her imprudence! how persuaded her husband that she had discovered her injustice to him during her pleasant nap! . . .

CHAPTER IX

[After touring the United States for two years as the leading actress in Fashion, *in* Armand, *the second of her plays to be staged, and in other presentations, Mrs. Mowatt and her husband decided to attempt the London stage. After a stormy voyage to England and a brief engagement in Manchester, Mrs. Mowatt opened in London in the popular drama* The Hunchback *in early 1848, and appeared to good audiences and generally favorable reviews in several other plays that spring.]*

. . . When the season was at its height, Armand was placed in rehearsal. It had first been perused and canvassed by four distinguished London critics. They were authors themselves, and three of them dramatic authors. The play was revised by one of their number; or rather, it was marked abundantly for revision. A speech was pointed out which bears strong resemblance to a passage in Byron's Sardanapalus. The imitation was an unintentional one. I proposed expunging the lines entirely, but was overruled by the judgment of my critics. I next attempted to alter them; but the amendment was not approved. They finally decided that the passage should stand undefended as it was originally written.

The play was put upon the stage after many laborious rehearsals. The scenery and stage appointments were all of the most costly character. The "cast" was unexceptionable. All the actors lent their hearty cooperation. The play could only fail through its own intrinsic want of merit.

I pass over the days of nervous unrest, of feverish anxiety, during its preparation. For an American, and a woman, to aim at double distinctions, as actress and dramatist, before a London tribunal, was, *to say the least*, a bold experiment. . . .

Armand was produced at the Theatre Royal, Marylebone, January 18, 1849. The theatre was crammed from pit to dome. The faces of well-known London literati were conspicuously scattered about the house. As soon as the curtain rose, this intelligence was brought to my dressing room. But for the note of Mr. Fox, I should probably have had another attack of "stage fright," and, by that fatal panic, insured the failure of the play. To be told from such a source that I had *"deserved success,"* sustained and inspired me.

At the close of the second act, the actors, who had assembled in a body around the wings to witness the representation, assured me that "the play was safe; the audience were in such a capital humor, and so *attentive."* To rivet the attention of an audience is always a gigantic step towards success. . . .

With what a thrill of delight I watched the green curtain fall upon the fifth act! After I once began to feel my full responsibilities as an artist, the nightly descent of this welcome green curtain became one of the ecstatic moments of my existence. . . .

Armand was enacted twenty-one nights. The title of the play in America had been Armand, or the Child of the People. This second title could not obtain a license in London, and was changed to the Peer and the Peasant. Various passages, which had been pronounced upon the stage in New York and Boston, were expunged by the English licenser, on account of their anti-monarchical tendency. They were necessarily omitted in London. Some of them were afterwards restored before a Dublin audience, and met with a most uproarious response. Armand was published in London immediately after its first representation. The copies nightly sold at the door of the theatre caused great annoyance to the dramatic representatives of the play. It is a singular fact, that if the eye of an actor chance to rest upon an individual in the boxes who is deeply absorbed in a book, and if the actor fancy that book is of the play then performing, he will almost invariably forget his part, though he may have enacted it correctly dozens of times. Sometimes the mere leaf-turning of books in the hands of the audience will throw a whole company into confusion, and the prompter's voice may be heard vainly attempting to plead the cause of the author.

As soon as I discovered this professional peculiarity, I endeavored to stop the sale of Armand, but unsuccessfully, as the English copyright had been sold.

Armand was reproduced before the close of the season, and I was offered a benefit, the proceeds of which were to be devoted to the purchase of a silver vase in commemoration of the London success of the American production. Every seat was engaged long before the appointed night. The largest amount that the theatre would hold when densely crowded being ascertained, the vase was purchased in advance. The presentation took place on the night of the benefit, and greatly added to the *éclat* of the occasion.

[While in London Mr. Mowatt again fell seriously ill; following medical advice, he journeyed to the West Indies in hopes that the warm climate would help him recover. Mrs. Mowatt remained behind. The theatrical season had begun and she had engagements to fulfill—and they needed money. Her play, Fashion, *was staged in December 1850 to generally good reviews by the critics. Mr. Mowatt returned to England, still gravely ill.]*

CHAPTER X

AFTER four months' sojourn in Malvern we returned to London. Towards the close of our stay Mr. Mowatt had grown rapidly worse. He almost entirely lost the use of his limbs. The strong arms of a friend were needed to bear him from his sofa to the carriage. All his energies, physical and mental, appeared suddenly to fail. Night brought to his sufferings no oblivious balm, morning no invigorating relief.

At this crisis, the entreaties of friends induced us to call in the celebrated Dr. D———n, the discoverer and promulgator of the chrono-thermal practice of medicine. We were already personally acquainted with him and his lovely wife—and were familiar with certain of his cures, which almost deserve the name of marvellous. With his coming departing hope dawned anew, and once more painted the bow of promise upon our future. His skill procured the sufferer almost instantaneous relief—arresting the disease which was beyond mortal cure.

The invalid was now confined entirely to his bed, but the spirit of pain had been exorcised. A holy calm diffused itself about that death bed, as though the breathings of good angels enveloped it with a heavenly aura. The veil of eternity was falling around it—not in funereal blackness that speaks of annihilation, but in the golden and purple folds of promise, descending from the "new heavens." To him who lay upon that couch, in purified patience of spirit, Death was a smiling angel of invitation, throwing open the crystal portals of the future, and joyfully beckoning the new guest into mansions of more perfect life—a life of holier uses—more ineffable joys—more conscious individuality—more angelic progression. Very often, with placid brow and in serene tones, he spoke of the coming change. His faith was so full of living, quickening *certainty*, that it rebuked the tears whose rebellious fall would have profaned such a death bed. He had not dwelt in the suburbs of the Holy City, but entered into its innermost temple. The doctrines of the New Church had not been received into his *memory* merely, but had come forth into his daily *life*, and been inscribed upon his heart. A never-wavering trust had cast out fear, and given to the foot of the Summoner the sound of music. . . .

My long illness had commenced in the spring—winter was approaching. As soon as my perfect restoration became known, I had numerous offers for theatrical engagements. Then, for the first time, Mr. Mowatt disclosed to me that by far the larger portion of all we possessed, the hard earnings of a long period of exertion, had, for business purposes, been left in the hands of the manager of the Olympic Theatre.

In his ruin it had been swept away. It became needful that I should resume my labors the instant I felt able. I pass over what this intelligence was to me. Life in all its bitter necessities—its hard requirements—had brought no extremity that tried me as did this.

My most advantageous offers were in the provinces. I must leave my vigils beside a couch which I still believed might be the bed of death, to wear the mockery of glittering robes in the frigid atmosphere of a theatre.

I sought a private interview with Dr. D———n, and entreated him to disclose to me his patient's true condition. The doctor's reluctance to comply with my request was almost answer sufficient. I told him frankly our exact situation, and implored him not to conceal from me the truth. I shall never forget or cease to be grateful for the feeling which he exhibited. His answer was, "I have seen so many wonders effected by a proper medical treatment, that I am never inclined to say that a recovery is *impossible*. In the case of Mr. Mowatt, I fear that it is improbable. No one can decide how long he may live. It may be a few months, and it may be much longer."

"Might the time be even shorter?"

"It *might* be; but he appears so much better that I do not anticipate any immediate danger."

"And what must I do?"

"Any thing rather than excite him by opposition, if you would not produce fatal consequences."

"Do you mean to say that I must leave London and fulfil some of these engagements? for the most advantageous one, the one he entreats me to accept, is in Dublin."

"Yes; if he is bent upon it, you must go."

I dreaded nothing so much as beholding "cares for the morrow" reenter, with disturbing influence, the now peaceful mind of one whose morrows on earth were numbered. Without further hesitation, I told him I would go. Richly did his reply reward the struggle for self-government which enabled me to make the decision.

The Dublin engagement was accepted for January. I was to remain absent but three weeks, and then hasten back to London. . . .

The moment of parting came. The suffering one left behind retained his smiling composure to the end. For me, I might well be thankful that his last words were a blessing; for I never heard the sound of his voice again. . . .

CHAPTER XI

OUR first care was to send to the theatre for letters. There was one from the invalid at home, dated Thursday morning and Thursday night. It was written in the same placid and hopeful strain as all the others which had cheered me during my absence. I noticed but one difference; the writing was singularly uneven, and on some lines there were but two words, as though they were traced by one who did not see, but only guessed at the space. This had, doubtless, been the case. Nothing in the tone of the letter betrayed a feebler state of body than usual.

On Saturday there was no letter. It was the first day since I left London that had brought no tones from the voice at a distance. Anxious pulses began to beat. Their throbbing was painfully quickened when Sunday came and went and brought no news. Monday morning I sent to the post office. The mail had not yet arrived—it was very late that day; and we learned that the mail due on the day previous had missed altogether. This accounted for my having no letters. I should certainly have two that day.

With renewed hope I went to my first rehearsal in that strange, cold, vast theatre—one of the largest in England. Mrs. Renshaw accompanied me. As we were passing the box office, on our way behind the scenes, the doorkeeper, seeing strange faces, inquired, "Is that Mrs. Mowatt?" On receiving my answer, he replied, "I have a great pile of letters for you, ma'am; there are several back mails this morning." and placed a large package of epistles in my eagerly-extended hands.

Very hurriedly I glanced over them to select the well-known writing. It was not there. Again I looked through the gathering mists that clouded my sight; there were many familiar hands, but one was missing. A note, in Mr. Davenport's writing, attracted my attention; that must give me information. I broke it open, and turned to the last lines before I had courage to glance at the first. They reassured me— the letter was dated Friday, and had probably been posted too late for that day's mail. He was paying Mr. Mowatt a visit, and wrote in his stead. The latter seemed somewhat weaker than usual, too weak to manage a pen—and, besides, he appeared inclined to sleep.

As I looked up from the letter, I perceived that the manager, Mr. Davis, was waiting to address me. Several of the company had assembled without my noticing them, and were scanning the stranger with inquisitive eyes. After exchanging a few words with Mr. Davis, whom I had seen but twice before, I inquired if I were delaying rehearsal.

"It is past the hour," he replied, "and every body is here; but if you wish to read your letters————" I interrupted him with, "I have read the only important one, and will not detain you."

He was leading the way to the stage, and I following. The package of letters seemed to burn my hands, and I glanced over them again. My eye caught sight of another note in Mr. Davenport's writing, and above the address the startling word, "immediate." I paused, too much alarmed to apologize to my conductor, and hastily tore open the letter. It was dated Saturday, and, after a gentle preparation, intimated that he feared Mr. Mowatt was worse. Mr. D———, with other friends, had passed the day at his bedside—he did not appear to suffer, but was very feeble. There was a P.S., dated 4 o'clock, stating that no change had taken place up to that hour. The writer's duties at the theatre, he said, would force him to leave at six.

I was folding the letter as composedly as I could, when I noticed a third letter in the same hand; and upon that, too, was the terrible word, "immediate." I opened it—the date was Sunday morning. It was strange that I should have opened them accidentally in the order of their dates. The first lines were all I read—they had told me the worst. The voice of consoling angels whispered, "God is not the God of the dead, but of the living; for all live unto him!"

I hardly know what took place; but I remember the gentle ministerings of the considerate manager and of my weeping attendant. As soon as I was able, we returned to our lodgings. . . .

We arrived in London late in the evening, after a journey the sadness of which I need not describe. For the next few weeks I took up my residence with friends now doubly endeared. . . .

I passed six weeks at the residences of various friends, and then prepared to resume my profession. Compliance with Mr. Mowatt's last wishes compelled me to remain in England until summer commenced. London was now full of distressing associations; I therefore made engagements for a tour in the provinces, to occupy the months which must pass before I could return to my own country, my own family. I travelled from city to city, accompanied only by Mrs. Renshaw, remaining a few weeks in each town, and acting every night; if that could be called *acting* which was but a soulless imitation of my former stage imbodiments. I could only coldly copy what I had done spontaneously in more inspired moments. I lost, for the time being, all power of original personation. . . .

During my engagement in Liverpool I was joined by Mr. S——h, a valued brother-in-law, who had just arrived from America. I passed a few weeks in London, bidding adieu to cherished friends, and, under my brother-in-law's protection, set sail for America, accompanied by Mrs. Renshaw. We embarked on the 9th July, 1851, in the steamship Pacific, commanded by Captain Nye. . . .

CHAPTER XII

TWO thirds of those memoirs have been penned in the quiet little chamber I have described—penned during intervals from suffering and a period of slow convalescence.

When I fully recover my health, (as the distinguished physician mentioned above, who has expended his skill upon me for nearly five months, is confident I shall do), I purpose taking a brief farewell of my profession in some of the principal cities of the Union. I desire to leave that profession as calmly and as deliberately as it was entered; for I shall bid it adieu with those objects, imperiously summoned by which I first bore the name of actress, happily accomplished. . . .

I have been for eight years an actress. In the exercise of my vocation I have visited many theatres throughout this land and in Great Britain. This fact, perhaps, gives me some right to speak upon the stage as an institution; upon its uses and abuses; for I speak (in all humility be it said) from actual knowledge and personal experience. My testimony has, at least, the value of being disinterested; for I was not bred to the stage; I entered upon it from the bosom of private life;

none who are linked to me by affinity of blood ever belonged to the profession; I am about to leave it of my own choice; and I bid it farewell in the midst of a career which, if it has reached its meridian, has not, as yet, taken the first downward inclination. I can have no object in defending the drama apart from the impulse to utter what I believe to be truth and an innate love and reverence for dramatic art. . . .

In the sacred Scriptures there is not a single passage which, by any fair inference, can be distorted into a condemnation of theatrical entertainments. And yet how many sincere and truth-loving Christians believe it to be their duty to raise a hue and cry against the stage! . . .

The parables are truths enveloped in fiction. The drama merely represents in action what the parable and similar fictions inculcate by written or oral teaching. The play is but the dramatized form of the poem, the novel, history, or the parable. And the mind is more vividly impressed by what it sees enacted than by what it hears related.

Take, for instance, the parable of the prodigal son. There can be no one so obtuse as not to admit the force and beauty of the illustration intended to be conveyed in it. Suppose that some dramatist, to enforce the lesson of paternal forgiveness upon minds which can be more deeply penetrated by visible symbols than by lecture, throws the parable into dramatic form, bringing out in appropriate language the whole moral of the story, and has it represented in a theatre. *Does the mere translation of the parable into represented action render it pernicious?* In this illustration we have the whole principle of the drama. . . .

Art is either right or it is wrong. The sanctioning voices of ages have pronounced it to be right. One branch of art includes the drama. Shall this branch be lopped off because the canker worm of evil has entered some of its fruit? Like sculpture, like painting, like music, like history, like the poem, the novel,—like every thing that ministers to faculties, which distinguish us from the brute creation,—the drama is either an instrument of good or evil, as it is rendered the one or the other by the use or abuse. This is the veriest truism. The theatre, like the press, is one of the most powerful organs for the diffusion of salutary or pernicious influences. Vicious books are often printed; but shall we, therefore, extirpate the press? Plays of questionable morality are sometimes enacted; but is that a cause for abolishing the stage—sacrificing for a temporary abuse the great and permanent use? . . .

But there has lately been a marked improvement in the class of plays offered to the public. That manager would be a bold one, who, at the Howard Athenaeum, in Boston, or at Niblo's in New York, would produce a play of decided immoral tendency. His theatre would soon be closed, even without any loud denunciations from its outraged supporters. The community would forsake the establishment, and leave the "beggarly account of empty boxes" to proclaim their disapproval. Numerous other theatres in this country, as in England, are becoming more and more cautious in the choice of plays to be enacted within their walls. In England, the voice of the licenser is a check upon the representation of immoral dramas; in this country, the voice of the people is a far more powerful organ than that of any royal licenser in exerting a similar control.

Passages, even in Shakspeare, which were listened to by audiences a few years ago without manifestations of displeasure, are now entirely omitted by actors, and, if spoken, would inevitably be hissed. I do not mean to assert that there are not passages left which ought to be expunged; but I believe that, in time, they will not be tolerated; and I know that it is the fault, not of the actor, but of the audience, if their ears are ever offended. The actor is supposed to speak only what is set down for him; and, according to the strict regulations of some theatres, he would be heavily fined if he deviated, upon his own responsibility, from the text. . . .

If I have somewhat warmly pleaded the cause of the stage and the actor, I hope my testimony has been given as though I stood in the courts of Areopagus, where no flowers of rhetoric were permitted to adorn and falsely color the pleader's simple statement. I have looked upon the citation of facts as my strongest arguments. These, I think, will be patiently heard and justly weighed by the impartial tribunal of the American public, before which I stand to add my feeble voice to those already raised against the wrongs received by the stage, the drama, and the profession.

To the members of that profession, whose labors and honors I shall so soon cease to share, I would say, in bidding them farewell, that there are many amongst them whom I esteem, some to whom I am warmly attached, and more whose career I shall watch with anxious interest. I would beg them to believe that I sympathize in their toils— I comprehend their sacrifices—I appreciate their exertions—I respect their virtues; and I cherish the hope, that, in ceasing to be ranked amongst their number, I shall not wholly be forgotten by them. . . .

Elizabeth Cady Stanton (1815-1902)

BORN in Johnstown, New York, in 1815, Elizabeth Cady Stanton was the fourth of six children of Daniel and Margaret Cady, of Scottish Presbyterian ancestry. She was both energetic and bright, and at the age of eleven her determination to achieve received special impetus when her only brother, a college student, died. She sought to fill his place through study and attention to the work of her father, a prominent lawyer and judge. Through her father, and at a girls' school in nearby Troy which had been opened by Emma Willard, the pioneer in education for women, she got an excellent education.

So many waves of religious and social reform were sweeping over the part of New York State where the family lived that it was soon called "the burned-over district." While at Emma Willard's school, Stanton was converted (for a time) by the dynamic Charles G. Finney, a famous revivalist preacher. At the home of her mother's cousin, the wealthy abolitionist leader Gerrit Smith, she heard the doctrines of the new militant phase of the antislavery movement being debated, and was present, with her new husband Henry B. Stanton, at the first world antislavery congress in London in 1840.

In Boston she mingled with the social and intellectual leaders of reform, and visited the Utopian community at nearby Brook Farm. In Albany she helped to agitate successfully for legislation to enable married women to inherit property and to hold it in their own names. When she settled in Seneca Falls, New York, she and a few friends, including a visitor, the distinguished Quaker antislavery leader Lucretia Mott, called the meeting in July 1848 which was to originate organized activity on behalf of woman's rights, a cause which from that point became her primary public interest. A few years later she took an active part in publicizing the cause of reform of woman's dress, through the costume created by her cousin Elizabeth Smith and named after their friend and coworker Amelia Bloomer.

Stanton pursued all these activities while she was keeping house and bringing up seven children. Although there was always hired help in her home, her intimate friend Susan B. Anthony, in addition to serving as the organizational genius of the woman's rights movement, often acted as housekeeper to free Stanton for writing manifestos, petitions, speeches, and articles. When the Stanton children were older, both women often took to the road, in more and more distant parts of the nation, to agitate for the adoption of suffrage for women— by then defined as the movement's primary goal. When, after inter-mittent conventions, the movement took formal shape as the National Woman Suffrage Association in 1869, Stanton became its first and only president.

Stanton and Anthony, however, entertained more radical views on marriage, divorce, and labor relations than many others seeking rights for women; the latter formed a more conservative organization, the American Woman Suffrage Association. When the two associa-tions eventually compromised and merged in 1890, Stanton served briefly as president of the united groups and was then succeeded by Anthony.

Despite these activities Stanton remained close to her children, especially her daughter Harriet Stanton Blatch and her son Theodore, each of whom followed her in pursuing the cause of woman's rights. She spent long periods abroad, visiting these two children and their families in England and France.

Stanton published her autobiography in 1898, when she was eighty-three years old, earlier having served as an author of the *History of Woman Suffrage* (vols. 1 and 2, 1881 and 1886), and *The Woman's Bible* (2 vols., 1895 and 1898). In those works, especially the former, the militancy which characterized her leadership of reform is more evident than in the autobiography. She made her home in New Jersey in later years, and died in New York in 1902.

Her autobiography presents her father, Judge Cady, as a figure who influenced her deeply, not only in childhood but in later years. What was the nature of this influence? Did it seem to shape her attitudes toward her husband? Toward other males? Toward her ambition and drive for achievement? What kinds of relationships did she have with other women, especially those who worked with her?

What sort of "self" does Stanton offer her readers? Does she seem to be focusing intensely on an exploration of her own individual identity, or is that identity something to be taken for granted, not demanding analysis? What is the general tone of her writing? Is her style of writing simple and direct, or more complex? How are tone and style related to the "self" she presents? Can one infer anything about her attitudes toward sexual relations or sexual expression from what she says, or does not say? What are her ultimate purposes in telling her life story in the way she tells it?

Eighty Years and More

*Elizabeth Cady Stanton**

I. CHILDHOOD

WITH several generations of vigorous, enterprising ancestors behind me, I commenced the struggle of life under favorable circumstances on the 12th day of November, 1815, the same year that my father, Daniel Cady, a distinguished lawyer and judge in the State of New York, was elected to Congress. Perhaps the excitement of a political campaign, in which my mother took the deepest interest, may have had an influence on my prenatal life and given me the strong desire that I have always felt to participate in the rights and duties of government.

My father was a man of firm character and unimpeachable integrity, and yet sensitive and modest to a painful degree. There were but two places in which he felt at ease—in the courthouse and at his own fireside. Though gentle and tender, he had such a dignified repose and reserve of manner that, as children, we regarded him with fear rather than affection.

My mother, Margaret Livingston, a tall, queenly looking woman, was courageous, self-reliant, and at her ease under all circumstances

*From *Eighty Years and More, (1815-1898) Reminiscences*, London: T. Fisher Unwin, 1898

and in all places. She was the daughter of Colonel James Livingston, who took an active part in the War of the Revolution.

My mother had the military idea of government, but her children, like their grandfather, were disposed to assume the responsibility of their own actions; thus the ancestral traits in mother and children modified, in a measure, the dangerous tendencies in each.

Our parents were as kind, indulgent, and considerate as the Puritan ideas of those days permitted, but fear, rather than love, of God and parents alike, predominated. Add to this our timidity in our intercourse with servants and teachers, our dread of the ever present devil, and the reader will see that, under such conditions, nothing but strong self-will and a good share of hope and mirthfulness could have saved an ordinary child from becoming a mere nullity.

The first event engraved on my memory was the birth of a sister when I was four years old. It was a cold morning in January when the brawny Scotch nurse carried me to see the little stranger, whose advent was a matter of intense interest to me for many weeks after. The large, pleasant room with the white curtains and bright wood fire on the hearth, where panada, catnip, and all kinds of little messes which we were allowed to taste were kept warm, was the center of attraction for the older children. I heard so many friends remark, "What a pity it is she's a girl!" that I felt a kind of compassion for the little baby. True, our family consisted of five girls and only one boy, but I did not understand at that time that girls were considered an inferior order of beings.

To form some idea of my surroundings at this time, imagine a two-story white frame house with a hall through the middle, rooms on either side, and a large back building with grounds on the side and rear, which joined the garden of our good Presbyterian minister, the Rev. Simon Hosack, of whom I shall have more to say in another chapter. Our favorite resorts in the house were the garret and cellar. In the former were barrels of hickory nuts, and, on a long shelf, large cakes of maple sugar and all kinds of dried herbs and sweet flag; spinning wheels, a number of small white cotton bags filled with bundles, marked in ink, "silk," "cotton," "flannel," "calico," etc., as well as ancient masculine and feminine costumes. Here we would crack the nuts, nibble the sharp edges of the maple sugar, chew some favorite herb, play ball with the bags, whirl the old spinning wheels, dress up in our ancestors' clothes, and take a bird's-eye view of the surrounding country from an enticing scuttle hole. This was forbidden ground, but, nevertheless, we often went there on the sly, which only made the little escapades more enjoyable.

The cellar of our house was filled, in winter, with barrels of apples, vegetables, salt meats, cider, butter, pounding barrels, wash-tubs, etc., offering admirable nooks for playing hide and seek. Two tallow candles threw a faint light over the scene on certain occasions. This cellar was on a level with a large kitchen where we played blind man's buff and other games when the day's work was done. These two rooms are the center of many of the merriest memories of my childhood days.

I can recall three colored men, Abraham, Peter, and Jacob, who acted as menservants in our youth. In turn they would sometimes play on the banjo for us to dance, taking real enjoyment in our games. They are all at rest now with "Old Uncle Ned in the place where the good niggers go." Our nurses, Lockey Danford, Polly Bell, Mary Dunn, and Cornelia Nickeloy—peace to their ashes—were the only shadows on the gayety of these winter evenings; for their chief delight was to hurry us off to bed, that they might receive their beaux or make short calls in the neighborhood. My memory of them is mingled with no senti-ment of gratitude or affection. In expressing their opinion of us in after years, they said we were a very troublesome, obstinate, disobedient set of children. I have no doubt we were in constant rebellion against their petty tyranny. Abraham, Peter, and Jacob viewed us in a different light, and I have the most pleasant recollections of their kind services.

Our nursery, a large room over a back building, had three barred windows reaching nearly to the floor. Two of these opened on a gently slanting roof over a veranda. In our night robes, on warm summer evenings we could, by dint of skillful twisting and compressing, get out between the bars, and there, snugly braced against the house, we would sit and enjoy the moon and stars and what sounds might reach us from the streets, while the nurse, gossiping at the back door, imagined we were safely asleep.

About this time we entered the Johnstown Academy, where we made the acquaintance of the daughters of the hotel keeper and the county sheriff. They were a few years my senior, but, as I was ahead of them in all my studies, the difference of age was somewhat equalized and we became fast friends. This acquaintance opened to us two new sources of enjoyment—the freedom of the hotel during "court week" (a great event in village life) and the exploration of the county jail. We made frequent visits to the jail and became deeply concerned about the fate of the prisoners, who were greatly pleased with our expressions of sympathy and our gifts of cake and candy. In time we became interested in the trials and sentences of prisoners, and would go to the courthouse and listen to the proceedings. Sometimes we would slip into the hotel where the judges and lawyers dined, and help our little friend wait on table. To be allowed to carry plates of bread and butter, pie and cheese I counted a high privilege. But more especially I enjoyed listening to the conversations in regard to the probable fate of our friends the prisoners in jail. On one occasion I projected a few remarks into a conversation between two lawyers, when one of them turned abruptly to me and said, "Child, you'd better attend to your business; bring me a glass of water." I replied indignantly, "I am not a servant; I am here for fun."

The winter gala days are associated, in my memory, with hanging up stockings and with turkeys, mince pies, sweet cider, and sleighrides by moonlight. My earliest recollections of those happy days, when schools were closed, books laid aside, and unusual liberties allowed, center in that large cellar kitchen to which I have already referred. There we spent many winter evenings in uninterrupted enjoyment. A large fireplace with huge logs shed warmth and cheerfulness around. In one corner sat Peter sawing his violin, while our youthful neighbors danced with us and played blindman's buff almost every evening during the vacation. The most interesting character in this game was a black boy called Jacob (Peter's lieutenant), who made things lively for us by always keeping one eye open—a wise precaution to guard himself from danger, and to keep us on the jump. Hickory nuts, sweet cider, and *olie-koeks* (a Dutch name for a fried cake with raisins inside) were our refreshments when there came a lull in the fun.

As St. Nicholas was supposed to come down the chimney, our stockings were pinned on a broomstick, laid across two chairs in front of the fireplace. We retired on Christmas Eve with the most pleasing anticipations of what would be in our stockings next morning. The thermometer in that latitude was often twenty degrees below zero, yet, bright and early, we would run downstairs in our bare feet over the cold floors to carry stockings, broom, etc. to the nursery. The gorgeous presents that St. Nicholas now distributes show that he, too, has been growing up with the country. The boys and girls of 1897 will laugh when they hear of the contents of our stockings in 1823. There was a little paper of candy, one of raisins, another of nuts, a red apple, an *olie-koek*, and a bright silver quarter of a dollar in the toe. If a child had been guilty of any erratic performances during the year, which was often my case, a long stick would protrude from the stocking; if particularly good, an illustrated catechism or the New Testament would appear, showing that the St. Nicholas of that time held decided views on discipline and ethics.

During the day we would take a drive over the snowclad hills and valleys in a long red lumber sleigh. All the children it could hold made the forests echo with their songs and laughter. The sleigh bells and Peter's fine tenor voice added to the chorus seemed to chant, as we passed, "Merry Christmas" to the farmers' children and to all we met on the highway.

Our next great fete was on the anniversary of the birthday of our Republic. The festivities were numerous and protracted, beginning then, as now, at midnight with bonfires and cannon; while the day was ushered in with the ringing of bells, tremendous cannonading, and a continuous popping of fire-crackers and torpedoes. Then a procession of soldiers and citizens marched through the town, an oration was delivered, the Declaration of Independence read, and a great dinner given in the open air under the trees in the grounds of the old courthouse. Each toast was announced with the booming of cannon. For all the calamities of the nation I believed King George responsible. At home and at school we were educated to hate the English. When we remember that, every Fourth of July, the Declaration was read with emphasis, and the orator of the day rounded all his glowing periods with denunciations of the mother country, we need not wonder at the national hatred of everything English. Our patriotism in those early days was measured by our dislike of Great Britain.

Other pleasures were, roaming in the forests and sailing on the mill pond. One day, when there were no boys at hand and several girls were impatiently waiting for a sail on a raft, my sister and I volunteered to man the expedition. We always acted on the assumption that what we had seen done, we could do. Accordingly we all jumped on the raft, loosened it from its moorings, and away we went with the current. Navigation on that mill pond was performed with long poles, but, unfortunately, we could not lift the poles, and we soon saw we were drifting toward the dam. But we had the presence of mind to sit down and hold fast to the raft. Fortunately, we went over right side up and gracefully glided down the stream, until rescued by the ever watchful Peter. I did not hear the last of that voyage for a long time. I was called the captain of the expedition, and one of the boys wrote a composition, which he read in school, describing the adventure and emphasizing the ignorance of the laws of navigation shown by the officers in command. I shed tears many times over that performance.

II. SCHOOL DAYS

WHEN I was eleven years old, two events occurred which changed considerably the current of my life. My only brother, who had just graduated from Union College, came home to die. A young man of great talent and promise, he was the pride of my father's heart. We early felt that this son filled a larger place in our father's affections and future plans than the five daughters together. Well do I remember how tenderly he watched my brother in his last illness, the sighs and tears he gave vent to as he slowly walked up and down the hall, and, when the last sad moment came, and we were all assembled to say farewell in the silent chamber of death, how broken were his utterances as he knelt and prayed for comfort and support. I still recall, too, going into the large darkened parlor to see my brother, and finding the casket, mirrors, and pictures all draped in white, and my father seated by his side, pale and immovable. As he took no notice of me, after standing a long while, I climbed upon his knee, when he mechanically put his arm about me and, with my head resting against his beating heart, we both sat in silence, he thinking of the wreck of all his hopes in the loss of a dear son, and I wondering what could be said or done to fill the void in his breast. At length he heaved a deep sigh and said: "Oh, my daughter, I wish you were a boy!" Throwing my arms about his neck, I replied: "I will try to be all my brother was."

Then and there I resolved that I would not give so much time as heretofore to play, but would study and strive to be at the head of all my classes and thus delight my father's heart. All that day and far into the night I pondered the problem of boyhood. I thought that the chief thing to be done in order to equal boys was to be learned and courageous. So I decided to study Greek and learn to manage a horse. Having formed this conclusion I fell asleep. My resolutions, unlike many such made at night, did not vanish with the coming light. I arose early and hastened to put them into execution. They were resolutions never to be forgotten—destined to mold my character anew. As soon as I was dressed I hastened to our good pastor, Rev. Simon Hosack, who was always early at work in his garden.

"Doctor," said I, "which do you like best, boys or girls?"

"Why, girls, to be sure; I would not give you for all the boys in Christendom."

"My father," I replied, "prefers boys; he wishes I was one, and I intend to be as near like one as possible. I am going to ride on horseback and study Greek. Will you give me a Greek lesson now, doctor? I want to begin at once."

"Yes, child," said he, throwing down his hoe, "come into my library and we will begin without delay."

He entered fully into the feeling of suffering and sorrow which took possession of me when I discovered that a girl weighed less in the scale of being than a boy, and he praised my determination to prove the contrary. The old grammar which he had studied in the University of Glasgow was soon in my hands, and the Greek article was learned before breakfast.

Then came the sad pageantry of death, the weeping of friends, the dark rooms, the ghostly stillness, the exhortation to the living to prepare for death, the solemn prayer, the mournful chant, the funeral cortege, the solemn, tolling bell, the burial. How I suffered during those sad days! What strange undefined fears of the unknown took possession of me! For months afterward, at the twilight hour, I went with my father to the new-made grave. Near it stood two tall poplar trees, against one of which I leaned, while my father threw himself on the grave, with outstretched arms, as if to embrace his child. At last the frosts and storms of November came and threw a chilling barrier between the living and the dead, and we went there no more.

During all this time I kept up my lessons at the parsonage and made rapid progress. I surprised even teacher, who thought me capable of doing anything. I learned to drive, and to leap a fence and ditch on horseback. I taxed every power, hoping some day to hear my father say: "Well, a girl is as good as a boy, after all." But he never said it. When the doctor came over to spend the evening with us, I would whisper in his ear: "Tell my father how fast I get on," and he would tell him, and was lavish in his praises. But my father only paced the room, sighed, and showed that he wished I were a boy; and I, not knowing why he felt thus, would hide my tears of vexation on the the doctor's shoulder.

Soon after this I began to study Latin, Greek, and mathematics with a class of boys in the Academy, many of whom were much older than I. For three years one boy kept his place at the head of the class, and I always stood next. Two prizes were offered in Greek. I strove for one and took the second. How well I remember my joy in receiving that prize. There was no sentiment of ambition, rivalry, or triumph over my companions, nor feeling of satisfaction in receiving this honor in the presence of those assembled on the day of the exhibition. One thought alone filled my mind. "Now," said I, "my father will be satisfied with me." So, as soon as we were dismissed, I ran down the hill, rushed breathless into his office, laid the new Greek Testament, which was my prize, on his table and exclaimed: "There, I got it!" He took up the book, asked me some questions about the class, the teachers, the spectators, and, evidently pleased, handed it back to me. Then, while I stood looking and waiting for him to say something which would show that he recognized the equality of the daughter with the son, he kissed me on the forehead and exclaimed, with a sigh, "Ah, you should have been a boy!"

I can truly say, after an experience of seventy years, that all the cares and anxieties, the trials and disappointments of my whole life, are light, when balanced with my sufferings in childhood and youth from the theological dogmas which I sincerely believed, and the gloom connected with everything associated with the name of religion, the church, the parsonage, the graveyard, and the solemn, tolling bell. The church, which was bare, with no furnace to warm us, no organ to gladden our hearts, no choir to lead our songs of praise in harmony, was sadly lacking in all attractions for the youthful mind. The preacher, shut up in an octagonal box high above our heads, gave us sermons over an hour long, and the chorister, in a similar box below him, intoned line after line of David's Psalms, while, like a flock of sheep at the heels of their shepherd, the congregation, without regard to time or tune, straggled after their leader.

To be restless, or to fall asleep under such solemn circumstances was a sure evidence of total depravity, and of the machinations of the devil striving to turn one's heart from God and his ordinances. As I was guilty of these shortcomings and many more, I early believed myself a veritable child of the Evil One, and suffered endless fears lest he should come some night and claim me as his own. To me he was a personal, ever-present reality, crouching a dark corner of the nursery. Ah! how many times I have stolen out of bed, and sat shivering on the stairs, where the hall lamp and the sound of voices from the parlor would, in a measure, mitigate my terror.

As my father's office joined the house, I spent there much of my time, when out of school, listening to the clients stating their cases, talking with the students, and reading the laws in regard to woman. In our Scotch neighborhood many men still retained the old feudal ideas of women and property. Fathers, at their death, would will the bulk of their property to the eldest son, with the proviso that the mother was to have a home with him. Hence it was not unusual for the mother, who had brought all the property into the family, to be made an unhappy dependent on the bounty of an uncongenial daughter-in-law and a dissipated son. The tears and complaints of the women who came to my father for legal advice touched my heart and early drew my attention to the injustice and cruelty of the laws. As the practice of the law was my father's business, I could not exactly understand why he could not alleviate the sufferings of these women. So, in order to enlighten me, he would take down his books and show me the inexorable statutes. The students, observing my interest, would amuse themselves by reading to me all the worst laws they could find, over which I would laugh and cry at turns. One Christmas morning I went into the office to show them, among other of my presents, a new coral necklace and bracelets. They all admired the jewelry and then began to tease me with hypothetical cases of future ownership. "Now," said Henry Bayard, "if in due time you should be my wife, those ornaments would be mine; I could take them and lock them up, and you could never wear them except with my permission. I could even exchange them for a box of cigars, and you could watch them evaporate in smoke."

Until I was sixteen years old, I was a faithful student in Johnstown Academy with a class of boys. Though I was the only girl in the higher classes of mathematics and the languages, yet, in our plays, all the girls and boys mingled freely together. In running races, sliding downhill, and snowballing, we made no distinction of sex. True, the boys would carry the school books and pull the sleighs up hill for their favorite girls, but equality was the general basis of our school relations. I dare say the boys did not make their snowballs quite so hard when pelting the girls, nor wash their faces with the same vehemence as they did each other's, but there was no public evidence of partiality. However, if any boy was too rough or took advantage of a girl smaller than himself, he was promptly thrashed by his fellows. There was an unwritten law and public sentiment in that little Academy world that enabled us to study and play together with the greatest freedom and harmony.

From the academy the boys of my class went to Union College at Schenectady. When those with whom I had studied and contended for prizes for five years came to bid me good-by, and I learned of the barrier that prevented me from following in their footsteps—"no girls admitted here"—my vexation and mortification knew no bounds. I remember, now, how proud and handsome the boys looked in their new clothes, as they jumped into the old stage coach and drove off, and how lonely I felt when they were gone and I had nothing to do, for the plans for my future were yet undetermined. Again I felt more keenly than ever the humiliation of the distinctions made on the ground of sex.

III. GIRLHOOD

MRS. WILLARD'S Seminary at Troy was the fashionable school in my girlhood, and in the winter of 1830, with upward of a hundred other girls, I found myself an active participant in all the joys and sorrows of that institution. When in family council it was decided to send me to that intellectual Mecca, I did not receive the announcement with unmixed satisfaction, as I had fixed my mind on Union College. The thought of a school without boys, who had been to me such a stimulus both in study and play, seemed to my imagination dreary and profitless.

The one remarkable feature of my journey to Troy was the railroad from Schenectady to Albany, the first ever laid in this country.* The manner of ascending a high hill going out of the city would now strike engineers as stupid to the last degree. The passenger cars were pulled up by a train, loaded with stones, descending the hill. The more rational way of tunneling through the hill or going around it had not yet dawned on our Dutch ancestors. At every step of my journey to Troy I felt that I was treading on my pride, and thus in a hopeless frame of mind I began my boarding-school career. I had already studied everything that was taught there except French, music, and dancing, so I devoted myself to these accomplishments. As I had a good voice I enjoyed singing, with a guitar accompaniment, and, having a good ear for time, I appreciated the harmony in music and motion and took great delight in dancing. The large house, the society of so many girls, the walks about the city, the novelty of everything made the new life more enjoyable than I had anticipated. To be sure I missed the boys, with whom I had grown up, played with

*However, the first scheduled passenger service on a railroad in the United States had taken place the previous year at Charleston, South Carolina.

for years, and later measured my intellectual powers with, but, as they became a novelty, there was new zest in occasionally seeing them. After I had been there a short time, I heard a call one day: "Heads out!" I ran with the rest and exclaimed, "What is it?" expecting to see a giraffe or some other wonder from Barnum's Museum.* "Why, don't you see those boys?" said one. "Oh," I replied, "is that all? I have seen boys all my life." When visiting family friends in the city, we were in the way of making the acquaintance of their sons, and as all social relations were strictly forbidden, there was a new interest in seeing them. As they were not allowed to call upon us or write notes, unless they were brothers or cousins, we had, in time, a large number of kinsmen.

There was an intense interest to me now in writing notes, receiving calls, and joining the young men in the streets for a walk, such as I had never known when in constant association with them at school and in our daily amusements. Shut up with girls, most of them older than myself, I heard many subjects discussed of which I had never thought before, and in a manner it were better I had never heard. The healthful restraint always existing between boys and girls in conversation is apt to be relaxed with either sex alone. In all my intimate association with boys up to that period, I cannot recall one word or act for criticism, but I cannot say the same of the girls during the three years I passed at the seminary in Troy. My own experience proves to me that it is a grave mistake to send boys and girls to separate institutions of learning, especially at the most impressible age. The stimulus of sex promotes alike a healthy condition of the intellectual and the moral faculties and gives to both a development they never can acquire alone.

Mrs. Willard, having spent several months in Europe, did not return until I had been at the seminary some time. I well remember her arrival, and the joy with which she was greeted by the teachers and pupils who had known her before. She was a splendid-looking woman, then in her prime, and fully realized my idea of a queen. I doubt whether any royal personage in the Old World could have received her worshipers with more grace and dignity than did this far-famed daughter of the Republic. She was one of the remarkable women of that period, and did a great educational work for her sex. She gave free

---

*An anachronism. Phineas T. Barnum, the great showman, did not open his American Museum in New York City until 1842, twelve years after Mrs. Stanton's arrival at Emma Willard's academy.

scholarships to a large number of promising girls, fitting them for teachers, with a proviso that, when the opportunity arose, they should, in turn, educate others.

The next happening in Troy that seriously influenced my character was the advent of the Rev. Charles G. Finney, a pulpit orator, who, as a terrifier of human souls, proved himself the equal of Savonarola. He held a protracted meeting in the Rev. Dr. Beaman's church, which many of my schoolmates attended. The result of six weeks of untiring effort on the part of Mr. Finney and his confreres was one of those intense revival seasons that swept over the city and through the seminary like an epidemic, attacking in its worst form the most susceptible. Owing to my gloomy Calvinistic training in the old Scotch Presbyterian church, and my vivid imagination, I was one of the first victims. We attended all the public services, beside the daily prayer and experience meetings held in the seminary. Our studies, for the time, held a subordinate place to the more important duty of saving our souls.

To state the idea of conversion and salvation as then understood, one can readily see from our present standpoint that nothing could be more puzzling and harrowing to the young mind. The revival fairly started, the most excitable were soon on the anxious seat. There we learned the total depravity of human nature and the sinner's awful danger of everlasting punishment. This was enlarged upon until the most innocent girl believed herself a monster of iniquity and felt certain of eternal damnation. Then God's hatred of sin was emphasized and his irreconcilable position toward the sinner so justified that one felt like a miserable, helpless, forsaken worm of the dust in trying to approach him, even in prayer.

Having brought you into a condition of profound humility, the only cardinal virtue for one under conviction, in the depths of your despair you were told that it required no herculean effort on your part to be transformed into an angel, to be reconciled to God, to escape endless perdition. The way to salvation was short and simple. We had naught to do but to repent and believe and give our hearts to Jesus, who was ever ready to receive them. How to do all this was the puzzling question. Talking with Dr. Finney one day, I said:

"I cannot understand what I am to do. If you should tell me to go to the top of the church steeple and jump off, I would readily do it, if thereby I could save my soul; but I do not know how to go to Jesus."

"Repent and believe," said he," that is all you have to do to be happy here and hereafter."

"I am very sorry," I replied, "for all the evil I have done, and I believe all you tell me, and the more sincerely I believe, the more unhappy I am."

With the natural reaction from despair to hope many of us imagined ourselves converted, prayed and gave our experiences in the meetings, and at times rejoiced in the thought that we were Christians—chosen children of God—rather than sinners and outcasts.

But Dr. Finney's terrible anathemas on the depravity and deceitfulness of the human heart soon shortened our newborn hopes. His appearance in the pulpit on these memorable occasions is indelibly impressed on my mind. I can see him now, his great eyes rolling around the congregation and his arms flying about in the air like those of a windmill. One evening he described hell and the devil and the long procession of sinners being swept down the rapids, about to make the awful plunge into the burning depths of liquid fire below, and the rejoicing hosts in the inferno coming up to meet them with the shouts of the devils echoing through the vaulted arches. He suddenly halted, and, pointing his index finger at the supposed procession, he exclaimed:

"There, do you not see them!"

I was wrought up to such a pitch that I actually jumped up and gazed in the direction to which he pointed, while the picture glowed before my eyes and remained with me for months afterward.

To change the current of my thoughts, a trip was planned to Niagara, and it was decided that the subject of religion was to be tabooed altogether. Accordingly our party, consisting of my sister, her husband, my father and myself, started in our private carriage, and for six weeks I heard nothing on the subject. About this time Gall and Spurzheim published their works on phrenology,* followed by Combe's "Constitution of Man," his "Moral Philosophy," and many other liberal works, all so rational and opposed to the old theologies that they produced a profound impression on my brother-in-law's mind. As we had these books with us, reading and discussing by the way, we all became deeply interested in the new ideas. Thus, after many months of weary wandering in the intellectual labyrinth of "The Fall Of Man,"

---

*Phrenology, a "science" popular that day, held that aspects of an individual's character and mental abilities were revealed by the shape of the skull, and especially by the location of bumps or indentations at specific points on the head.

"Original Sin," "Total Depravity," "God's Wrath," "Satan's Triumph," "The Crucifixion," "The Atonement," and "Salvation by Faith," I found my way out of the darkness into the clear sunlight of Truth. My religious superstitions gave place to rational ideas based on scientific facts, and in proportion, as I looked at everything from a new standpoint, I grew more and more happy, day by day. . . .

After leaving school, until my marriage, I had the most pleasant years of my girlhood. With frequent visits to a large circle of friends and relatives in various towns and cities, the monotony of home life was sufficiently broken to make our simple country pleasures always delightful and enjoyable. An entirely new life now opened to me. The old bondage of fear of the visible and the invisible was broken and, no longer subject to absolute authority, I rejoiced in the dawn of a new day of freedom in thought and action. . . .

IV. LIFE AT PETERBORO

THE year, with us, was never considered complete without a visit to Peterboro, N.Y., the home of Gerrit Smith. Though he was a reformer and was very radical in many of his ideas, yet, being a man of broad sympathies, culture, wealth, and position, he drew around him many friends of the most conservative opinions. He was a man of fine presence, rare physical beauty, most affable and courteous in manner, and his hospitalities were generous to an extreme, and dispensed to all classes of society.

Every year representatives from the Oneida tribe of Indians visited him. His father had early purchased of them large tracts of land, and there was a tradition among them that, as an equivalent for the good bargains of the father, they had a right to the son's hospitality, with annual gifts of clothing and provisions. The slaves, too, had heard of Gerrit Smith, the abolitionist, and of Peterboro as one of the safe points *en route* for Canada. His mansion was, in fact, one of the stations on the "underground railroad" for slaves escaping from bondage. Hence they, too, felt that they had a right to a place under his protecting roof. On such occasions the barn and the kitchen floor were utilized as chambers for the black man from the southern plantation and the red man from his home in the forest. . . .

These were the times when the anti-slavery question was up for hot discussion. In all the neighboring towns conventions were held in which James G. Birney, a Southern gentleman who had emancipated his slaves, Charles Stuart of Scotland, and George Thompson of

England, Garrison, Phillips, May, Beriah Green, Foster, Abby Kelly, Lucretia Mott, Douglass, and others took part. Here, too, John Brown, Sanborn, Morton, and Frederick Douglass met to talk over that fatal movement on Harper's Ferry. On the question of temperance, also, the people were in a ferment. Dr. Cheever's pamphlet, "Deacon Giles' Distillery," was scattered far and wide, and, as he was sued for libel, the question was discussed in the courts as well as at every fireside. Then came the Father Matthew and Washingtonian movements, and the position of the Church on these questions intensified and embittered the conflict. This brought the Cheevers, the Pierponts, the Delevans, the Nortons, and their charming wives to Peterboro. It was with such company and varied discussions on every possible phase of political, religious, and social life that I spent weeks every year. . . .*

It was in Peterboro, too, that I first met one who was then considered the most eloquent and impassioned orator on the anti-slavery platform, Henry B. Stanton. He had come over from Utica with Alvan Stewart's beautiful daughter, to whom report said he was engaged; but, as she soon after married Luther R. Marsh, there was a mistake somewhere. However, the rumor had its advantages. Regarding him as not in the matrimonial market, we were all much more free and easy in our manners with him than we would otherwise have been. A series of anti-slavery conventions was being held in Madison County, and there I had the pleasure of hearing him for the first time. As I had a passion for oratory, I was deeply impressed with his power. He was not so smooth and eloquent as Phillips, but he could make his audience both laugh and cry; the latter, Phillips himself said he never could do. Mr. Stanton was then in his prime, a fine-looking, affable young man, with remarkable conversational talent, and was ten years my senior, with the advantage that that number of years necessarily gives. . . .

One morning, as we came out from breakfast, Mr. Stanton joined me on the piazza, where I was walking up and down enjoying the balmy air and the beauty of the foliage. "As we have no conventions," said he, "on hand, what do you say to a ride on horseback this morning?" I readily accepted the suggestion, ordered the horses, put on my habit, and away we went. The roads were fine and we took a long ride. As we were returning home we stopped often to admire the scenery and, perchance, each other. When walking slowly through a beautiful grove, he laid his hand on the horn of the saddle and, to my

* Here Mrs. Stanton brings together events that took place between the early 1830s and the late 1850s.

surprise, made one of those charming revelations of human feeling which brave knights have always found eloquent words to utter, and to which fair ladies have always listened with mingled emotions of pleasure and astonishment. . . .

V. OUR WEDDING JOURNEY

MY engagement was a season of doubt and conflict—doubt as to the wisdom of changing a girlhood of freedom and enjoyment for I knew not what, and conflict because the step I proposed was in opposition to the wishes of my family. Whereas, heretofore, friends were continually suggesting suitable matches for me and painting the marriage relation in the most dazzling colors, now that state was represented as beset with dangers and disappointments, and men, of all God's creatures as the most depraved and unreliable. Hard pressed, I broke my engagement, after months of anxiety and bewilderment; suddenly I decided to renew it, as Mr. Stanton was going to Europe as a delegate to the World's Anti-slavery Convention, and we did not wish the ocean to roll between us.

Thursday, May 10, 1840, I determined to take the fateful step, without the slightest preparation for a wedding or a voyage; but Mr. Stanton, coming up the North River, was detained on "Marcy's Overslaugh," a bar in the river where boats were frequently stranded for hours. This delay compelled us to be married on Friday, which is commonly supposed to be a most unlucky day. But as we lived together, without more than the usual matrimonial friction, for nearly a half a century, had seven children, all but one of whom are still living, and have been well sheltered, clothed, and fed, enjoying sound minds in sound bodies, no one need be afraid of going through the marriage ceremony on Friday for fear of bad luck. The Scotch clergyman who married us, being somewhat superstitious, begged us to postpone it until Saturday; but, as we were to sail early in the coming week, that was impossible. That point settled, the next difficulty was to persuade him to leave out the word "obey" in the marriage ceremony. As I obstinately refused to obey one with whom I supposed I was entering into an equal relation, that point, too, was conceded.* A few friends were invited to be present and, in a simple

---

*Mrs. Stanton was apparently one of the first women to refuse to "obey" as a part of the standard marriage service of one of the major religious denominations.

white evening dress, I was married. . . .

Sister Madge, who had stood by me bravely through all my doubts and anxieties, went with us to New York and saw us on board the vessel. My sister Harriet and her husband, Daniel C. Eaton, a merchant in New York city, were also there. He and I had had for years a standing game of "tag" at all our partings, and he vowed to send me "tagged" to Europe. I was equally determined that he should not. Accordingly, I had a desperate chase after him all over the vessel, but in vain. He had the last "tag" and escaped. As I was compelled, under the circumstances, to conduct the pursuit with some degree of decorum, and he had the advantage of height, long limbs, and freedom from skirts, I really stood no chance whatever. However, as the chase kept us all laughing, it helped to soften the bitterness of parting.

Fairly at sea, I closed another chapter of my life, and my thoughts turned to what lay in the near future. James G. Birney, the anti-slavery nominee for the presidency of the United States, joined us in New York, and was a fellow-passenger on the *Montreal* for England. He and my husband were delegates to the World's Anti-slavery Convention, and both interested themselves in my anti-slavery education. They gave me books to read, and, as we paced the deck day by day, the question was the chief theme of our conversation.

Mr. Birney was a polished gentleman of the old school, and was excessively proper and punctilious in manner and conversation. I soon perceived that he thought I needed considerable toning down before reaching England. I was quick to see and understand that his criticisms of others in a general way and the drift of his discourses on manners and conversation had a nearer application than he intended I should discover, though he hoped I would profit by them. I was always grateful to anyone who took an interest in my improvement, so I laughingly told him, one day, that he need not make his criticisms any longer in that roundabout way, but might take me squarely in hand and polish me up as speedily as possible. Sitting in the saloon at night after a game of chess, in which, perchance, I had been the victor, I felt complacent and would sometimes say:

"Well, what have I said or done to-day open to criticism?"

So, in the most gracious manner, he replied on one occasion:

"You went to the masthead in a chair, which I think very unladylike. I heard you call your husband 'Henry' in the presence of strangers, which is not permissible in polite society. You should always say 'Mr. Stanton.' You have taken three moves back in this game." . . .

As he found even more fault with my husband, we condoled with each other and decided that our friend was rather hypercritical and that we were as nearly perfect as mortals need be for the wear and tear of ordinary life. Being both endowed with a good degree of self-esteem, neither the praise nor the blame of mankind was overpowering to either of us. As the voyage lasted eighteen days—for we were on a sailing vessel—we had time to make some improvement, or, at least, to consider all friendly suggestions. . . .

But all things must end in this mortal life, and our voyage was near its termination, when we were becalmed on the Southern coast of England and could not make more than one knot an hour. When within sight of the distant shore, a pilot boat came along and offered to take anyone ashore in six hours. I was so delighted at the thought of reaching land that, after much persuasion, Mr. Stanton and Mr. Birney consented to go. Accordingly we were lowered into the boat in an armchair, with a luncheon consisting of a cold chicken, a loaf of bread, and a bottle of wine with just enough wind to carry our light craft toward our destination. . . .

As we had no luggage with us, our detention by customs officers was brief, and we were soon conducted to a comfortable little hotel, which we found in the morning was a bower of roses. I had never imagined anything so beautiful as the drive up to Exeter on the top of a coach, with four stout horses, trotting at the rate of ten miles an hour. It was the first day of June, and country was in all its glory. The foliage was of the softest green, the trees were covered with blossoms, and shrubs with flowers. The roads were perfect; the large, fine-looking coachman, with his white gloves and reins, his rosy face and lofty bearing and the postman in red, blowing his horn as we passed through every village, made the drive seem like a journey in fairyland. We had heard that England was like a garden of flowers, but we were wholly unprepared for such wealth of beauty. . . .

The next day brought us to London. When I first entered our lodging house in Queen Street, I thought it the gloomiest abode I had ever seen. The arrival of a delegation of ladies, the next day, from Boston and Philadelphia, changed the atmosphere of the establishment, and filled me with delightful anticipations of some new and charming acquaintances, which I fully realized in meeting Emily Winslow, Abby Southwick, Elizabeth Neal, Mary Grew, Abby Kimber, Sarah Pugh, Lucretia Mott. There had been a split in the American anti-slavery ranks, and delegates came from both branches, and, as they were equally represented at our lodgings, I became familiar with the whole controversy. The potent element which caused the division was the woman question, and as the Garrisonian branch maintained the right of women to speak and vote in the conventions, all my sympathies were with Garrisonians, though Mr. Stanton and Mr. Birney belonged to the other branch, called political abolitionists. To me there was no question so important as the emancipation of women from the dogmas of the past, political, religious, and social. It struck me as very remarkable that abolitionists, who felt so keenly the wrongs of the slave, should be so oblivious to the equal wrongs of their own mothers, wives, and sisters, when, according to the common law, both classes occupied a similar legal status.

Our chief object in visiting England at this time was to attend the World's Anti-slavery Convention, to meet June 12, 1840, in Freemasons' Hall, London. Delegates from all the anti-slavery societies of civilized nations were invited, yet, when they arrived, those representing associations of women were rejected. Though women were members of the National Anti-slavery Society, accustomed to speak and vote in all its conventions, and to take an equally active part with men in the whole anti-slavery struggle, and were there as delegates from associations of men and women, as well as those distinctively of their own sex, yet all alike were rejected because they were women. Women, according to English prejudices at that time, were excluded by Scriptural texts from sharing equal dignity and authority with men in all reform associations; hence it was to English minds pre-eminently unfitting that women should be admitted as equal members to a World's convention. The question was hotly debated through an entire day. My husband made a very eloquent speech in favor of admitting the women delegates.

When we consider that Lady Byron, Anna Jameson, Mary Howitt, Mrs. Hugo Reid, Elizabeth Fry, Amelia Opie, Ann Green Phillips, Lucretia Mott, and many remarkable women, speakers and leaders in the Society of Friends, were all compelled to listen in silence to the masculine platitudes on woman's sphere, one may form some idea of the indignation of unprejudiced friends, and especially that of such women as Lydia Maria Child, Maria Chapman, Deborah Weston, Angelina and Sarah Grimké, and Abby Kelly, who were impatiently waiting and watching on this side, in painful suspense, to hear how their delegates were received. . . .

The clerical portion of the convention was most violent in its opposition. The clergymen seemed to have God and his angels especially in their care and keeping, and were in agony lest the women should do or say something to shock the heavenly hosts. . . .

It was really pitiful to hear narrow-minded bigots, pretending to be teachers and leaders of men, so cruelly remanding their own mothers, with the rest of womankind, to absolute subjection to the ordinary masculine type of humanity. I always regretted that the women themselves had not taken part in the debate before the convention was fully organized and the question of delegates settled. It seemed to me then, and does now, that all delegates with credentials from recognized societies should have had a voice in the organization of the convention, though subject to exclusion afterward. However, the women sat in a low curtained seat like a church choir, and modestly listened to the French, British, and American Solons for twelve of the longest days in June, as did, also, our grand Garrison and Rogers in the gallery. They scorned a convention that ignored the rights of the very women who had fought side by side, with them in the anti-slavery conflict. "After battling so many long years," said Garrison, " for the liberties of African slaves, I can take no part in a convention that strikes down the most sacred rights of all women." After coming three thousand miles to speak on the subject nearest his heart, he nobly shared the enforced silence of the rejected delegates. It was a great act of self-sacrifice that should never be forgotten by women. . . .

As the convention adjourned, the remark was heard on all sides, "It is about time some demand was made for new liberties for women." As Mrs. Mott and I walked home, arm in arm, commenting on the incidents of the day, we resolved to hold a convention as soon as we returned home, and form a society to advocate the rights of women. . . .

These were the first women I had ever met who believed in the equality of the sexes and who did not believe in the popular orthodox religion. The acquaintance of Lucretia Mott, who was a broad, liberal thinker on politics, religion, and all questions of reform, opened to me a new world of thought. As we walked about to see the lights of London, I embraced every opportunity to talk with her. It was intensely gratifying to hear all that, through years of doubt, I had dimly thought, so freely discussed by other women, some of them no older than myself—women, too, of rare intelligence, cultivation, and refinement. After six weeks' sojourn under the same roof with Lucretia Mott, whose conversation was uniformly on a high plane, I felt that I knew her too well to sympathize with the orthodox Friends, who denounced her as a dangerous woman because she doubted certain dogmas they fully believed. . . .

[Between June and December, 1840, the Stantons visited France, returned to England, spent time sightseeing in Scotland and Ireland, and attended many reform meetings. By now they had a wide circle of friends and acquaintances among British social and political reformers. They then sailed for home.]

VI. MOTHERHOOD

AFTER spending the holidays in New York city, we started for Johnstown in a "stage sleigh, conveying the United States mail," drawn by spanking teams of four horses, up the Hudson River valley. We were three days going to Albany, stopping over night at various points; a journey now performed in three hours. The weather was clear and cold, the sleighing fine, the scenery grand, and our traveling companions most entertaining, so the trip was very enjoyable. From Albany to Schenectady we went in the railway cars; then another sleighride of thirty miles brought us to Johnstown. My native hills, buried under two feet of snow, tinted with the last rays of the setting sun, were a beautiful and familiar sight. . . .

Our trunks unpacked, wardrobes arranged in closets and drawers, the excitement of seeing friends over, we spent some time in making plans for the future.

My husband, after some consultation with my father, decided to enter his office and commence the study of the law. As this arrangement kept me under the parental roof, I had two added years of pleasure, walking, driving, and riding on horseback with my sisters. Madge and Kate were dearer to me than ever, as I saw the inevitable separation awaiting us in the near future.

The puzzling questions of theology and poverty that had occupied so much of my thoughts, now gave place to the practical one, "what to do with a baby." Though motherhood is the most important of all the professions,—requiring more knowledge than any other department in human affairs,—yet there is not sufficient attention given to the preparation for this office. . . .

. . . I had recently visited our dear friends, Theodore and Angelina Grimké-Weld, and they warned me against books on this subject. They had been so misled by one author, who assured them that the stomach of a child could only hold one tablespoonful, that they nearly starved their firstborn to death. Though the child dwindled, day by day, and, at the end of a month, looked like a little old man, yet they still stood by the distinguished author. Fortunately, they both went off, one day, and left the child with Sister "Sarah," who thought she would make an experiment and see what a child's stomach could hold, as she had grave doubts about the tablespoonful theory. To her surprise the baby took a pint bottle full of milk, and had the sweetest sleep thereon he had known in his earthly career. After that he was permitted to take what he wanted, and "the author" was informed of his libel on the infantile stomach.

So here, again, I was entirely afloat, launched on the seas of doubt without chart or compass. The life and well-being of the race seemed to hang on the slender thread of such traditions as were handed down by ignorant mothers and nurses. One powerful ray of light illuminated the darkness; it was the work of Andrew Combe on "Infancy." . . . I read several chapters to the nurse. Although, out of her ten children, she had buried five, she still had too much confidence in her own wisdom and experience to pay much attention to any new idea that might be suggested to her. Among other things, Combe said that a child's bath should be regulated by the thermometer, in order to be always of the same temperature. She ridiculed the idea, and said her elbow was better than any thermometer, and, when I insisted on its use, she would invariably, with a smile of derision, put her elbow in first, to show how exactly it tallied with the thermometer. When I insisted that the child should not be bandaged, she rebelled outright, and said she would not take the responsibility of nursing a child without a bandage. I said, "Pray, sit down, dear nurse, and let us reason together. Do not think I am setting up my judgment against yours, with all your experience. I am simply trying to act on the opinions of a distinguished physician, who says there should be no pressure on a child anywhere; that the limbs and body should be free; that it is cruel to bandage an infant from hip to armpit, as is usually done in America; or both body and legs, as is done in Europe; or strap them to boards, as is done by savages on both continents. Can you give me one good reason, nurse, why a child should be bandaged?

"Yes," she said emphatically, "I can give you a dozen."

"I only asked for one," I replied.

"Well," said she, after much hesitation, "the bones of a newborn infant are soft, like cartilage, and, unless you pin them up snugly, there is danger of their falling apart."

"It seems to me," I replied, "you have given the strongest reason why they should be carefully guarded against the slightest pressure. It is very remarkable that kittens and puppies should be so well put together that they need no artificial bracing, and the human family be left wholly to the mercy of a bandage. Suppose a child was born where you could not get a bandage, what then? Now I think this child will remain intact without a bandage, and, if I am willing to take the risk, why should you complain?"

"Because," she said, "if the child should die, it would injure my name as a nurse. I therefore wash my hands of all these new-fangled notions."

So she bandaged the child every morning, and I as regularly took it off. . . .

Besides the obstinacy of the nurse, I had the ignorance of physicians to contend with. When the child was four days old we discovered that the collar bone was bent. The physician, wishing to get a pressure on the shoulder, braced the bandage round the wrist. "Leave that," he said, "ten days, and then it will be all right." Soon after he left I noticed that the child's hand was blue, showing that the circulation was impeded. "That will never do," said I; "nurse, take it off." "No, indeed," she answered, "I shall never interfere with the doctor." So I took it off myself, and sent for another doctor, who was said to know more of surgery. He expressed great surprise that the first physician called should have put on so severe a bandage. "That," said he, "would do for a grown man, but ten days of it on a child would make him a cripple." However, he did nearly the same thing, only fastening it round the hand instead of the wrist. I soon saw that the ends of the fingers were all purple, and that to leave that on ten days would be as dangerous as the first. So I took that off.

"What a woman!" exclaimed the nurse. "What do you propose to do?"

"Think out something better, myself; so brace me up with some pillows and give the baby to me."

She looked at me aghast and said, "You'd better trust the doctors, or your child will be a helpless cripple."

"Yes," I replied, "he would be, if we had left either of those bandages on, but I have an idea of something better."

"Now," said I, talking partly to myself and partly to her, "what we want is a little pressure on that bone; that is what both those men aimed at. How can we get it without involving the arm, is the question?"

"I am sure I don't know," said she, rubbing her hands and taking two or three brisk turns round the room.

"Well, bring me three strips of linen, four double." I then folded one, wet in arnica and water, and laid it on the collar bone, put two other bands, like a pair of suspenders, over the shoulders, crossing them both in front and behind, pinning the ends to the diaper, which gave the needed pressure without impeding the circulation anywhere. As I finished she gave me a look of budding confidence, and seemed satisfied that all was well. Several times, night and day, we wet the compress and readjusted the bands, until all appearances of inflammation had subsided.

At the end of ten days the two sons of Æsculapius appeared and made their examination and said all was right, whereupon I told them how badly their bandages worked and what I had done myself. They smiled at each other, and one said:

"Well, after all, a mother's instinct is better than a man's reason."

"Thank you, gentlemen, there was no instinct about it. I did some hard thinking before I saw how I could get a pressure on the shoulder without impeding the circulation, as you did."

Thus, in the supreme moment of a young mother's life, when I needed tender care and support, I felt the whole responsibility of my child's supervision; but though uncertain at every step of my own knowledge, I learned another lesson in self-reliance. I trusted neither men nor books absolutely after this, either in regard to the heavens above or the earth beneath, but continued to use my "mother's instinct," if "reason" is too dignified a term to apply to woman's thoughts. My advice to every mother is, above all other arts and sciences, study first what relates to babyhood, as there is no department of human action in which there is such lamentable ignorance. . . .

VII. BOSTON AND CHELSEA

IN the autumn of 1843 my husband was admitted to the bar and commenced the practice of law in Boston with Mr. Bowles, brother-in-law of the late General John A. Dix. This gave me the opportunity to make many pleasant acquaintances among the lawyers in Boston, and to meet, intimately, many of the noble men and women among reformers, whom I had long worshiped at a distance. . . .

I was a frequent visitor at the home of William Lloyd Garrison. Though he had a prolonged battle to fight in the rough outside world, his home was always a haven of rest. Mrs. Garrison was a sweet-tempered, conscientious woman, who tried, under all circumstances, to do what was right. . . . Though always in straitened circumstances, the Garrisons were very hospitable. It was next to impossible for Mr. Garrison to meet a friend without inviting him to his house, especially at the close of a convention.

I was one of twelve at one of his impromptu tea parties. We all took it for granted that his wife knew we were coming, and that her preparations were already made. Surrounded by half a dozen children, she was performing the last act in the opera of Lullaby, wholly unconscious of the invasion downstairs. But Mr. Garrison was equal to every emergency, and, after placing his guests at their ease in the parlor, he hastened to the nursery, took off his coat, and rocked the baby until his wife had disposed of the remaining children. Then they had a consultation about the tea, and when, basket in hand, the good man sallied forth for the desired viands, Mrs. Garrison, having made a hasty toilet, came down to welcome her guests. She was as genial and self-possessed as if all things had been prepared. She made no apologies for what was lacking in the general appearance of the house nor in the variety of the menu—it was sufficient for her to know that Mr. Garrison was happy in feeling free to invite his friends. The impromptu meal was excellent, and we had a most enjoyable evening. I have no doubt that Mrs. Garrison had more real pleasure than if she had been busy all day making preparations and had been tired out when her guests arrived.

The anti-slavery conventions and fairs, held every year during the holidays, brought many charming people from other States, and made Boston a social center for the coadjutors of Garrison and Phillips. These conventions surpassed any meetings I had ever attended; the speeches were eloquent and the debates earnest and forcible. Garrison and Phillips were in their prime, and slavery was a question of national interest. The hall in which the fairs were held, under the auspices of Mrs. Chapman and her cohorts, was most artistically decorated. There one could purchase whatever the fancy could desire, for English friends, stimulated by the appeals of Harriet Martineau and Elizabeth Pease, used to send boxes of beautiful things, gathered from all parts of the Eastern Continent. There, too, one could get a most *recherché* luncheon in the society of the literati of Boston; for, however indifferent many were to slavery *per se*, they enjoyed these fairs, and all classes flocked there till far into the night. It was a kind of ladies' exchange for the holiday week, where each one was sure to meet her friends. The fair and the annual convention, coming in succession, intensified the interest in both. I never grew weary of the conventions, though I attended all the sessions, lasting, sometimes, until eleven o'clock at night. The fiery eloquence of the abolitionists, the amusing episodes that occurred when some crank was suppressed and borne out on the shoulders of his brethren, gave sufficient variety to the proceedings to keep the interest up to high-water mark. . . .

Mrs. Oliver Johnson and I spent two days at the Brook Farm Community when in the height of its prosperity. There I met the Ripleys, who were, I believe the backbone of the experiment,—William Henry Channing, Bronson Alcott, Charles A. Dana, Frederick Cabot, William Chase, Mrs. Horace Greeley, who was spending a few days there, and many others, whose names I cannot recall. Here was a charming family of intelligent men and women, doing their own farm and house work, with lectures, readings, music, dancing, and games when desired; realizing, in a measure, Edward Bellamy's beautiful vision of the equal conditions of the human family in the year 2000. . . .

In 1843 my father moved to Albany, to establish my brothers-in-law, Mr. Wilkeson and Mr. McMartin, in the legal profession. That made Albany the family rallying point for a few years. This enabled me to spend several winters at the Capital and to take an active part in the discussion of the Married Woman's Property Bill, then pending in the legislature. William H. Seward, Governor of the State from 1839 to 1843, recommended the Bill, and his wife, a woman of rare intelligence, advocated it in society. Together we had the opportunity of talking with many members, both of the Senate and the Assembly, in social circles, as well as in their committee rooms. Bills were pending from 1836 until 1848, when the measure finally passed.

My second son was born in Albany, in March, 1844, under more favorable auspices than the first, as I knew, then, what to do with a baby. Returning to Chelsea we commenced housekeeping, which afforded me another chapter of experience. A new house, newly furnished, with beautiful views of Boston Bay, was all I could desire. Mr. Stanton announced to me, in starting, that his business would occupy all his time, and that I must take entire charge of the housekeeping. So, with two good servants and two babies under my sole supervision, my time was pleasantly occupied. . . .

Our house was pleasantly situated on the Chelsea Hills, commanding a fine view of Boston, the harbor, and surrounding country. There, on the upper piazza, I spent some of the happiest days of my life, enjoying in turn; the beautiful outlook, my children, and my books.

Here, under the very shadow of Bunker Hill Monument, my third son was born. Shortly after this Gerrit Smith and his wife came to spend a few days with us, so this boy, much against my will, was named after my cousin. I did not believe in old family names unless they were peculiarly euphonious. I had a list of beautiful names for sons and daughters, from which to designate each newcomer; but, as yet, not one on my list had been used. However, I put my foot down, at No. 4, and named him Theodore, and, thus far, he has proved himself a veritable "gift from God," doing his uttermost, in every way possible, to fight the battle of freedom for woman. . . .

As my husband's health was delicate, and the New England winters proved too severe for him, we left Boston, with many regrets, and sought a more genial climate in Central New York.

VIII. THE WOMAN'S RIGHTS CONVENTION

IN the spring of 1847 we moved to Seneca Falls. Here we spent sixteen years of our married life, and here our other children—two sons and two daughters—were born. . . .

In Seneca Falls my life was comparatively solitary, and the change from Boston was somewhat depressing. There, all my immediate friends were reformers, I had near neighbors, a new home with all the modern conveniences, and well-trained servants. Here our residence was on the outskirts of the town, roads very often muddy and no sidewalks most of the way, Mr. Stanton was frequently from home, I had poor servants, and an increasing number of children. To keep a house and grounds in good order, purchase every article for daily use, keep the wardrobes of half a dozen human beings in proper trim, take the children to dentists, shoemakers, and different schools, or find teachers at home, altogether made sufficient work to keep one brain busy, as well as all the hands I could impress into the service. Then, too, the novelty of housekeeping had passed away, and much that was once attractive in domestic life was now irksome. I had so many cares that the company I needed for intellectual stimulus was a trial rather than a pleasure. . . .

Up to this time life had glided by with comparative ease, but now the real struggle was upon me. My duties were too numerous and varied, and none sufficiently exhilarating or intellectual to bring into play my higher faculties. I suffered with mental hunger, which, like an empty stomach, is very depressing. I had books, but no stimulating companionship. To add to my general dissatisfaction at the change from Boston, I found that Seneca Falls was a malarial region, and in due time all the children were attacked with chills and fever which, under homeopathic treatment in those days, lasted three months.* The servants were afflicted in the same way. Cleanliness, order, the love of the beautiful and artistic, all faded away in the struggle to accomplish what was absolutely necessary from hour to hour. Now I understood, as I never had before, how women could sit down and rest in the midst of general disorder. Housekeeping, under such conditions, was impossible, so I packed our clothes, locked up the house, and went to that harbor of safety, home, as I did ever after in stress of weather.

I now fully understood the practical difficulties most women had to contend with in the isolated household, and the impossibility of woman's best development if in contact, the chief part of her life, with servants and children. Fourier's phalansterie community life and cooperative households had a new significance for me.* Emerson says, "A healthy discontent is the first step to progress." The general discontent I felt with woman's portion as wife, mother, housekeeper, physician, and spiritual guide, the chaotic conditions into which everything fell without her constant supervision, and the wearied, anxious look of the majority of women impressed me with a strong feeling that some active measures should be taken to remedy the wrongs of society in general, and of women in particular. My experience at the World's Anti-slavery Convention, all I had read of the legal status of women, and the oppression I saw everywhere, together swept

*Homeopathy was a system of medical practice that had originated in Europe in the early nineteenth century. In it, illnesses were treated with small doses of drugs that produced somewhat the same effects as the symptoms of the illness. Such dosages tended to do much less damage to the patient than the bleeding and purging that were important parts of standard medical practice in that day, and sometimes the patient received an effective drug, such as quinine, which was probably used to treat Mrs. Stanton's malarial children and servants.

*Charles Fourier (1772-1837), French Utopian socialist, devised a highly structured communal system that won hundreds of converts, many of them prominent people, in nineteenth-century America. Brook Farm in Roxbury, Massachusetts, visited by Mrs. Stanton (see above), was at first more loosely organized but was then converted to the Fourierist system for a short time before it ended.

across my soul, intensified now by many personal experiences. It seemed as if all the elements had conspired to impel me to some onward step. I could not see what to do or where to begin—my only thought was a public meeting for protest and discussion.

In this tempest-tossed condition of mind I received an invitation to spend the day with Lucretia Mott, at Richard Hunt's, in Waterloo. There I met several members of different families of Friends, earnest, thoughtful women. I poured out, that day, the torrent of my long-accumulating discontent, with such vehemence and indignation that I stirred myself, as well as the rest of the party, to do and dare anything. My discontent, according to Emerson, must have been healthy, for it moved us all to prompt action, and we decided, then and there, to call a "Woman's Rights Convention." We wrote the call that evening and published it in the *Seneca County Courier* the next day, the 14th of July, 1848, giving only five days' notice, as the convention was to be held on the 19th and 20th. The call was inserted without signatures,—in fact it was a mere announcement of a meeting,—but the chief movers and managers were Lucretia Mott, Mary Ann McClintock, Jane Hunt, Martha C. Wright, and myself. The convention, which was held two days in the Methodist Church, was in every way a grand success. The house was crowded at every session, the speaking good, and a religious earnestness dignified all the proceedings. . . .

. . . No words could express our astonishment on finding, a few days afterward, that what seemed to us so timely, so rational, and so sacred, should be a subject for sarcasm and ridicule to the entire press of the nation. With our Declaration of Rights and Resolutions for a text, it seemed as if every man who could wield a pen prepared a homily on "woman's sphere." All the journals from Maine to Texas seemed to strive with each other to see which could make our movement appear the most ridiculous. The anti-slavery papers stood by us manfully and so did Frederick Douglass, both in the convention and in his paper, *The North Star*, but so pronounced was the popular voice against us, in the parlor, press, and pulpit, that most of the ladies who had attended the convention and signed the declaration, one by one, withdrew their names and influence and joined our persecutors. Our friends gave us the cold shoulder and felt themselves disgraced by the whole proceeding.

If I had had the slightest premonition of all that was to follow that convention, I fear I should not have had the courage to risk it, and I must confess that it was with fear and trembling that I consented to attend another, one month afterward, in Rochester. Fortunately, the first one seemed to have drawn all the fire, and of the second but little was said. But we had set the ball in motion, and now, in quick succession, conventions were held in Ohio, Indiana, Massachusetts, Pennsylvania, and in the City of New York, and have been kept up nearly every year since.

The most noteworthy of the early conventions were those held in Massachusetts, in which such men as Garrison, Phillips, Channing, Parker, and Emerson took part. It was one of these that first attracted the attention of Mrs. John Stuart Mill, and drew from her pen that able article on "The Enfranchisement of Woman," in the *Westminster Review* of October, 1852.

The same year of the convention, the Married Woman's Property Bill, which had given rise to some discussion on woman's rights in New York, had passed the legislature. This encouraged action on the part of women, as the reflection naturally arose that, if the men who make the laws were ready for some onward step, surely the women themselves should express some interest in the legislation. Ernestine L. Rose, Paulina Wright (Davis), and I had spoken before committees of the legislature years before, demanding equal property rights for women. We had circulated petitions for the Married Woman's Property Bill for many years, and so also had the leaders of the Dutch aristocracy, who desired to see their life-long accumulations descend to their daughters and grandchildren rather than pass into the hands of dissipated, thriftless sons-in-law. Judge Hertell, Judge Fine, and Mr. Geddes of Syracuse prepared and championed the several bills, at different times, before the legislature. Hence the demands made in the convention were not entirely new to the reading and thinking public of New York—the first State to take any action on the question. . . .*

With these new duties and interests, and a broader outlook on human life, my petty domestic annoyances gradually took a subordinate place. Now I began to write articles for the press, letters to conventions held in other States, and private letters to friends, to arouse them to thought on this question. . . .

. . . Now my mind, as well as my hands, was fully occupied, and instead of mourning, as I had done, over what I had lost in leaving Boston, I tried in every way to make the most of life in Seneca Falls. Seeing that elaborate refreshments prevented many social gatherings, I often gave an evening entertainment without any. I told the

*Pennsylvania also enacted a married women's property law in early 1848.

young people, whenever they wanted a little dance or a merry time, to make our house their rallying point, and I would light up and give them a glass of water and some cake. In that way we had many pleasant informal gatherings. Then, in imitation of Margaret Fuller's Conversationals, we started one which lasted several years. We selected a subject each week on which we all read and thought; each, in turn, preparing an essay ten minutes in length.

These were held, at different homes, Saturday of each week. On coming together we chose a presiding officer for the evening, who called the meeting to order, and introduced the essayist. That finished, he asked each member, in turn, what he or she had read or thought on the subject, and if any had criticisms to make on the essay. Everyone was expected to contribute something. Much information was thus gained, and many spicy discussions followed. All the ladies, as well as the gentlemen, presided in turn, and so became familiar with parliamentary rules. The evening ended with music, dancing, and a general chat. In this way we read and thought over a wide range of subjects and brought together the best minds in the community. Many young men and women who did not belong to what was considered the first circle,—for in every little country village there is always a small clique that constitutes the aristocracy,—had the advantages of a social life otherwise denied them. I think that all who took part in this Conversation Club would testify to its many good influences. . . .

IX. SUSAN B. ANTHONY

THE reports of the conventions held in Seneca Falls and Rochester, N.Y., in 1848, attracted the attention of one destined to take a most important part in the new movement—Susan B. Anthony, who, for her courage and executive ability, was facetiously called by William Henry Channing, the Napoleon of our struggle. At this time she was teaching in the academy at Canajoharie, a little village in the beautiful valley of the Mohawk. . . .

But, before long, conflicts in the outside world disturbed our young teacher. The multiplication table and spelling book no longer enchained her thoughts; larger questions began to fill her mind. About the year 1850 Susan B. Anthony hid her ferrule away. Temperance, anti-slavery, woman suffrage—three pregnant questions,—presented themselves, demanding her consideration. Higher, ever higher, rose their appeals, until she resolved to dedicate her energy and thought to the burning needs of the hour. Owing to early experience of the disabilities of her sex, the first demand for equal rights for women found echo in Susan's heart. . . .

At this stage of her development I met my future friend and coadjutor for the first time. How well I remember the day! George Thompson and William Lloyd Garrison having announced an anti-slavery meeting in Seneca Falls, Miss Anthony came to attend it. These gentlemen were my guests. Walking home, after the adjourn-ment, we met Mrs. Bloomer and Miss Anthony on the corner of the street, waiting to greet us. There she stood, with her good, earnest face and genial smile, dressed in gray delaine, hat and all the same color, relieved with pale blue ribbons, the perfection of neatness and sobri-ety. I liked her thoroughly, and why I did not at once invite her home with me to dinner, I do not know. She accuses me of that neglect, and has never forgiven me, as she wished to see and hear all she could of our noble friends. I suppose my mind was full of what I had heard, or my coming dinner, or the probable behavior of three mischievous boys who had been busily exploring the premises while I was at the meeting. . . .

It is often said, by those who know Miss Anthony best, that she has been my good angel, always pushing and goading me to work, and that but for her pertinacity I should never have accomplished the little I have. On the other hand it has been said that I forged the thunder-bolts and she fired them. Perhaps all this is, in a measure, true. With the cares of a large family I might, in time, like too many women, have become wholly absorbed in a narrow family selfishness, had not my friend been continually exploring new fields for missionary labors. Her description of a body of men on any platform, complacently deciding questions in which woman had an equal interest, without an equal voice, readily roused me to a determination to throw a firebrand into the midst of their assembly.

Thus, whenever I saw that stately Quaker girl coming across my lawn, I knew that some happy convocation of the sons of Adam was to be set by the ears, by one of our appeals or resolutions. The little portmanteau, stuffed with facts, was opened, and there we had what the Rev. John Smith and Hon. Richard Roe had said: false interpreta-tions of Bible texts, the statistics of women robbed of their property, shut out of some college, half paid for their work, the reports of some disgraceful trial; injustice enough to turn any woman's thoughts from stockings and puddings. Then we would get out our pens and write articles for papers, or a petition to the legislature; indite letters to the faithful, here and there; stir up the women in Ohio, Pennsylvania, or Massachusetts; call on *The Lily, The Una, The Liberator, The Standard* to remember our wrongs as well as those of the slave. We never met without issuing a pronunciamento on some question. In thought and sympathy we were one, and in the division of labor we exactly complemented each other. In writing we did better work than either could alone. While she is slow and analytical in composition, I am rapid and synthetic. I am the better writer, she the better critic. She supplied the facts and statistics, I the philosophy and rhetoric, and, together, we have made arguments that have stood unshaken through the storms of long years; arguments that no one has answered. Our speeches may be considered the united product of our two brains.

So entirely one are we that, in all our associations, ever side by side on the same platform, not one feeling of envy or jealousy has ever shadowed our lives. We have indulged freely in criticism of each other when alone, and hotly contended whenever we have differed, but in our friendship of years there has never been the break of one hour. To the world we always seem to agree and uniformly reflect each other. Like husband and wife, each has the feeling that we must have no differences in public. . . .

X. MY FIRST SPEECH BEFORE A LEGISLATURE

WOMEN had been willing so long to hold a subordinate position, both in private and public affairs, that a gradually growing feeling of rebellion among them quite exasperated the men, and their manifestations of hostility in public meetings were often as ridiculous as humiliating. . . .

I soon convinced Miss Anthony that the ballot was the key to the situation; that when we had a voice in the laws we should be welcome to any platform. . . .

From the year 1850 conventions were held in various States, and their respective legislatures were continually besieged; New York was thoroughly canvassed by Miss Anthony and others. Appeals, calls for meetings, and petitions were circulated without number. In 1854 I prepared my first speech for the New York legislature. That was a great event in my life. I felt so nervous over it, lest it should not be worthy the occasion, that Miss Anthony suggested that I should slip up to Rochester and submit it to the Rev. William Henry Channing, who was preaching there at that time. I did so, and his opinion was so favorable as to the merits of my speech that I felt quite reassured. My father felt equally nervous when he saw, by the Albany *Evening Journal*, that I was to speak at the Capitol, and asked me to read my speech to him also. Accordingly, I stopped at Johnstown on my way to Albany, and, late one evening, when he was alone in his office, I entered and took my seat on the opposite side of his table. On no occasion, before or since, was I ever more embarrassed—an audience of one, and that the one of all others whose approbation I most desired, whose disapproval I most feared. I knew he condemned the whole movement, and was deeply grieved at the active part I had taken. Hence I was fully aware that I was about to address a wholly unsympathetic audience. However, I began, with a dogged determination to give all the power I could to my manuscript, and not to be discouraged or turned from my purpose by any tender appeals or adverse criticisms. I described the widow in the first hours of her grief, subject to the intrusions of the coarse minions of the law, taking inventory of the household goods, of the old armchair in which her loved one had breathed his last, of the old clock in the corner that told the hour he passed away. I threw all the pathos I could into my voice and language at this point, and, to my intense satisfaction, I saw tears filling my father's eyes. I cannot express the exultation I felt, thinking that now he would see, with my eyes, the injustice women suffered under the laws he understood so well.

Feeling that I had touched his heart I went on with renewed confidence, and, when I had finished, I saw he was thoroughly magnetized. With beating heart I waited for him to break the silence. He was evidently deeply pondering over all he had heard, and did not speak for a long time. I believed I had opened to him a new world of thought. He had listened long to the complaints of women, but from the lips of his own daughter they had come with a deeper pathos and power. At last, turning abruptly, he said: "Surely you have had a happy, comfortable life, with all your wants and needs supplied; and yet that speech fills me with self-reproach; for one might naturally ask, how can a young woman, tenderly brought up, who has had no bitter personal experience, feel so keenly the wrongs of her sex? Where did you learn this lesson?" "I learned it here," I replied, "in your office, when a child, listening to the complaints women made to you. They who have sympathy and imagination to make the sorrows of others their own can readily learn all the hard lessons of life from the experience of others." "Well, well!" he said, "you have made your points clear and strong; but I think I can find you even more cruel laws than those you have quoted." He suggested some improvements in my speech, looked up other laws, and it was one o'clock in the morning before we kissed each other good-night. How he felt on the question after that I do not know, as he never said anything in favor of or against it. He gladly gave me any help I needed, from time to time, in looking up the laws, and was very desirous that whatever I gave to the public should be carefully prepared.

Miss Anthony printed twenty thousand copies of this address, laid it on the desk of every member of the legislature, both in the Assembly and Senate, and, in her travels that winter, she circulated it throughout the State. I am happy to say I never felt so anxious about the fate of a speech since. . . .

XI. REFORMS AND MOBS

THERE was one bright woman among the many in our Seneca Falls literary circle to whom I would give more than a passing notice—Mrs. Amelia Bloomer, who represented three novel phases of woman's life. She was assistant postmistress; an editor of a reform paper advocating temperance and woman's rights; and an advocate of the new costume which bore her name!

In 1849 her husband was appointed postmaster, and she became his deputy, was duly sworn in, and, during the administration of Taylor and Fillmore, served in that capacity. When she assumed her duties the improvement in the appearance and conduct of the office was generally acknowledged. A neat little room adjoining the public office became a kind of ladies' exchange, where those coming from different parts of the town could meet to talk over the news of the day and read the papers and magazines that came to Mrs. Bloomer as editor of *The Lily*. Those who enjoyed the brief reign of a woman in the post office can readily testify to the void felt by the ladies of the village when Mrs. Bloomer's term expired and a man once more reigned in her stead. However, she still edited *The Lily*, and her office remained a fashionable center for several years. Although she wore the bloomer dress, its originator was Elizabeth Smith Miller, the only daughter of Gerrit Smith. In the winter of 1852 Mrs. Miller came to visit me in Seneca Falls, dressed somewhat in the Turkish style—short skirt, full trousers of fine black broadcloth; a Spanish cloak, of the same material, reaching to the knee; beaver hat and feathers and dark furs;

altogether a most becoming costume and exceedingly convenient for walking in all kinds of weather. To see my cousin, with a lamp in one hand and a baby in the other, walk upstairs with ease and grace, while, with flowing robes, I pulled myself up with difficulty, lamp and baby out of the question, readily convinced me that there was sore need of reform in woman's dress, and I promptly donned a similar attire. What incredible freedom I enjoyed for two years! Like a captive set free from his ball and chain; I was always ready for a brisk walk through sleet and snow and rain, to climb a mountain, jump over a fence, work in the garden, and, in fact, for any necessary locomotion.

Bloomer is now a recognized word in the English language. Mrs. Bloomer, having *The Lily* in which to discuss the merits of the new dress, the press generally took up the question, and much valuable information was elicited on the physiological results of woman's fashionable attire; the crippling effect of tight waists and long skirts, the heavy weight on the hips, and high heels, all combined to throw the spine out of plumb and lay the foundation for all manner of nervous diseases. But, while all agreed that some change was absolutely necessary for the health of woman, the press stoutly ridiculed those who were ready to make the experiment.

A few sensible women, in different parts of the country, adopted the costume, and farmers' wives especially proved its convenience. It was also worn by skaters, gymnasts, tourists, and in sanitariums. But, while the few realized its advantages, the many laughed it to scorn, and heaped such ridicule on its wearers that they soon found that the physical freedom enjoyed did not compensate for the persistent persecution and petty annoyances suffered at every turn. To be rudely gazed at in public and private, to be the conscious subjects of criticism, and to be followed by crowds of boys in the streets, were all, to the very last degree, exasperating. A favorite doggerel that our tormentors chanted, when we appeared in public places, ran thus:

> "Heigh! ho! in rain and snow,
> The bloomer now is all the go.
> Twenty tailors take the stitches,
> Twenty women wear the breeches.
> Heigh! ho! in rain and snow,
> The bloomer now is all the go."

The singers were generally invisible behind some fence or attic window. Those who wore the dress can recall countless amusing and annoying experiences. The patience of most of us was exhausted in about two years; but our leader, Mrs. Miller, bravely adhered to the costume for nearly seven years, under the most trying circumstances. While her father was in Congress, she wore it at many fashionable dinners and receptions in Washington. She was bravely sustained, however, by her husband, Colonel Miller, who never flinched in escorting his wife and her coadjutors, however inartistic their costumes might be. To tall, gaunt women with large feet and to those who were short and stout, it was equally trying. . . .

In the winter of 1861, just after the election of Lincoln, the abolitionists decided to hold a series of conventions in the chief cities of the North. All their available speakers were pledged for active service. The Republican party, having absorbed the political abolitionists within its ranks by its declared hostility to the extension of slavery, had come into power with overwhelming majorities. Hence the Garrisonian abolitionists, opposed to all compromises, felt that this was the opportune moment to rouse the people to the necessity of holding that party to its declared principles, and pushing it, if possible, a step or two forward.

I was invited to accompany Miss Anthony and Beriah Green to a few points in Central New York. But we soon found, by the concerted action of Republicans all over the country, that anti-slavery conventions would not be tolerated. Thus Republicans and Democrats made common cause against the abolitionists. The John Brown raid, the year before, had intimidated Northern politicians as much as Southern slaveholders, and the general feeling was that the discussion of the question at the North should be altogether suppressed.

From Buffalo to Albany our experience was the same, varied only by the fertile resources of the actors and their surroundings. Thirty years of education had somewhat changed the character of Northern mobs. They no longer dragged men through the streets with ropes around their necks, nor broke up women's prayer meetings; they no longer threw eggs and brickbats at the apostles of reform, nor dipped them in barrels of tar and feathers, they simply crowded the halls, and, with laughing, groaning, clapping, and cheering, effectually interrupted the proceedings. Such was our experience during the two days we attempted to hold a convention in St. James' Hall, Buffalo. As we paid for the hall, the mob enjoyed themselves, at our expense, in more ways than one. Every session, at the appointed time, we took our places on the platform, making, at various intervals of silence, renewed efforts to speak. Not succeeding, we sat and conversed with each other and the many friends who crowded the platform and anterooms. . . .

These Buffalo rowdies were headed by ex-Justice Hinson, aided by younger members of the Fillmore and Seymour families, and the chief of police and fifty subordinates, who were admitted to the hall free, for the express purpose of protecting our right of free speech, but who, in defiance of the mayor's orders, made not the slightest effort in our defense. At Lockport there was a feeble attempt in the same direction. At Albion neither hall, church, nor schoolhouse could be obtained, so we held small meetings in the dining room of the hotel. At Rochester, Corinthian Hall was packed long before the hour advertised. This was a delicately appreciative, jocose mob. . . . Here, too, all attempts to speak were futile. At Port Byron a generous sprinkling of cayenne pepper on the stove soon cut short all constitutional arguments and paeans to liberty.

And so it was all the way to Albany. The whole State was aflame with the mob spirit, and from Boston and various points in other States the same news reached us. As the legislature was in session, and we were advertised in Albany, a radical member sarcastically moved "That as Mrs. Stanton and Miss Anthony were about to move on Albany, the militia be ordered out for the protection of the city." Happily, Albany could then boast of a Democratic mayor, a man of courage and conscience, who said the right of free speech should never be trodden under foot where he had the right to prevent it. And grandly did that one determined man maintain order in his jurisdiction. Through all the sessions of the convention Mayor Thatcher sat on the platform, his police stationed in different parts of the hall and outside the building, to disperse the crowd as fast as it collected. If a man or boy hissed or made the slightest interruption, he was immediately ejected. And not only did the mayor preserve order in the meetings, but, with a company of armed police, he escorted us, every time, to and from the Delevan House. The last night Gerrit Smith addressed the mob from the steps of the hotel, after which they gave him three cheers and dispersed in good order. . . .

XII. VIEWS ON MARRIAGE AND DIVORCE

THE widespread discussion we are having, just now, on the subject of marriage and divorce, reminds me of an equally exciting one in 1860. A very liberal bill, introduced into the Indiana legislature by

Robert Dale Owen, and which passed by a large majority, roused much public thought on the question, and made that State free soil for unhappy wives and husbands. A similar bill was introduced into the legislature of New York by Mr. Ramsey, which was defeated by four votes, owing, mainly, to the intense opposition of Horace Greeley. He and Mr. Owen had a prolonged discussion, in the New York *Tribune*, in which Mr. Owen got decidedly the better of the argument. . . .

As we were holding a woman suffrage convention in Albany, at the time appointed for the hearing, Ernestine L. Rose and Lucretia Mott briefly added their views on the question. Although Mrs. Mott had urged Mrs. Rose and myself to be as moderate as possible in our demands, she quite unconsciously made the most radical utterance of all, in saying that marriage was a question beyond the realm of legislation, that must be left to the parties themselves. . . .

The discussion on the question of marriage and divorce occupied one entire session of the convention, and called down on us severe criticisms from the metropolitan and State Press. So alarming were the comments on what had been said that I began to feel that I had inadvertently taken out the underpinning from the social system. Enemies were unsparing in their denunciations, and friends ridiculed the whole proceeding. I was constantly called on for a definition of marriage and asked to describe home life as it would be when men changed their wives every Christmas. Letters and newspapers poured in upon me, asking all manner of absurd questions, until I often wept with vexation. So many things, that I had neither thought nor said, were attributed to me that, at times, I really doubted my own identity.

However, in the progress of events the excitement died away, the earth seemed to turn on its axis as usual, women were given in marriage, children were born, fires burned as brightly as ever at the domestic altars, and family life, to all appearances, was as stable as usual. . . .

XIII. WOMEN AS PATRIOTS

ON April 15, 1861, the President of the United States called out seventy-five thousand militia, and summoned Congress to meet July 4, when four hundred thousand men were called for, and four hundred millions of dollars were voted to suppress the Rebellion. . . .

After consultation with Horace Greeley, William Lloyd Garrison, Governor Andrews, and Robert Dale Owen, Miss Anthony and I decided to call a meeting of women in Cooper Institute and form a

Woman's Loyal League, to advocate the immediate emancipation and enfranchisement of the Southern slaves, as the most speedy way of ending the War. . . .

It was agreed that the practical work to be done to secure freedom for the slaves was to circulate petitions through all the Northern States. For months these petitions were circulated diligently everywhere, as the signatures show—some signed on fence posts, plows, the anvil, the shoemaker's bench—by women of fashion and those in the industries, alike in the parlor and the kitchen; by statesmen, professors in colleges, editors, bishops; by sailors, and soldiers, and the hard-handed children of toil, building railroads and bridges, and digging canals, and in mines in the bowels of the earth. Petitions, signed by three hundred thousand persons, can now be seen in the national archives in the Capitol at Washington. Three of my sons spent weeks in our office in Cooper Institute, rolling up the petitions from each State separately, and inscribing on the outside the number of names of men and women contained therein. We sent appeals to the President the House of Representatives, and the Senate, from time to time, urging emancipation and the passage of the proposed Thirteenth, Fourteenth, and Fifteenth Amendments to the National Constitution. During these eventful months we received many letters from Senator Sumner, saying, "Send on the petitions as fast as received; they give me opportunities for speech." . . .

The leading journals vied with each other in praising the patience and prudence, the executive ability, the loyalty, and the patriotism of the women of the League, and yet these were the same women who, when demanding civil and political rights, privileges, and immunities for themselves, had been uniformly denounced as "unwise," "imprudent," "fanatical," and "impracticable." During the six years they held their own claims in abeyance to those of the slaves of the South, and labored to inspire the people with enthusiasm for the great measures of the Republican party, they were highly honored as "wise, loyal, and clear-sighted." But when the slaves were emancipated, and these women asked that they should be recognized in the reconstruction as citizens of the Republic, equal before the law, all these transcendent virtues vanished like dew before the morning sun. And thus it ever is: so long as woman labors to second man's endeavors and exalt his sex above her own, her virtues pass unquestioned; but when she dares to demand rights and privileges for herself, her motives, manners, dress, personal appearance, and character are subjects for ridicule and detraction. . . .

Miss Anthony and I were the first to see the full significance of the word "male" in the Fourteenth Amendment, and we at once sounded the alarm, and sent out petitions for a constitutional amendment to "prohibit the States from disfranchising any of their citizens on the ground of sex." Miss Anthony, who had spent the year in Kansas, started for New York the moment she saw the proposition before Congress to put the word "male" into the national Constitution, and made haste to rouse the women in the east to the fact that the time had come to begin vigorous work again for woman's enfranchisement.

Leaving Rochester, October 11, she called on Martha Wright at Auburn; Phebe Jones and Lydia Mott at Albany; Mmes. Rose, Gibbons, Davis, at New York city; Lucy Stone and Antoinette Brown Blackwell in New Jersey; Stephen and Abby Foster at Worcester; Mmes. Severance, Dall, Nowell, Dr. Harriot K. Hunt, Dr. M.E. Zakrzewska, and Messrs. Phillips and Garrison in Boston, urging them to join in sending protests to Washington against the pending legislation. Mr. Phillips at once consented to devote five hundred dollars from the "Jackson Fund" to commence the work. Miss Anthony and I spent all our Christmas holidays in writing letters and addressing appeals and petitions to every part of the country, and, before the close of the session of 1865-66, petitions with ten thousand signatures were poured into Congress. . . .

XIV. PIONEER LIFE IN KANSAS—OUR NEWSPAPER, "THE REVOLUTION"

IN 1867 the proposition to extend the suffrage to women and to colored men was submitted to the people of the State of Kansas, and, among other Eastern speakers, I was invited to make a campaign through the State. As the fall elections were pending, there was great excitement everywhere. Suffrage for colored men was a Republican measure, which the press and politicians of that party advocated with enthusiasm.

As woman suffrage was not a party question, we hoped that all parties would favor the measure; that we might, at last, have one green spot on earth where women could enjoy full liberty as citizens of the United States. Accordingly, in July, Miss Anthony and I started, with high hopes of a most successful trip, and, after an uneventful journey of one thousand five hundred miles, we reached the sacred soil where John Brown and his sons had helped to fight the battles that made Kansas a free State.

Lucy Stone, Mr. Blackwell, and Olympia Brown had preceded us and opened the campaign with large meetings in all the chief cities. Miss Anthony and I did the same. Then it was decided that, as we were to go to the very borders of the State, where there were no railroads, we must take carriages, and economize our forces by taking different routes. I was escorted by ex-Governor Charles Robinson. We had a low, easy carriage, drawn by two mules, in which we stored about a bushel of tracts, two valises, a pail for watering the mules, a basket of apples, crackers, and other such refreshments as we could purchase on the way. Some things were suspended underneath the carriage, some packed on behind, and some under the seat and at our feet. It required great skill to compress the necessary baggage into the allotted space. As we went to the very verge of civilization, wherever two dozen voters could be assembled, we had a taste of pioneer life. We spoke in log cabins, in depots, unfinished schoolhouses, churches, hotels, barns, and in the open air. . . .

The friends of woman suffrage were doomed to disappointment. Those in the East, on whom they relied for influence through the liberal newspapers, were silent, and we learned, afterward, that they used what influence they had to keep the abolitionists and Republicans of the State silent, as they feared the discussion of the woman question would jeopardize the enfranchisement of the black man. However, we worked untiringly and hopefully, not seeing through the game of the politicians until nearly the end of the canvass, when we saw that our only chance was in getting the Democratic vote. Accordingly, George Francis Train, then a most effective and popular speaker, was invited into the State to see what could be done to win the Democracy. He soon turned the tide, strengthened the weak-kneed Republicans and abolitionists, and secured a large Democratic vote.

For three months we labored diligently, day after day, enduring all manner of discomforts in traveling, eating, and sleeping. As there were no roads or guideposts, we often lost our way. In going through canons and fording streams it was often so dark that the Governor was obliged to walk ahead to find the way, taking off his coat so that I could see his white shirt and slowly drive after him. Though seemingly calm and cool, I had a great dread of these night adventures, as I was in constant fear of being upset on some hill and rolled into the water. The Governor often complimented me on my courage, when I was fully aware of being tempest-tossed with anxiety. I am naturally very timid, but, being silent under strong emotions of either pleasure or pain, I am credited with being courageous in the hour of danger. . . .

In spite of the discomforts we suffered in the Kansas campaign, I was glad of the experience. It gave me added self-respect to know that I could endure such hardships and fatigue with a great degree of cheerfulness. . . .

. . . The seed sown in Kansas in 1867 is now bearing its legitimate fruits. There was not a county in the State where meetings were not held or tracts scattered with a generous hand. If the friends of our cause in the East had been true and had done for woman what they did for the colored man, I believe both propositions would have been carried; but with a narrow policy, playing off one against the other, both were defeated. A policy of injustice always bears its own legitimate fruit in failure. . . .

The question settled in Kansas, we returned, with George Francis Train, to New York. He offered to pay all the expenses of the journey and meetings in all the chief cities on the way, and see that we were fully and well reported in their respective journals. After prolonged consultation Miss Anthony and I thought best to accept the offer and we did so. Most of our friends thought it a grave blunder, but the result proved otherwise. Mr. Train was then in his prime—a large, fine-looking man, a gentleman in dress and manner, neither smoking, chewing, drinking, nor gormandizing. He was an effective speaker and actor, as one of his speeches, which he illustrated, imitating the poor wife at the washtub and the drunken husband reeling in, fully showed. He gave his audience charcoal sketches of everyday life rather than argument. He always pleased popular audiences, and even the most fastidious were amused with his caricatures. As the newspapers gave several columns to our meetings at every point through all the States, the agitation was widespread and of great value. To be sure our friends, on all sides, fell off, and those especially who wished us to be silent on the question of woman's rights, declared "the cause too sacred to be advocated by such a charlatan as George Francis Train." We thought otherwise, as the accession of Mr. Train increased the agitation twofold. . . .

Reaching New York, Mr. Train made it possible for us to establish a newspaper, which gave another impetus to our movement. The *Revolution*, published by Susan B. Anthony and edited by Parker Pillsbury and myself, lived two years and a half and was then consolidated with the New York *Christian Enquirer*, edited by the

Rev. Henry Bellows, D.D. I regard the brief period in which I edited the *Revolution* as one of the happiest of my life, and I may add the most useful.

XV. WESTWARD HO!

IN the month of June, 1871, Miss Anthony and I went to California, holding suffrage meetings in many of the chief cities from New York to San Francisco, where we arrived about the middle of July, in time to experience the dry, dusty season.

We tarried, on the way, one week in Salt Lake City. It was at the time of the Godby secession, when several hundred Mormons abjured that portion of the faith of their fathers which authorized polygamy. A decision had just been rendered by the United States Supreme Court declaring the first wife and her children the only legal heirs. Whether this decision hastened the secession I do not know; however, it gave us the advantage of hearing all the arguments for and against the system. Those who were opposed to it said it made slaves of men. To support four wives and twenty children was a severe strain on any husband. The women who believed in polygamy had much to say in its favor, especially in regard to the sacredness of motherhood during the period of pregnancy and lactation; a lesson of respect for that period being religiously taught all Mormons.

We were very thankful for the privilege granted us of speaking to the women alone in the smaller Tabernacle. Our meeting opened at two o'clock and lasted until seven, giving us five hours of uninterrupted conversation. Judge McKeon had informed me of the recent decisions and the legal aspects of the questions, which he urged me to present to them fully and frankly, as no one had had such an opportunity before to speak to Mormon women alone. So I made the most of my privilege. I gave a brief history of the marriage institution in all times and countries, of the matriarchate, when the mother was the head of the family and owned the property and children; of the patriarchate, when man reigned supreme and woman was enslaved; of polyandry, polygamy, monogamy, and prostitution. We had a full and free discussion of every phase of the question, and we all agreed that we were still far from having reached the ideal position for woman in marriage, however satisfied man might be with his various experiments. Though the Mormon women, like all others, stoutly defend their own religion, yet they are no more satisfied than other sect. All women are dissatisfied with their position as inferiors, and their dissatisfaction increases in exact ratio with their intelligence and development. . . .

The journey over the Rocky Mountains was more interesting and wonderful than I had imagined. A heavy shower the morning we reached the alkali plains made the trip through that region, where travelers suffer so much, quite endurable. Although we reached California in its hot, dry season, we found the atmosphere in San Francisco delightful, fanned with the gentle breezes of the Pacific, cooled with the waters of its magnificent harbor. The Golden Gate does indeed open to the eye of the traveler one of the most beautiful harbors in the world. . . .

California was on the eve of an important election, and John A. Bingham of Ohio and Senator Cole were stumping the State for the Republican party. At several points we had the use of their able arguments as applied to woman. As Mr. Bingham's great speech was on the Thirteenth, Fourteenth, and Fifteenth Amendments, every principle he laid down literally enfranchised the women of the nation. I met the Ohio statesman one morning at breakfast, after hearing him the night before. I told him his logic must compel him to advocate woman suffrage. With a most cynical smile he said "he was not the puppet of logic, but the slave of practical politics." . . .

At Stockton we met a party of friends just returning from the Yosemite, who gave us much valuable information for the journey. Among other things, I was advised to write to Mr. Hutchins, the chief authority there, to have a good, strong horse in readiness to take me down the steep and narrow path into the valley. We took the same driver and carriage which our friends had found trustworthy, and started early in the morning. The dust and heat made the day's journey very wearisome, but the prospect of seeing the wonderful valley made all hardships of little consequence. Quite a large party were waiting to mount their donkeys and mules when we arrived. One of the attendants, a man about as thin as a stair rod, asked me if I was the lady who had ordered a strong horse; I being the stoutest of the party, he readily arrived at that conclusion, so my steed was promptly produced. But I knew enough of horses and riding to see at a glance that he was a failure, with his low withers and high haunches, for descending steep mountains. In addition to his forward pitch, his back was immensely broad. Miss Anthony and I decided to ride astride and had suits made for that purpose; but alas! my steed was so broad that I could not reach the stirrups, and the moment we began to descend,

I felt as if I were going over his head. So I fell behind, and, when the party had all gone forward, I dismounted, though my slender guide assured me there was no danger, he "had been up and down a thousand times." But, as I had never been at all, his repeated experiences did not inspire me with courage. I decided to walk. That, the guide said, was impossible. "Well," said I, by way of compromise, "I will walk as far as I can, and when I reach the impossible, I will try that ill-constructed beast. I cannot see what you men were thinking of when you selected such an animal for this journey." And so we went slowly down, arguing the point whether it were better to ride or walk; to trust one's own legs, or, by chance, be precipitated thousands of feet down the mountain side.

It was a hot August day; the sun, in the zenith, shining with full power. My blood was at boiling heat with exercise and vexation. Alternately sliding and walking, catching hold of rocks and twigs, drinking at every rivulet, covered with dust, dripping with perspiration, skirts, gloves, and shoes in tatters, for four long hours I struggled down to the end, when I laid myself out on the grass, and fell asleep, perfectly exhausted, having sent the guide to tell Mr. Hutchins that I had reached the valley, and, as I could neither ride nor walk, to send a wheelbarrow, or four men with a blanket to transport me to the hotel. That very day the Mariposa Company had brought the first carriage into the valley, which, in due time, was sent to my relief. Miss Anthony, who, with a nice little Mexican pony and narrow saddle, had made her descent with grace and dignity, welcomed me on the steps of the hotel, and laughed immoderately at my helpless plight. . . .

In the spring I went to Nebraska, and Miss Anthony and I again made a Western tour, sometimes together and sometimes by different routes. A constitutional convention was in session in Lincoln, and it was proposed to submit an amendment to strike the word "male" from the Constitution. Nebraska became a State in March, 1867, and took "Equality before the law" as her motto. Her Territorial legislature had discussed, many times, proposed liberal legislation for women, and her State legislature had twice considered propositions for women's enfranchisement. . . .

After I had addressed the convention, some of the members called on me to discuss the points of my speech. All the gentlemen were serious and respectful with one exception. A man with an unusually small head, diminutive form, and crooked legs tried, at my expense, to be witty and facetious. During a brief pause in the conversation he brought his chair directly before me and said, in a mocking tone, "Don't you think that the best thing a woman can do is to perform well her part in the role of wife and mother? My wife presented me with eight beautiful children; is not this a better life-work than that of exercising the right of suffrage?"

I had had my eye on this man during the whole interview, and saw that the other members were annoyed at his behavior. I decided, when the opportune moment arrived, to give him an answer not soon to be forgotten; so I promptly replied to his question, as I slowly viewed him from head to foot, "I have met few men, in my life, worth repeating eight times." The members burst into a roar of laughter, and one of them, clapping him on the shoulder, said: "There, sonny, you have read and spelled; you better go." This scene was heralded in all the Nebraska papers, and, wherever the little man went, he was asked why Mrs. Stanton thought he was not worth repeating eight times. . . .

XVI. WRITING "THE HISTORY OF WOMAN SUFFRAGE"

THE four years following the Centennial* were busy, happy ones, of varied interests and employments, public and private. Sons and daughters graduating from college, bringing troops of young friends to visit us; the usual matrimonial entanglements, with all their promises of celestial bliss intertwined with earthly doubts and fears; weddings, voyages to Europe, business ventures—in this whirl of plans and projects our heads, hearts, and hands were fully occupied. Seven boys and girls dancing round the fireside, buoyant with all life's joys opening before them, are enough to keep the most apathetic parents on the watch-towers by day and anxious even in dreamland by night. My spare time, if it can be said that I ever had any, was given during these days to social festivities. The inevitable dinners, teas, picnics, and dances with country neighbors, all came round in quick succession. We lived, at this time, at Tenafly, New Jersey, not far from the publisher of the *Sun*, Isaac W. England, who also had seven boys and girls as full of frolic as our own. Mrs. England and I entered into

---

*At the Centennial Celebration of American Independence, held in Philadelphia on July 4, 1876, Mrs. Stanton and her allies, refused permission to participate as a woman's group, submitted a written Woman's Declaration of Rights to the presiding officer and then read it aloud to a crowd from a nearby platform.

all their games with equal zest. The youngest thought half the fun was to see our enthusiasm in "blindman's buff," "fox and geese," and "bean bags." It thrills me with delight, even now, to see these games! . . .

In addition to the domestic cares which a large family involved, Mrs. Gage, Miss Anthony, and I were already busy collecting material for "The History of Woman Suffrage." This required no end of correspondence. Then my lecturing trips were still a part of the annual programme. Washington conventions, too, with calls, appeals, resolutions, speeches and hearings before the Committees of Congress and State legislatures, all these came round in the year's proceedings as regularly as pumpkin pies for Thanksgiving, plum pudding for Christmas, and patriotism for Washington's birthday. Those who speak for glory or philanthropy are always in demand for college commencements and Fourth of July orations, hence much of Miss Anthony's eloquence, as well as my own, was utilized in this way. . . .

On November 12, 1880, I was sixty-five years old, and, pursuant to my promise, I then began my diary. It was a bright, sunny day, but the frost king was at work; all my grand old trees, that stood like sentinels, to mark the boundary of my domain, were stripped of their foliage, and their brilliant colors had faded into a uniform brown; but the evergreens and the tall, prim cedars held their own, and, when covered with snow, their exquisite beauty brought tears to my eyes. One need never be lonely mid beautiful trees.

My thoughts were with my absent children—Harriot in France, Theodore in Germany, Margaret with her husband and brother Gerrit, halfway across the continent, and Bob still in college. I spent the day writing letters and walking up and down the piazza, and enjoyed, from my windows, a glorious sunset. Alone, on birthdays or holidays, one is very apt to indulge in sad retrospections. The thought of how much more I might have done for the perfect development of my children than I had accomplished, depressed me. I thought of all the blunders in my own life and in their education. Little has been said of the responsibilities of parental life; accordingly little or nothing has been done. I had such visions of parental duties that day that I came to the conclusion that parents never could pay the debt they owe their children for bringing them into this world of suffering, unless they can insure them sound minds in sound bodies, and enough of the good things of this life to enable them to live without a continual struggle for the necessaries of existence. . . .

The arrival of Miss Anthony and Mrs. Gage, on November 20, banished all family matters from my mind. What planning, now, for volumes, chapters, footnotes, margins, appendices, paper, and type; of engravings, title, preface, and introduction! I had never thought that the publication of a book required the consideration of such endless details. We stood appalled before the mass of material, growing higher and higher with every mail, and the thought of all the reading involved made us feel as if our lifework lay before us. Six weeks of steady labor all day, and often until midnight, made no visible decrease in the pile of documents. However, before the end of the month we had our arrangements all made with publishers and engravers, and six chapters in print. When we began to correct proof we felt as if something was accomplished. Thus we worked through the winter and far into the spring, with no change except the Washington Convention and an occasional evening meeting in New York city. . . .

In May, 1881, the first volume of our History appeared; it was an octavo, containing 871 pages, with good paper, good print, handsome engravings, and nicely bound. I welcomed it with the same feeling of love and tenderness as I did my firstborn. I took the same pleasure in hearing it praised and felt the same mortification in hearing it criticised. . . . In fact, we received far more praise and less blame than we anticipated. We began the second volume in June. . . .

Toward the end of October, Miss Anthony returned, after a rest of two months, and we commenced work again on the second volume of the History. November 2 being election day, the Republican carriage, decorated with flags and evergreens, came to the door for voters. As I owned the house and paid the taxes, and as none of the white males was home, I suggested that I might go down and do the voting, whereupon the gentlemen who represented the Republican committee urged me, most cordially, to do so. Accompanied by my faithful friend, Miss Anthony, we stepped into the carriage and went to the poll, held in the hotel where I usually went to pay taxes. When we entered the room it was crowded with men. I was introduced to the inspectors by Charles Everett, one of our leading citizens, who said: "Mrs. Stanton is here, gentlemen, for the purpose of voting. As she is a taxpayer, of sound mind, and of legal age, I see no reason why she should not exercise this right of citizenship."

The inspectors were thunderstruck. I think they were afraid that I was about to capture the ballot box. One placed his arms round it, with one hand close over the aperture where the ballots were slipped in, and said, with mingled surprise and pity, "Oh, no, madam! Men only are allowed to vote." I then explained to him that, in accordance with the Constitution of New Jersey, women had voted in New Jersey down to 1801, when they were forbidden the further exercise of the right by an arbitrary act of the legislature, and, by a recent amendment to the national Constitution, Congress had declared that "all persons born or naturalized in the United States, and subject to the jurisdiction thereof, are citizens of the United States and of the State wherein they reside" and are entitled to vote. I told them that I wished to cast my vote, as a citizen of the United States, for the candidates for United States offices. Two of the inspectors sat down and pulled their hats over their eyes, whether from shame or ignorance I do not know. The other held on to the box, and said "I know nothing about the Constitutions, State or national. I never read either; but I do know that in New Jersey, women have not voted in my day, and I cannot accept your ballot." So I laid my ballot in his hand, saying that I had the same right to vote that any man present had, and on him must rest the responsibility of denying me my rights of citizenship. . . .

XVII. IN THE SOUTH OF FRANCE

HAVING worked diligently through nearly two years on the second volume of "The History of Woman Suffrage," I looked forward with pleasure to a rest, in the Old World, beyond the reach and sound of my beloved Susan and the woman suffrage movement. On May 27, 1892,* I sailed with my daughter Harriot on the *Chateau Leoville* for Bordeaux. The many friends who came to see us off brought fruits and flowers, boxes of candied ginger to ward off seasickness, letters of introduction, and light literature for the voyage. We had all the daily and weekly papers, secular and religious, the new monthly magazines, and several novels. We thought we would do an immense amount of reading, but we did very little. Eating, sleeping, walking on deck, and watching the ever-changing ocean are about all that most people care to do. The sail down the harbor that bright, warm evening was beautiful, and, we lingered on deck in the moonlight until a late hour. . . .

We had a smooth, pleasant, uneventful voyage, until the last night, when, on nearing the French coast, the weather became dark and stormy. The next morning our good steamer pushed slowly and carefully up the broad, muddy Gironde and landed us on the bustling quays of Bordeaux, where my son Theodore stood waiting to receive us. As we turned to say farewell to our sturdy ship—gazing up at its black iron sides besprinkled with salty foam—a feeling of deep

*An error. It was in 1882.

thankfulness took possession of us, for she had been faithful to her trust, and had borne us safely from the New World to the Old, over thousands of miles of treacherous sea. . . .

It was a bright, cool day on which we took the train for Toulouse, and we enjoyed the delightful run through the very heart of old Gascony and Languedoc. It was evident that we were in the South, where the sun is strong, for, although summer had scarcely begun, the country already wore a brown hue. But the narrow strips of growing grain, the acres of grape vines, looking like young currant bushes, and the fig trees scattered here and there, looked odd to the eye of a native of New York. . . .

Laura Curtis Bullard, in her sketch of me in "Our Famous Women," says: "In 1882, Mrs. Stanton went to France, on a visit to her son Theodore, and spent three months at the convent of La Sagesse, in the city of Toulouse." This is quite true; but I have sometimes tried to guess what her readers thought I was doing for three months in a convent. Weary of the trials and tribulations of this world, had I gone there to prepare in solitude for the next? Had I taken the veil in my old age? Or, like high-church Anglicans and Roman Catholics, had I made this my retreat? Not at all. My daughter wished to study French advantageously, my son lived in the mountains hard by, and the garden of La Sagesse, with its big trees, clean gravel paths, and cool shade, was the most delightful spot.

In this religious retreat I met, from time to time, some of the most radical and liberal-minded residents of the South. Toulouse is one of the most important university centers of France, and bears with credit the proud title of "the learned city." With two distinguished members of the faculty, the late Dr. Nicholas Joly and Professor Moliner of the law school, I often had most interesting discussions on all the great questions of the hour. That three heretics—I should say, six, for my daughter, son, and his wife often joined the circle—could thus sit in perfect security, and debate, in the most unorthodox fashion, in these holy precincts, all the reforms, social, political, and religious, which the United States and France need in order to be in harmony with the spirit of the age, was a striking proof of the progress the world has made in freedom of speech. The time was when such acts would have cost us our lives, even if we had been caught expressing our heresies in the seclusion of our own homes. But here, under the oaks of a Catholic convent, with the gray-robed sisters all around us, we could point out the fallacies of Romanism itself, without fear or trembling. Glorious Nineteenth Century, what conquests are thine! . . .

At Jacournassy, the country seat of Mme. Berry, whose daughter my son Theodore married, I spent a month full of surprises. How everything differed from America, and even from the plain below! The peasants, many of them at least, can neither speak French nor understand it. Their language is a patois, resembling both Spanish and Italian, and they cling to it with astonishing pertinacity. Their agricultural implements are not less quaint than their speech. The plow is a long beam with a most primitive share in the middle, a cow at one end, and a boy at the other. The grain is cut with a sickle and threshed with a flail on the barn floor, as in Scripture times. Manure is scattered over the fields with the hands. . . .

One of the sources of amusement, during my sojourn at Jacournassy, was of a literary nature. My son Theodore was then busy collecting the materials for his book entitled "The Woman Question in Europe," and every post brought in manuscripts and letters from all parts of the continent, written in almost every tongue known to Babel. So just what I came abroad to avoid, I found on the very threshold where I came to rest. We had good linguists at the chateau, and every document finally came forth in English dress, which, however, often needed much altering and polishing. This was my part of the work. . . .

The scenery in the Black Mountains is very grand, and reminds one of the lofty ranges of mountains around the Yosemite Valley in California. In the distance are the snow-capped Pyrenees, producing a solemn beauty, a profound solitude. We used to go every evening where we could see the sun set and watch the changing shadows in the broad valley below. Another great pleasure here was watching the gradual development of my first grandchild, Elizabeth Cady Stanton, born at Paris, on the 3d of May, 1882. She was a fine child; though only three months old her head was covered with dark hair, and her large blue eyes looked out with intense earnestness from beneath her well-shaped brow. . . .

On August 20, I returned to Toulouse and our quiet convent. The sisters gave me a most affectionate welcome and I had many pleasant chats, sitting in the gardens, with the priests and professors. . . .

Theodore, his wife, and baby, and Mr. Blatch, a young Englishman, came to visit us. The sisters and school children manifested great delight in the baby, and the former equal pleasure in Mr. Blatch's marked attention to my daughter, as babies and courtships were unusual tableaux in a convent. . . .

We gave a farewell dinner at the Tivollier Hotel to some of our friends. With speeches and toasts we had a merry time. Professor Joly was the life of the occasion. He had been a teacher in France for forty years and had just retired on a pension. I presented to him "The History of Woman Suffrage," and he wrote a most complimentary review of it in one of the leading French journals. Every holiday must have its end. Other duties called me to England. So, after a hasty good-by to Jacournassy and La Sagesse, to the Black Mountains and Toulouse, to Languedoc and the South, we took train one day in October, just as the first leaves began to fall, and, in fourteen hours, were at Paris. I had not seen the beautiful French capital since 1840. My sojourn within its enchanting walls was short,—too short,—and I woke one morning to find myself, after an absence of forty-two years, again on the shores of England, and before my eyes were fairly open, grim old London welcomed me back. But the many happy hours spent in "merry England" during the winter of 1882-83 have not effaced from my memory the months in Languedoc.

Reaching London in the fogs and mists of November, 1882, the first person I met, after a separation of many years, was our revered and beloved friend William Henry Channing. The tall, graceful form was somewhat bent; the sweet, thoughtful face somewhat sadder; the crimes and miseries of the world seemed heavy on his heart. With his refined, nervous organization, the gloomy moral and physical atmosphere of London was the last place on earth where that beautiful life should have ended. I found him in earnest conversation with my daughter and the young Englishman she was soon to marry, advising them not only as to the importance of the step they were about to take, but as to the minor points to be observed in the ceremony. At the appointed time a few friends gathered in Portland Street Chapel, and as we approached the altar our friend appeared in surplice and gown, his pale, spiritual face more tender and beautiful than ever. This was the last marriage service he ever performed, and it was as pathetic as original. His whole appearance was so in harmony with the exquisite sentiments he uttered, that we who listened felt as if, for the time being, we had entered with him into the Holy of Holies. . . .

[Mrs. Stanton then spent the ensuing year in Great Britain, traveling, sightseeing, visiting fellow reformers, and attending reform meetings. It was her first return to these scenes since 1840, when she had attended the World Antislavery Convention in London on her honeymoon.]

XVIII. WOMAN AND THEOLOGY

RETURNING from Europe in the autumn of 1883, after visiting a large circle of relatives and friends, I spent six weeks with my cousin, Elizabeth Smith Miller, at her home at Geneva, on Seneca Lake.

Through Miss Frances Lord, a woman of rare culture and research, my daughter and I had become interested in the school of theosophy, and read "Isis Unveiled," by Madame Blavatsky, Sinnett's works on the "Occult World," and "The Perfect Way," by Anna Kingsford. Full of these ideas, I soon interested my cousins in the subject, and we resolved to explore, as far as possible, some of these Eastern mysteries, of which we had heard so much. We looked in all directions to find some pilot to start us on the right course. We heard that Gerald Massey was in New York city, lecturing on "The Devil," "Ghosts," and "Evil Spirits" generally, so we invited him to visit us and give a course of lectures in Geneva. But, unfortunately, he was ill, and could not open new fields of thought to us at that time, though we were very desirous to get a glimpse into the unknown world, and hold converse with the immortals. As I soon left Geneva with my daughter, Mrs. Stanton Lawrence, our occult studies were, for a time, abandoned.

My daughter and I often talked of writing a story, she describing the characters and their environments and I attending to the philosophy and soliloquies. As I had no special duties in prospect, we decided that this was the time to make our experiment. Accordingly we hastened to the family homestead at Johnstown, New York, where we could be entirely alone. Friends on all sides wondered what had brought us there in the depth of winter. But we kept our secret, and set ourselves to work with diligence, and after three months our story was finished to our entire satisfaction. We felt sure that everyone who read it would be deeply interested and that we should readily find a publisher. We thought of "Our Romance" the first thing in the morning and talked of it the last thing at night. But alas! friendly critics who read our story pointed out its defects, and in due time we reached their conclusions, and the unpublished manuscript now rests in a pigeonhole of my desk. We had not many days to mourn our disappointment, as Madge was summoned to her Western home, and Miss Anthony arrived armed and equipped with bushels of documents for vol. iii. of "The History of Woman Suffrage." The summer and autumn of 1884 Miss Anthony and I passed at Johnstown, working diligently on the History, indulging only in an occasional drive, a stroll round the town in the evening, or a ride in the open street cars. . . .

In May, 1885, we left Johnstown and took possession of our house at Tenafly, New Jersey. It seemed very pleasant, after wandering in the Old World and the New, to be in my own home once more, surrounded by the grand trees I so dearly loved; to see the gorgeous sunsets, the twinkling fireflies; to hear the whippoorwills call their familiar note, while the June bugs and the mosquitoes buzz outside the nets through which they cannot enter. Many people complain of the mosquito in New Jersey, when he can so easily be shut out of the family circle by nets over all the doors and windows. I had a long piazza, encased in netting, where paterfamilias, with his pipe, could muse and gaze at the stars unmolested.

June brought Miss Anthony and a box of fresh documents for another season of work on vol. iii. of our History. We had a flying visit from Miss Eddy of Providence, daughter of Mrs. Eddy who gave fifty thousand dollars to the woman suffrage movement, and a granddaughter of Francis Jackson of Boston, who also left a generous bequest to our reform. We found Miss Eddy a charming young woman with artistic tastes. She showed us several pen sketches she had made of some of our reformers, that were admirable likenesses.

Mr. Stanton's "Random Recollections" were published at this time and were well received. A dinner was given him, on his eightieth birthday (June 27, 1885), by the Press Club of New York city, with speeches and toasts by his lifelong friends. As no ladies were invited I can only judge from the reports in the daily papers, and what I could glean from the honored guest himself, that it was a very interesting occasion.

In April rumors of a domestic invasion, wafted on every Atlantic breeze, warned us that our children were coming from England and France—a party of six. Fortunately, the last line of the History was written, so Miss Anthony, with vol. iii. and bushels of manuscripts, fled to the peaceful home of her sister Mary at Rochester. The expected party sailed from Liverpool the 26th of May, on the *America*. After being out three days the piston rod broke and they were obliged to return. My son-in-law, W. H. Blatch, was so seasick and disgusted that he remained in England, and took a fresh start two months later, and had a swift passage without any accidents. The rest were transferred to the *Germanic*, and reached New York the 12th of June. Different divisions of the party were arriving until midnight. Five people and twenty pieces of baggage! The confusion of such an invasion quite upset the even tenor of our days, and it took some time for people and trunks to find their respective niches. However crowded elsewhere, there was plenty of room in our hearts, and we were unspeakably happy to have our flock all around us once more.

I had long heard so many conflicting opinions about the Bible— some saying it taught woman's emancipation and some her subjection—that, during this visit of my children, the thought came to me that it would be well to collect every biblical reference to women in one small compact volume, and see on which side the balance of influence really was. . . .

A happy coincidence enabled me at last to begin this work. While my daughter, Mrs. Stanton Blatch, was with me, our friend Miss Frances Lord, on our earnest invitation, came to America to visit us. She landed in New York the 4th of August, 1886. As it was Sunday she could not telegraph, hence there was no one to meet her, and, as we all sat chatting on the front piazza, suddenly, to our surprise and delight, she drove up. After a few days' rest and general talk of passing events, I laid the subject so near my heart before her and my daughter. They responded promptly and heartily, and we immediately set to work. I wrote to every woman who I thought might join such a committee, and Miss Lord ran through the Bible in a few days, marking each chapter that in any way referred to women. We found that the work would not be so great as we imagined, as all the facts and teachings in regard to women occupied less than one-tenth of the whole Scriptures. We purchased some cheap Bibles, cut out the texts, pasted them at the head of the page, and underneath, wrote our commentaries as clearly and concisely as possible. We did not intend to have sermons or essays, but brief comments, to keep "The Woman's Bible" as small as possible.

Miss Lord and I worked several weeks together, and Mrs. Blatch and I, during the winter of 1887, wrote all our commentaries on the Pentateuch. But we could not succeed in forming the committee, nor, after writing innumerable letters, make the women understand what we wanted to do. I still have the commentaries of the few who responded, and the letters of those who declined—a most varied and amusing bundle of manuscripts in themselves. Some said the Bible had no special authority with them; that, like the American Constitution, it could be interpreted to mean anything—slavery, when we protected that "Institution," and freedom, when it existed no longer. Others said that woman's sphere was clearly marked out in the Scriptures, and all attempt at emancipation was flying in the face of Providence. Others said they considered all the revisions made by men thus far, had been so many acts of sacrilege, and they did hope women would not add their influence, to weaken the faith of the people in the divine origin of the Holy Book, for, if men and women could change it in one particular, they could in all. On the whole the correspondence was discouraging.

Later Miss Lord became deeply interested in psychical researches, and I could get no more work out of her. And as soon as we had finished the Pentateuch, Mrs. Blatch declared she would go no farther; that it was the driest history she had ever read, and most derogatory to women. . . .

On October 27, 1886, with my daughter, nurse, and grandchild, I again sailed for England. Going out of the harbor in the clear early morning, we had a fine view of Bartholdi's statue of Liberty Enlightening the World. We had a warm, gentle rain and a smooth sea most of the way, and, as we had a stateroom on deck, we could have the portholes open, and thus get all the air we desired. With novels and letters, chess and whist the time passed pleasantly, and, on the ninth day, we landed in Liverpool.

[Mrs. Stanton's trip abroad lasted eighteen months, during which she spent about six months in Paris, living in an apartment— which, to her surprise, she thoroughly enjoyed—and living an active social life, filled with visits from both American friends and new French acquaintances.]

XIX. THE INTERNATIONAL COUNCIL OF WOMEN

PURSUANT to the idea of the feasibility and need of an International Council of Women, mentioned in a preceding chapter, it was decided to celebrate the fourth decade of the woman suffrage movement in the United States by calling together such a council. At its nineteenth annual convention, held in January, 1887, the National Woman Suffrage Association resolved to assume the entire responsibility of holding a council, and to extend an invitation, for that purpose, to all associations of women in the trades, professions, and reforms, as well as those advocating political rights. Early in June, 1887, a call was issued for such a council to convene under the auspices of the National Woman Suffrage Association at Washington, D.C., on March 25, 1888. The grand assemblage of women, coming from all the countries of the civilized globe, proved that the call for such a council was opportune, while the order and dignity of the proceedings proved the women worthy the occasion. No one doubts now the wisdom of that initiative step nor the added power women have gained over popular thought through the International Council.

As the proceedings of the convention were fully and graphically reported in the *Woman's Tribune* at that time, and as its reports were afterward published in book form, revised and corrected by Miss Anthony, Miss Foster, and myself, I will merely say that our most sanguine expectations as to its success were more than realized. The large theater was crowded for an entire week, and hosts of able women spoke, as if specially inspired, on all the vital questions of the hour. Although the council was called and conducted by the suffrage association, yet various other societies were represented. . . .

One of the best speeches at the council was made by Helen H. Gardener. It was a criticism of Dr. Hammond's position in regard to the inferior size and quality of woman's brain. As the doctor had never had the opportunity of examining the brains of the most distinguished women, and, probably, those only of paupers and criminals, she felt he had no data on which to base his conclusions. Moreover, she had the written opinions of several leading physicians, that it was quite impossible to distinguish the male from the female brain.

The hearing at the Capitol, after the meeting of the council, was very interesting, as all the foreign delegates were invited to speak each in the language of her own country; to address their alleged representatives in the halls of legislation was a privilege they had never enjoyed at home. It is very remarkable that English women have never made the demand for a hearing in the House of Commons, nor even for a decent place to sit, where they hear the debates and see the fine proportions of the representatives. The delegates had several brilliant receptions at the Riggs House, and at the houses of Senator Stanford of California and Senator Palmer of Michigan. Miss Anthony and I spent two months in Washington, that winter. . . .

The winter of 1888-89 I was to spend with my daughter in Omaha. I reached there in time to witness the celebration of the completion of the first bridge between that city and Council Bluffs. There was a grand procession in which all the industries of both towns were represented, and which occupied six hours in passing. We had a desirable position for reviewing the pageant, and very pleasant company to interpret the mottoes, symbols, and banners. The bridge practically brings the towns together, as electric street cars now run from one to the other in ten minutes. Here, for the first time, I saw the cable cars running up hill and down without any visible means of locomotion. . . .

My seventy-third birthday I spent with my son Gerrit Smith Stanton, on his farm near Portsmouth, Iowa. As we had not met in several years, it took us a long time, in the network of life, to pick up all the stitches that had dropped since we parted. I amused myself darning stockings and drawing plans for an addition to his house. But in the spring my son and his wife came to the conclusion that they had had enough of the solitude of farm life and turned their faces eastward. . . .

Owing to the illness of my son-in-law, Frank E. Lawrence, he and my daughter went to California to see if the balmy air of San Diego would restore his health, and so we gave up housekeeping in Omaha, and, on April 20, 1889, in company with my eldest son I returned East and spent the summer at Hempstead, Long Island, with my son Gerrit and his wife. . . .

In September, 1889, my daughter, Mrs. Stanton Lawrence, came East to attend a school of physical culture, and my other daughter, Mrs. Stanton Blatch, came from England to enjoy one of our bracing winters. Unfortunately we had rain instead of snow, and fogs instead of frost. However, we had a pleasant reunion at Hempstead. After a few days in and about New York visiting friends, we went to Geneva and spent several weeks in the home of my cousin, the daughter of Gerrit Smith. . . .

From Geneva we went to Buffalo, but, as I had a bad cold and a general feeling of depression, I decided to go to the Dansville Sanatorium and see what Doctors James and Kate Jackson could do for me. I was there six weeks and tried all the rubbings, pinchings, steamings; the Swedish movements of the arms, hands, legs, feet; dieting, massage, electricity, and, though I succeeded in throwing off only five pounds of flesh, yet I felt like a new being. It is a charming place to be in—the home is pleasantly situated and the scenery very fine. The physicians are all genial, and a cheerful atmosphere pervades the whole establishment. . . .

From Dansville my daughters and I went on to Washington to celebrate the seventieth birthday of Miss Anthony, who has always been to them as a second mother. Mrs. Blatch made a speech at the celebration, and Mrs. Lawrence gave a recitation. First came a grand supper at the Riggs House. The dining room was beautifully decorated; in fact, Mr. and Mrs. Spofford spared no pains to make the occasion one long to be remembered. May Wright Sewall was the mistress of ceremonies. She read the toasts and called on the different speakers. Phoebe Couzins, Rev. Anna Shaw, Isabella Beecher Hooker, Matilda Joslyn Gage, Clara B. Colby, Senator Blair of New Hampshire, and many others responded. I am ashamed to say that we kept up the festivities till after two o'clock. Miss Anthony, dressed in dark velvet and point lace, spoke at the close with great pathos. Those of us who were there will not soon forget February 15, 1890.

After speaking before committees of the Senate and House, I gave the opening address at the annual convention. Mrs. Stanton Blatch spoke a few minutes on the suffrage movement in England, after which we hurried off to New York, and went on board the *Aller*, one of the North German Lloyd steamers, bound for Southampton....

[Mrs. Stanton spent the next eighteen months in England with her daughter's family, carrying on her usual round of activities. The following few years, on her return to the United States, were filled with both enjoyment of family and friends and frequent public appearances.]

XX. MY EIGHTIETH BIRTHDAY

WITHOUT my knowledge or consent, my lifelong friend, Susan B. Anthony, who always seems to appreciate homage tendered to me more highly than even to herself, made arrangements for the celebration of my eightieth birthday, on the 12th day of November, 1895. She preferred that this celebration should be conducted by the National Council of Women, composed of a large number of organizations representing every department of woman's labor, though, as the enfranchisement of woman had been my special life work, it would have been more appropriate if the celebration had been under the auspices of the National Woman's Suffrage Association.

Mrs. Mary Lowe Dickinson, President of the National Council of Women, assumed the financial responsibility and the extensive correspondence involved, and with rare tact, perseverance, and executive ability made the celebration a complete success. In describing this occasion I cannot do better than to reproduce, in part, Mrs. Dickinson's account, published in *The Arena:*

"In the month of June, 1895, the National Council of Women issued the following invitation:

"'Believing that the progress made by women in the last half century may be promoted by a more general notice of their achievements, we propose to hold, in New York city, a convention for this purpose. As an appropriate time for such a celebration, the eightieth birthday of Elizabeth Cady Stanton has been chosen. Her half century of pioneer work for the rights of women makes her name an inspiration for such an occasion and her life a fitting object for the homage of all women.

"'This National Council is composed of twenty organizations; these and all other societies interested are invited to co-operate in grateful recognition of the debt the present generation owes to the pioneers of the past. From their interest in the enfranchisement of women, the influence of Mrs. Stanton and her coadjutor, Miss Anthony, has permeated all departments of progress and made them a common center round which all interested in woman's higher development may gather.' . . .

"... No woman present could fail to be impressed with what we owe to the women of the past, and especially to this one woman who was the honored guest of the occasion. And no young woman could desire to forget the picture of this aged form as, leaning upon her staff, Mrs. Stanton spoke to the great audience of over six thousand, as she had spoken hundreds of times before in legislative halls, and whenever her word could influence the popular sentiment in favor of justice for all mankind."

My birthday celebration, with all the testimonials of love and friendship I received, was an occasion of such serious thought and deep feeling as I had never before experienced. Having been accustomed for half a century to blame rather than praise, I was surprised with such a manifestation of approval; I could endure any amount of severe criticism with complacency, but such an outpouring of homage and affection stirred me profoundly. . . .

The birthday celebration was to me more than a beautiful pageant; more than a personal tribute. It was the dawn of a new day for the Mothers of the Race! The harmonious co-operation of so many different organizations, with divers interests and opinions, in one grand jubilee was, indeed, a heavenly vision of peace and hope; a prophecy that with the exaltation of Womanhood would come new Life, Light, and Liberty to all mankind.

Linda Brent (pseudonym of Harriet Jacobs)
(1813-1897)

THE author of *Incidents in the Life of a Slave Girl,* which was published in 1861, was a woman named Harriet Jacobs who had escaped from slavery in North Carolina nineteen years earlier and who was then forty-eight. Since 1842 Jacobs had been living and working in New York, Boston, and other places, and had assisted her brother John in his antislavery office and reading room in Rochester, New York. She had been befriended by two families for whom she worked, the abolitionists Isaac and Amy Post of Rochester and the well-known author and editor Nathaniel P. Willis and his second wife, Cornelia Grinnell Willis, of New York, as well as the antislavery author and editor Lydia Maria Child. After the passage of the Fugitive Slave Law of 1850 had made Jacobs' life as an escaped slave increasingly precarious, Mrs. Willis purchased her freedom from her owner; Mrs. Post encouraged her to write about her life in slavery, and when Jacobs finished her narrative, Mrs. Child edited it for publication.

After publication of the narrative, however, its authenticity was questioned and it came to be viewed as an unreliable source. Jacobs was little-known except to her friends, her employers, and a small circle of abolitionists, and she did not wish to identify herself publicly as the willing mistress of a Southern white man by whom she had had two illegitimate children, even though she blamed her situation on the warping effects of slavery. Hence she wrote under an assumed name and disguised the names of other individuals and places. These devices led historians and other later critics to suspect that the book was largely the work of Mrs. Child or some other abolitionist, since "Linda Brent" had not been identified and since in at least one other case a slave narrative had turned out to be more fiction than fact.

Not until the historian Jean Fagin Yellin recently unearthed a connection between Jacobs and Edenton, North Carolina, and, with the aid of other researchers, discovered the actual identities of the people about whom Jacobs wrote, was it clear that *Incidents in the Life of a Slave Girl* was firmly based in fact. Her oppressor in the narrative, Dr. Flint, turned out to be a Dr. James Norcom; her lover, Mr. Sands, was in real life the lawyer Samuel Tredwell Sawyer; and her employers in New York, Mr. and Mrs. Bruce, were the Willises spoken of above.

Moreover, not until Yellin identified letters Jacobs had written to the press and discovered and analyzed others of her letters in manuscript collections could it be shown that Jacobs was fully capable of writing her own story. In her Introduction, Lydia Maria Child declared that her own editorial revisions to the book were "mainly for purposes of condensation and orderly arrangement," and that "with trifling exceptions, the ideas and the language are her [Jacob's] own." The precise amount of editorial intervention can never be established, and the reader may suspect that many of the story's rhetorical flourishes were added at Mrs. Child's behest, if not by her hand, but there is now good reason to believe that the incidents in the book are those supplied by Harriet Jacobs.

Incidents tells its own story of the brutalities, including sexual exploitation, of slavery. It also reveals the solid support black families and their friends could give each other under dangerous conditions, as well as the occasional unexpected altruism shown by whites to blacks, in ways that constituted an active, if small-scale, subversion of the slave system.

Such a story, one of the very few narratives told by a woman who had escaped from slavery, and one filled with such a wealth of convincing detail, served the antislavery cause well. Abolitionists capitalized on some of the obvious conflicts between Romantic ideals and slavery's usages. On the one hand, American men paid tribute to an idealized femininity and women welcomed it, while both celebrated the innocence of childhood. On the other, slaveholders were sometimes guilty of sadistic punishment or sexual exploitation of defenseless women, as well as of selling their victims' children, some of whom were the owners' own offspring. Such cruel ironies could arouse those who otherwise tolerated slavery as an unhappy but intractable reality.

In addition to its direct attack on slavery, Jacobs' narrative also serves as a critique of some of the pretensions of American democracy and as a contribution to feminist thought and action. As the escaped slave Frederick Douglass had earlier done in his own narrative, Jacobs demonstrated her essential humanity, her intelligence, and her claim to citizenship despite her origins at the bottom of the American social order. Like Mowatt and Stanton, she asserted in effect, through this poignant literary statement, that her psychological history was a matter of importance.

During the Civil War Jacobs did relief work among "contrabands"—slaves freed by the processes of war—in Washington, and as the war ended in 1865 she returned to Edenton, North Carolina, to bring supplies to the family members and friends who were still there. She and her daughter went to England to raise funds for the aid of orphans and the aged in Savannah; later she ran a boarding house in Cambridge, Massachusetts, and spent her latter years in Washington with her daughter. Her brother and son had gone as gold miners first to California and then Australia; the former returned to the United States but the latter apparently died in Australia. She herself died in 1897.

One question that confronts the reader is whether Jacobs' indictment of slavery tends to warp the value of her story as a human document. One way to approach that problem is to study the kind of details of life, events, and personal relationships presented by the author. Are they one-dimensional, or do they reveal some of the expected variety of attitudes, behavior, and personalities among both whites and blacks? Does her tale of seduction, secret hiding places, and escape sound as if romantic imagination had been applied too liberally to it, or do the happenings of everyday life add a strong sense of reality? Does Jacobs offer a sense of "self" that goes beyond complaint or apology to a positive affirmation of her identity?

Incidents in the Life of a Slave Girl

Linda Brent (Harriet Jacobs)

Edited by Lydia Maria Child

I. CHILDHOOD

I WAS born a slave; but I never knew it till six years of happy childhood had passed away. My father was a carpenter, and considered so intelligent and skilful in his trade, that, when buildings out of the common line were to be erected, he was sent for from long distances, to be head workman. On condition of paying his mistress two hundred dollars a year, and supporting himself, he was allowed to work at his trade, and manage his own affairs. His strongest wish was to purchase his children; but, though he several times offered his hard earnings for that purpose, he never succeeded. In complexion my parents were a light shade of brownish yellow, and were termed mulattoes. They lived together in a comfortable home; and, though we were all slaves, I was so fondly shielded that I never dreamed I was a piece of merchandise, trusted to them for safe keeping, and liable to be

* From *Incidents in the Life of a Slave Girl*. Written by Herself. Edited by L. Maria Child. Boston: Published for the author, 1861.

demanded of them at any moment. I had one brother, William, who was two years younger than myself—a bright, affectionate child. I had also a great treasure in my maternal grandmother, who was a remarkable woman in many respects. She was the daughter of a planter in South Carolina, who, at his death, left her mother and his three children free, with money to go to St. Augustine, where they had relatives. It was during the Revolutionary War; and they were captured on their passage, carried back, and sold to different purchasers. Such was the story my grandmother used to tell me; but I do not remember all the particulars. She was a little girl when she was captured and sold to the keeper of a large hotel. I have often heard her tell how hard she fared during childhood. But as she grew older she evinced so much intelligence, and was so faithful, that her master and mistress could not help seeing it was for their interest to take care of such a valuable piece of property. She became an indispensable personage in the household, officiating in all capacities, from cook and wet nurse to seamstress. She was much praised for her cooking; and her nice crackers became so famous in the neighborhood that many people were desirous of obtaining them. In consequence of numerous requests of this kind, she asked permission of her mistress to bake crackers at night, after all the household work was done; and she obtained leave to do it, provided she would clothe herself and her children from the profits. Upon these terms, after working hard all day for her mistress, she began her midnight bakings, assisted by her two oldest children. The business proved profitable; and each year she laid by a little, which was saved for a fund to purchase her children. Her master died, and the property was divided among his heirs. The widow had her dower in the hotel, which she continued to keep open. My grandmother remained in her service as a slave; but her children were divided among her master's children. As she had five, Benjamin, the youngest one, was sold, in order that each heir might have an equal portion of dollars and cents. There was so little difference in our ages that he seemed more like my brother than my uncle. He was a bright, handsome lad, nearly white; for he inherited the complexion my grandmother had derived from Anglo-Saxon ancestors. Though only ten years old, seven hundred and twenty dollars were paid for him. His sale was a terrible blow to my grandmother; but she was naturally hopeful, and she went to work with renewed energy, trusting in time to be able to purchase some of her children. She had laid up three hundred dollars, which her mistress one day begged as a loan, promising to pay her soon. The reader probably knows that no promise or writing given to a slave is legally binding; for, according to Southern laws, a slave, *being* property, can *hold* no property. When my grandmother lent her hard earnings to her mistress, she trusted solely to her honor. The honor of a slaveholder to a slave!

To this good grandmother I was indebted for many comforts. My brother Willie and I often received portions of the crackers, cakes, and preserves, she made to sell; and after we ceased to be children we were indebted to her for many more important services.

Such were the unusually fortunate circumstances of my early childhood. When I was six years old, my mother died; and then, for the first time, I learned by the talk around me, that I was a slave. My mother's mistress was the daughter of my grandmother's mistress. She was the foster sister of my mother; they were both nourished at my grandmother's breast. In fact, my mother had been weaned at three months old, that the babe of the mistress might obtain sufficient food. They played together as children; and when they became women, my mother was a most faithful servant to her white foster sister. On her death-bed her mistress promised that her children should never suffer for any thing; and during her lifetime she kept her word. They all spoke kindly of my dead mother, who had been a slave merely in name, but in nature was noble and womanly. I grieved for her, and my young mind was troubled with the thought who would now take care of me and my little brother. I was told that my home was now to be with her mistress; and I found it a happy one. No toilsome or disagreeable duties were imposed upon me. My mistress was so kind to me that I was always glad to do her bidding, and proud to labor for her as much as my young years would permit. I would sit by her side for hours, sewing diligently, with a heart as free from care as that of any free-born white child. When she thought I was tired, she would send me out to run and jump; and away I bounded, to gather berries or flowers to decorate her room. Those were happy days—too happy to last. The slave child had no thought for the morrow; but there came that blight which too surely waits on every human being born to be a chattel.

When I was nearly twelve years old, my kind mistress sickened and died. As I saw the cheek grow paler, and the eye more glassy, how earnestly I prayed in my heart that she might live! I loved her; for she had been almost like a mother to me. My prayers were not answered. She died, and they buried her in the little churchyard, where, day after day, my tears fell upon her grave. . . .

After a brief period of suspense, the will of my mistress was read, and we learned that she had bequeathed me to her sister's daughter, a child of five years old. So vanished our hopes. My mistress had taught me the precepts of God's Word: "Thou shalt love thy neighbor as thyself." "Whatsoever ye would that men should do unto you, do ye even so unto them." But I was her slave, and I suppose she did not recognize me as her neighbor. I would give much to blot out from my memory that one great wrong. As a child, I loved my mistress; and, looking back on the happy days I spent with her, I try to think with less bitterness of this act of injustice. While I was with her, she taught me to read and spell; and for this privilege, which so rarely falls to the lot of a slave, I bless her memory.

She possessed but few slaves; and at her death those were all distributed among her relatives. Five of them were my grandmother's children, and had shared the same milk that nourished her mother's children. Notwithstanding my grandmother's long and faithful service to her owners, not one of her children escaped the auction block. These God-breathing machines are no more, in the sight of their masters, than the cotton they plant, or the horses they tend.

II. THE NEW MASTER AND MISTRESS

DR. FLINT, a physician in the neighborhood, had married the sister of my mistress, and I was now the property of their little daughter. It was not without murmuring that I prepared for my new home; and what added to my unhappiness, was the fact that my brother William was purchased by the same family. My father, by his nature, as well as by the habit of transacting business as a skilful mechanic, had more of the feelings of a freeman than is common among slaves. My brother was a spirited boy; and being brought up under such influences, he early detested the name of master and mistress. One day, when his father and his mistress both happened to call him at the same time, he hesitated between the two; being perplexed to know which had the strongest claim upon his obedience. He finally concluded to go to his mistress. When my father reproved him for it, he said, "You both called me, and I didn't know which I ought to go to first."

"You are *my* child," replied our father, "and when I call you, you should come immediately, if you have to pass through fire and water."

Poor Willie! He was now to learn his first lesson of obedience to a master. Grandmother tried to cheer us with hopeful words, and they found an echo in the credulous hearts of youth.

When we entered our new home we encountered cold looks, cold words, and cold treatment. We were glad when the night came. On my narrow bed I moaned and wept, I felt so desolate and alone.

I had been there nearly a year, when a dear little friend of mine was buried. I heard her mother sob, as the clods fell on the coffin of her only child, and I turned away from the grave, feeling thankful that I still had something left to love. I met my grandmother, who said, "Come with me, Linda;" and from her tone I knew that something sad had happened. She led me apart from the people, and then said, "My child, your father is dead." Dead! How could I believe it? He had died so suddenly I had not even heard that he was sick. I went home with my grandmother. My heart rebelled against God, who had taken from me mother, father, mistress, and friend. The good grandmother tried to comfort me. "Who knows the ways of God?" said she. "Perhaps they have been kindly taken from the evil days to come." Years afterwards I often thought of this. She promised to be a mother to her grandchildren, so far as she might be permitted to do so; and strengthened by her love, I returned to my master's. . . .

The next day I followed his remains to a humble grave beside that of my dear mother. There were those who knew my father's worth, and respected his memory. . . .

Little attention was paid to the slaves' meals in Dr. Flint's house. If they could catch a bit of food while it was going, well and good. I gave myself no trouble on that score, for on my various errands I passed my grandmother's house, where there was always something to spare for me. I was frequently threatened with punishment if I stopped there; and my grandmother, to avoid detaining me, often stood at the gate with something for my breakfast or dinner. I was indebted to *her* for all my comforts, spiritual or temporal. It was *her* labor that supplied my scanty wardrobe. I have a vivid recollection of the linsey-woolsey dress given me every winter by Mrs. Flint. How I hated it! It was one of the badges of slavery. . . .

My grandmother's mistress had always promised her that, at her death, she should be free; and it was said that in her will she made good the promise. But when the estate was settled, Dr. Flint told the faithful old servant that, under existing circumstances, it was necessary she should be sold.

On the appointed day, the customary advertisement was posted up, proclaiming that there would be a "public sale of negroes, horses, &c." Dr. Flint called to tell my grandmother that he was unwilling to wound her feelings by putting her up at auction, and that he would prefer to dispose of her at private sale. My grandmother saw through his hypocrisy; she understood very well that he was ashamed of the job. She was a very spirited woman, and if he was base enough to sell her, when her mistress intended she should be free, she was determined the public should know it. She had for a long time supplied many families with crackers and preserves; consequently, "Aunt Marthy," as she was called, was generally known, and every body who knew her respected her intelligence and good character. Her long and faithful service in the family was also well known, and the intention of her mistress to leave her free. When the day of sale came, she took her place among the chattels, and at the first call she sprang upon the auction-block. Many voices called out, "Shame! Shame! Who is going to sell *you*, aunt Marthy? Don't stand there! That is no place for *you*." Without saying a word, she quietly awaited her fate. No one bid for her. At last, a feeble voice said, "Fifty dollars." It came from a maiden lady, seventy years old, the sister of my grandmother's deceased mistress. She had lived forty years under the same roof with my grandmother; she knew how faithfully she had served her owners, and how cruelly she had been defrauded of her rights; and she resolved to protect her. The auctioneer waited for a higher bid; but her wishes were respected; no one bid above her. She could neither read nor write; and when the bill of sale was made out, she signed it with a cross. But what consequence was that, when she had a big heart overflowing with human kindness? She gave the old servant her freedom.

At that time, my grandmother was just fifty years old. Laborious years had passed since then: and now my brother and I were slaves to the man who had defrauded her of her money, and tried to defraud her of her freedom. One of my mother's sisters, called Aunt Nancy, was also a slave in his family. She was a kind, good aunt to me; and supplied the place of both housekeeper and waiting maid to her mistress. She was, in fact, at the beginning and end of every thing. . . .

When I had been in the family a few weeks, one of the plantation slaves was brought to town, by order of his master. It was near night when he arrived, and Dr. Flint ordered him to be taken to the work house, and tied up to the joist, so that his feet would just escape the ground. In that situation he was to wait till the doctor had taken his tea. I shall never forget that night. Never before, in my life, had I heard hundreds of blows fall, in succession, on a human being. His piteous groans, and his "O, pray don't, massa," rang in my ear for months afterwards. There were many conjectures as to the cause of this terrible punishment. Some said master accused him of stealing corn; others said the slave had quarrelled with his wife, in the presence of the overseer, and had accused his master of being the father of her child. They were both black, and the child was very fair. . . .

III. THE SLAVES' NEW YEAR'S DAY

DR. FLINT owned a fine residence in town, several farms, and about fifty slaves, besides hiring a number by the year.

Hiring-day at the south takes place on the 1st of January. On the 2d, the slaves are expected to go to their new masters. On a farm, they work until the corn and cotton are laid. They then have two holidays. Some masters give them a good dinner under the trees. This over, they work until Christmas eve. If no heavy charges are meantime brought against them, they are given four or five holidays, whichever the master or overseer may think proper. Then comes New year's eve; and they gather together their little alls, or more properly speaking, their little nothings, and wait anxiously for the dawning of day. At the appointed hour the grounds are thronged with men, women, and children, waiting, like criminals, to hear their doom pronounced. The slave is sure to know who is the most humane, or cruel master, within forty miles of him.

It is easy to find out, on that day, who clothes and feeds his slaves well; for he is surrounded by a crowd, begging, "Please, massa, hire me this year. I will work *very* hard, massa."

If a slave is unwilling to go with his new master, he is whipped, or locked up in jail, until he consents to go, and promises not to run away during the year. Should he chance to change his mind, thinking it justifiable to violate an extorted promise, woe unto him if he is caught! The whip is used till the blood flows at his feet; and his stiffened limbs are put in chains, to be dragged in the field for days and days!

If he lives until the next year, perhaps the same man will hire him again, without even giving him an opportunity of going to the hiring-ground. After those for hire are disposed of, those for sale are called up.

On one of these sale days, I saw a mother lead seven children to the auction-block. She knew that *some* of them would be taken from her; but they took *all*. The children were sold to a slave-trader, and their mother was bought by a man in her own town. Before night her children were all far away. She begged the trader to tell her where he intended to take them; this he refused to do. How *could* he, when he knew he would sell them, one by one, wherever he could command the highest price! I met that mother in the street, and her wild, haggard face lives to-day in my mind. She wrung her hands in anguish, and exclaimed, "Gone! All gone! Why *don't* God kill me!" I had no words wherewith to comfort her. Instances of this kind are of daily, yea, of hourly occurrence.

Slaveholders have a method, peculiar to their institution, of getting rid of *old* slaves, whose lives have been worn out in their service. I knew an old woman, who for seventy years faithfully served her master. She had become almost helpless, from hard labor and disease. Her owners moved to Alabama, and the old black woman was left to be sold to any body who would give twenty dollars for her.

IV. THE SLAVE WHO DARED TO FEEL LIKE A MAN

TWO years had passed since I entered Dr. Flint's family, and those years had brought much of the knowledge that comes from experience, though they had afforded little opportunity for any other kinds of knowledge.

My grandmother had, as much as possible, been a mother to her orphan grandchildren. By perseverance and unwearied industry, she was now mistress of a snug little home, surrounded with the necessaries of life. She would have been happy could her children have shared them with her. There remained but three children and two grandchildren, all slaves. Most earnestly did she strive to make us feel that it was the will of God: that He had seen fit to place us under such circumstances; and though it seemed hard, we ought to pray for contentment.

It was a beautiful faith, coming from a mother who could not call her children her own. But I, and Benjamin, her youngest boy, condemned it. We reasoned that it was much more the will of God that we should be situated as she was. We longed for a home like hers. There we always found sweet balsam for our troubles. She was so loving, so sympathizing! She always met us with a smile, and listened with patience to all our sorrows. She spoke so hopefully, that unconsciously the clouds gave place to sunshine. There was a grand big oven there, too, that baked bread and nice things for the town, and we knew there was always a choice bit in store for us.

But, alas! even the charms of the old oven failed to reconcile us to our hard lot. . . .

If there was one pure, sunny spot for me, I believed it to be in Benjamin's heart, and in another's, whom I loved with all the ardor of a girl's first love. My owner knew of it, and sought in every way to render me miserable. He did not resort to corporal punishment, but to all the petty, tyrannical ways that human ingenuity could devise.

I remember the first time I was punished. It was in the month of February. My grandmother had taken my old shoes, and replaced them with a new pair. I needed them; for several inches of snow had fallen, and it still continued to fall. When I walked through Mrs. Flint's room, their creaking grated harshly on her refined nerves. She called me to her, and asked what I had about me that made such a horrid noise. I told her it was my new shoes. "Take them off," said she; "and if you put them on again, I'll throw them into the fire."

I took them off, and my stockings also. She then sent me a long distance, on an errand. As I went through the snow, my bare feet tingled. That night I was very hoarse; and I went to bed thinking the next day would find my sick, perhaps dead. What was my grief on waking to find myself quite well! . . .

One afternoon I sat at my sewing, feeling unusual depression of spirits. My mistress had been accusing me of an offense, of which I assured her I was perfectly innocent; but I saw, by the contemptuous curl of her lip, that she believed I was telling a lie.

I wondered for what wise purpose God was leading me through such thorny paths, and whether still darker days were in store for me. As I sat musing thus, the door opened softly, and William came in. "Well, brother," said I, "what is the matter this time?"

"O Linda, Ben and his master have had a dreadful time!" said he.

My first thought was that Benjamin was killed. "Don't be frightened, Linda, " said William; "I will tell you all about it."

It appeared that Benjamin's master had sent for him, and he did not immediately obey the summons. When he did, his master was angry, and began to whip him. He resisted. Master and slave fought, and finally the master was thrown. Benjamin had cause to tremble; for he had thrown to the ground his master—one of the richest men in town. I anxiously awaited the result. . . .

It is not necessary to state how he made his escape. Suffice it to say, he was on his way to New York when a violent storm overtook the vessel. The captain said he must put into the nearest port. This alarmed Benjamin, who was aware that he would be advertised in every port near his own town. His embarrassment was noticed by the captain. To port they went. There the advertisement met the captain's eye. Benjamin so exactly answered its description, that the captain laid hold on him, and bound him in chains. The storm passed, and they proceeded to New York. Before reaching that port Benjamin managed to get off his chains and throw them overboard. He escaped from the vessel, but was pursued, captured, and carried back to his master. . . .

That day seems but as yesterday, so well do I remember it. I saw him led though the streets in chains, to jail. His face was ghastly pale, yet full of determination. He had begged one of the sailors to go to his mother's house and ask her not to meet him. He said the sight of her distress would take from him all self-control. She yearned to see him, and she went; but she screened herself in the crowd, that it might be as her child had said. . .

[Benjamin remained in jail for six months, refusing to ask his master's pardon for trying to escape, and was then sold to a slave trader who was bound for New Orleans. His mother tried to purchase him through an intermediary, but before this could be done Benjamin escaped again on a ship whose destination was Baltimore.]

For once his white face did him a kindly service. They had no suspicion that it belonged to a slave; otherwise, the law would have been followed out to the letter, and the *thing* rendered back to slavery. The brightest skies are often overshadowed by the darkest clouds. Benjamin was taken sick, and compelled to remain in Baltimore three weeks. His strength was slow in returning; and his desire to continue his journey seemed to retard his recovery. How could he get strength without air and exercise? He resolved to venture on a short walk. A by-street was selected, where he though himself secure of not being met by any one that knew him; but a voice called out, "Halloo, Ben, my boy! what are you doing *here*?"

His first impulse was to run; but his legs trembled so that he could not stir. He turned to confront his antagonist, and behold, there stood his old master's next door neighbor! He thought it was all over with him now; but it proved otherwise. That man was a miracle. He possessed a goodly number of slaves, and yet was not quite deaf to that mystic clock, whose ticking is rarely heard in the slaveholder's breast.

"Ben, you are sick," said he. "Why, you look like a ghost. I guess I gave you something of a start. Never mind, Ben, I am not going to touch you. You had a pretty tough time of it, and you may go on your way rejoicing for all me. But I would advise you to get out of this place plaguy quick, for there are several gentlemen here from our town." He described the nearest and safest route to New York, and added, "I shall be glad to tell your mother I have seen you. Good-by, Ben."

Benjamin turned away, filled with gratitude, and surprised that the town he hated contained such a gem—a gem worthy of a purer setting.

This gentleman was a Northerner by birth, and had married a southern lady. On his return, he told my grandmother that he had seen her son, and of the service he had rendered him.

Benjamin reached New York safely, and concluded to stop there until he had gained strength enough to proceed further. It happened that my grandmother's only remaining son had sailed for the same city on business for his mistress. Through God's providence, the brothers met. You may be sure it was a happy meeting. "O Phil," exclaimed Benjamin, "I am here at last." Then he told him how near he came to dying, almost in sight of free land, and how he prayed that he might live to get one breath of free air. . . .

He begged my uncle Phillip not to return south; but stay and work with him, till they earned enough to buy those at home. His brother told him it would kill their mother if he deserted her in her trouble. . . .

Uncle Phillip came home, and the first words he uttered when he entered the house were, "Mother, Ben is free! I have seen him in New York." She stood looking at him with a bewildered air. "Mother, don't you believe it?" he said, laying his hand softly upon her shoulder. She raised her hands, and exclaimed, "God be praised! Let us thank him." She dropped on her knees, and poured forth her heart in prayer. Then Phillip must sit down and repeat to her every word Benjamin had said. He told her all; only he forbore to mention how sick and pale her darling looked. Why should he distress her when she could do him no good?

The brave old woman still toiled on, hoping to rescue some of her other children. After a while she succeeded in buying Phillip. She paid eight hundred dollars, and came home with the precious document that secured his freedom. . . .

V. THE TRIALS OF GIRLHOOD

DURING the first years of my service in Dr. Flint's family, I was accustomed to share some indulgences with the children of my mistress. Though this seemed to me no more than right, I was grateful for it, and tried to merit the kindness by the faithful discharge of my duties. But I now entered on my fifteenth year—a sad epoch in the life of a slave girl. My master began to whisper foul words in my ear. Young as I was, I could not remain ignorant of their import. I tried to treat them with indifference or contempt. The master's age, my extreme youth, and the fear that his conduct would be reported to my grandmother, made him bear this treatment for many months. He was a crafty man, and resorted to many means to accomplish his purposes. Sometimes he had stormy, terrific ways, that made his victims tremble; sometimes he assumed a gentleness that he thought must surely subdue. Of the two, I preferred his stormy moods, although they left me trembling. He tried his utmost to corrupt the pure principles my grandmother had instilled. He peopled my young mind with unclean images, such as only a vile monster could think of. I turned from him with disgust and hatred. . . .

. . . Even the little child, who is accustomed to wait on her mistress and her children, will learn before she is twelve-years-old, why it is that her mistress hates such and such a one among the slaves. Perhaps the child's own mother is among those hated ones. She listens to violent outbreaks of jealous passion, and cannot help understanding what is the cause. She will become prematurely knowing in evil things. Soon she will learn to tremble when she hears her master's footfall. She will be compelled to realize that she is no longer a child. If God has bestowed beauty upon her, it will prove her greatest curse. That which commands admiration in the white woman only hastens the degradation of the female slave. I know that some are too much brutalized by slavery to feel the humiliation of their position; but many slaves feel it most acutely, and shrink from the memory of it. I cannot tell how much I suffered in the presence of these wrongs, nor how I am still pained by the retrospect. My master met me at every turn, reminding me that I belonged to him, and swearing by heaven and earth that he would compel me to submit to him. If I went out for a breath of fresh air, after a day of unwearied toil, his footsteps dogged me. If I knelt by my mother's grave, his dark shadow fell on me even there. The light heart which nature had given me became heavy with sad forebodings. The other slaves in my master's house noticed the change. Many of them pitied me; but none dared to ask the cause. They had no need to inquire. They knew too well the guilty practices under that roof; and they were aware that to speak of them was an offence that never went unpunished.

I longed for some one to confide in. I would have given the world to have laid my head on my grandmother's faithful bosom, and told her all my troubles. But Dr. Flint swore he would kill me, if I was not as silent as the grave. Then, although my grandmother was all in all to me, I feared her as well as loved her. I had been accustomed to look up to her with a respect bordering upon awe. I was very young, and felt shamefaced about telling her such impure things, especially as I knew her to be very strict on such subjects. Moreover, she was a woman of high spirit. She was usually very quiet in her demeanor; but if her indignation was once roused, it was not very easily quelled. I had been told that she once chased a white gentleman with a loaded pistol, because he insulted one of her daughters. I dreaded the consequences of a violent outbreak; and both pride and fear kept me silent. But though I did not confide in my grandmother, and even evaded her vigilant watchfulness and inquiry, her presence in the neighborhood was some protection to me. Though she had been a slave, Dr. Flint was afraid of her. He dreaded her scorching rebukes. Moreover, she was known and patronized by many people; and he did not wish to have his villainy made public. It was lucky for me that I did not live on a distant plantation, but in a town not so large that the inhabitants were ignorant of each other's affairs. Bad as are the laws and customs in a slaveholding community, the doctor, as a professional man, deemed it prudent to keep up some outward show of decency. . . .

VI. THE JEALOUS MISTRESS

. . .MRS. FLINT possessed the key to her husband's character before I was born. She might have used this knowledge to counsel and to screen the young and the innocent among her slaves; but for them she had no sympathy. They were the objects of her constant suspicion and malevolence. She watched her husband with unceasing vigilance; but he was well practiced in means to evade it. What he could not find opportunity to say in words he manifested in signs. He invented more than were ever thought of in a deaf and dumb asylum. I let them pass, as if I did not understand what he meant; and many were the curses and threats bestowed on me for my stupidity. One day he caught me teaching myself to write. He frowned, as if he was not well pleased; but I suppose he came to the conclusion that such an accomplishment might help to advance his favorite scheme. Before long, notes were often slipped into my hand. I would return them, saying, "I can't read them, sir." "Can't you?" he replied; "then I must read them to you." He always finished the reading by asking, "Do you understand?" Sometimes he would complain of the heat of the tea room, and order his supper to be placed on a small table in the piazza. He would seat himself there with a well-satisfied smile, and tell me to stand by and brush away the flies. He would eat very slowly, pausing between the mouthfuls. These intervals were employed in describing the happiness I was so foolishly throwing away, and in threatening me with the penalty that finally awaited my stubborn disobedience. He boasted much of the forbearance he had exercised towards me and reminded me that there was limit to his patience. When I succeeded in avoiding opportunities for him to talk to me at home, I was ordered to come to his office, to do some errand. When there, I was obliged to stand and listen to such language as he saw fit to address to me. Sometimes I so openly expressed my contempt for him that he would become violently enraged, and I wondered why he did not strike me. Circumstanced as he was, he probably thought it was better policy to be forbearing. But the state of things grew worse and worse daily. In desperation I told him that I must and would apply to my grandmother for protection. He threatened me with death, and worse than death, if I made any complaint to her. Strange to say, I did not despair. I was naturally of a buoyant disposition, and always I had a hope of somehow getting out of his clutches. Like many a poor, simple slave before me, I trusted that some threads of joy would yet be woven into my dark destiny.

I had entered my sixteenth year, and every day it became more apparent that my presence was intolerable to Mrs. Flint. Angry words frequently passed between her and her husband. He had never punished me himself, and he would not allow anybody else to punish me. In that respect, she was never satisfied; but, in her angry moods, no terms were too vile for her to bestow upon me. Yet I, whom she detested so bitterly, had far more pity for her than he had, whose duty it was to make her life happy. I never wronged her, or wished to wrong her; and one word of kindness from her would have brought me to her feet.

After repeated quarrels between the doctor and his wife, he announced his intention to take his youngest daughter, then four years old, to sleep in his apartment. It was necessary that a servant should sleep in the same room, to be on hand if the child stirred. I was selected for that office, and informed for what purpose that arrangement had been made. By managing to keep within sight of people, as much as possible, during the day time, I had hitherto succeeded in eluding my master, though a razor was often held to my throat to force me to change this line of policy. At night I slept by the side of my great aunt, where I felt safe. He was too prudent to come into her room. She was an old woman, and had been in the family many years. Moreover, as a married man, and a professional man, he deemed it necessary to save appearances in some degree. But he resolved to remove the obstacle in the way of his scheme; and he thought he had planned it so that he should evade suspicion. He was well aware how much I prized my refuge by the side of my old aunt, and he determined to dispossess me of it. The first night the doctor had the little child in his room alone. The next morning, I was ordered to take my station as nurse the following night. A kind Providence interposed in my favor. During the day Mrs. Flint heard of this new arrangement, and a storm followed. I rejoiced to hear it rage.

After a while my mistress sent for me to come to her room. Her first question was, "Did you know you were to sleep in the doctor's room?"

"Yes, ma'am."

"Who told you?"

"My master."

"Will you answer truly all the questions I ask?"

"Yes, ma'am."

"Tell me, then, as you hope to be forgiven, are you innocent of what I have accused you?"

"I am."

She handed me a Bible, and said, "Lay your hand on your heart, kiss this holy book, and swear before God that you tell me the truth."

I took the oath she required, and I did it with a clear conscience.

"You have taken God's holy word to testify your innocence," said she. "If you have deceived me, beware! Now take this stool, sit down, look me directly in the face, and tell me all that has passed between your master and you."

I did as she ordered. As I went on with my account her color changed frequently, she wept, and sometimes groaned. She spoke in tones so sad, that I was touched by her grief. The tears came to my eyes; but I was soon convinced that her emotions arose from anger and wounded pride. She felt that her marriage vows were desecrated, her dignity insulted; but she had no compassion for the poor victim of her husband's perfidy. She pitied herself as a martyr; but she was incapable of feeling for the condition of shame and misery in which her unfortunate, helpless slave was placed.

Yet perhaps she had some touch of feeling for me; for when the conference was ended, she spoke kindly, and promised to protect me. I should have been much comforted by this assurance if I could have had confidence in it; but my experiences in slavery had filled me with distrust. She was not a very refined woman, and had not much control over her passions. I was an object of her jealousy, and, consequently, of her hatred; and I knew I could not expect kindness or confidence from her under the circumstances in which I was placed. I could not blame her. Slaveholders' wives feel as other women would under similar circumstances. The fire of her temper kindled from small sparks, and now the flame became so intense that the doctor was obliged to give up his intended arrangement.

I knew I had ignited the torch, and I expected to suffer for it afterwards; but I felt too thankful to my mistress for the timely aid she rendered me to care much about that. She now took me to sleep in a room adjoining her own. There I was an object of her especial care, though not of her especial comfort, for she spent many a sleepless night to watch over me. Sometimes I woke up, and found her bending over me. At other times she whispered in my ear, as though it was her husband who was speaking to me and listened to hear what I would answer. If she startled me, on such occasions, she would glide stealthily away; and the next morning she would tell me I had been talking in my sleep, and ask who I was talking to. At last, I began to be fearful for my life. It had been often threatened; and you can imagine, better than I can describe, what an unpleasant sensation it must produce to wake up in the dead of night and find a jealous woman bending over you. Terrible as this experience was, I had fears that it would give place to one more terrible.

My mistress grew weary of her vigils; they did not prove satisfactory. She changed her tactics. She now tried the trick of accusing my master of crime, in my presence, and gave my name as the author of the accusation. To my utter astonishment, he replied, "I don't believe it; but if she did acknowledge it, you tortured her into exposing me." Tortured into exposing him! Truly, Satan had no difficulty in distinguishing the color of his soul! I understood his object in making this false representation. It was to show me that I gained nothing by seeking the protection of my mistress; that the power was still all in his own hands. I pitied Mrs. Flint. She was a second wife, many years the junior of her husband; and the hoary-headed miscreant was enough to try the patience of a wiser and better woman. She was completely foiled, and knew not how to proceed. She would gladly have had me flogged for my supposed false oath; but, as I have already stated, the doctor never allowed any one to whip me. The old sinner was politic. The application of the lash might have led to remarks that would have exposed him in the eyes of his children and grandchildren. How often did I rejoice that I lived in a town where all the inhabitants knew each other! If I had been on a remote plantation, or lost among the multitude of a crowded city, I should not be a living woman at this day. . . .

VII. THE LOVER

THERE was in the neighborhood a young colored carpenter; a free born man. We had been well acquainted in childhood, and frequently met together afterwards. We became mutually attached, and he proposed to marry me. I loved him with all the ardor of a young girl's first love. But when I reflected that I was a slave, and that the laws gave no sanction to the marriage of such, my heart sank within me. My lover wanted to buy me; but I knew that Dr. Flint was too wilful and arbitrary a man to consent to that arrangement. From him, I was sure of experiencing all sorts of opposition, and I had nothing to hope from my mistress. She would have been delighted to have got rid of me, but not in that way. It would have relieved her mind of a burden if she could have seen me sold to some distant state, but if I was married near home I should be just as much in her husband's power as I had previously been,—for the husband of a slave has no power to protect her . . . .

This love-dream had been my support through many trials; and I could not bear to run the risk of having it suddenly dissipated. There was a lady in the neighborhood, a particular friend of Dr. Flint's, who often visited the house. I had a great respect for her, and she had always manifested a friendly interest in me. Grandmother thought she would have great influence with the doctor. I went to this lady, and told her my story. I told her I was aware that my lover's being a free-born man would prove a great objection; but he wanted to buy me; and if Dr. Flint would consent to that arrangement, I felt sure he would be willing to pay any reasonable price. She knew that Mrs. Flint disliked me; therefore I ventured to suggest that perhaps my mistress would approve of my being sold, as that would rid her of me. The lady listened with kindly sympathy, and promised to do her utmost to promote my wishes. She had an interview with the doctor, and I believe she pleaded my cause earnestly; but it was all to no purpose.

How I dreaded my master now! Every minute I expected to be summoned to his presence; but the day passed, and I heard nothing from him. The next morning, a message was brought to me: "Master wants you in his study." I found the door ajar, and I stood a moment gazing at the hateful man who claimed a right to rule me, body and soul. I entered, and tried to appear calm. I did not want him to know how my heart was bleeding. He looked fixedly at me, with an expression which seemed to say, "I have half a mind to kill you on the spot." At last he broke the silence, and that was relief to both of us.

"So you want to be married, do you?" said he, "and to a free nigger."

"Yes, sir."

"Well, I'll soon convince you whether I am your master, or the nigger fellow you honor so highly. If you *must* have a husband, you may take up with one of my slaves."

What a situation I should be in, as the wife of one of *his* slaves, even if my heart had been interested!

I replied, "Don't you suppose, sir, that a slave can have some preference about marrying? Do you suppose that all men are alike to her?"

"Do you love this nigger?" said he, abruptly.

"Yes, sir."

"How dare you tell me so!" he exclaimed, in great wrath. After a slight pause, he added, "I supposed you thought more of yourself; that you felt above the insults of such puppies."

I replied, "If he is a puppy I am a puppy, for we are both of the negro race. It is right and honorable for us to love each other. The man you call a puppy never insulted me, sir; and he would not love me if he did not believe me to be a virtuous woman."

He sprang upon me like a tiger, and gave me a stunning blow. It was the first time he had ever struck me; and fear did not enable me to control my anger. When I had recovered a little from the effects, I exclaimed, "You have struck me for answering you honestly. How I despise you!"

There was silence for some minutes. Perhaps he was deciding what should be my punishment; or, perhaps, he wanted to give me time to reflect on what I had said, and to whom I had said it. Finally, he asked, "Do you know what you have said?"

"Yes, sir; but your treatment drove me to it."

"Do you know that I have a right to do as I like with you,—that I can kill you, if I please?"

"You have tried to kill me, and I wish you had; but you have no right to do as you like with me."

"Silence!" he exclaimed, in a thundering voice. "By heavens, girl, you forget yourself too far! Are you mad? If you are, I will soon bring you to your senses. Do you think any other master would bear what I have borne from you this morning? Many masters would have killed you on the spot. How would you like to be sent to jail for your insolence?"

"I know I have been disrespectful, sir," I replied; "but you drove me to it; I couldn't help it. As for the jail, there would be more peace for me there than there is here."

"You deserve to go there," said he, "and to be under such treatment, that you would forget the meaning of the word *peace*. It would do you good. It would take some of your high notions out of you. But I am not ready to send you there yet, notwithstanding your ingratitude for all my kindness and forbearance. You have been the plague of my life. I have wanted to make you happy, and I have been repaid with the basest ingratitude; but though you have proved yourself incapable of appreciating my kindness, I will be lenient towards you, Linda. I will give you one more chance to redeem your character. If you behave yourself and do as I require, I will forgive you and treat you as I always have done; but if you disobey me, I will punish you as I would the meanest slave on my plantation. Never let me hear that fellow's name mentioned again. If I ever know of your speaking to him I will cowhide you both; and if I catch him lurking about my premises, I will shoot him as soon as I would a dog. Do you hear what I say? I'll teach you a lesson about marriage and free niggers! Now go, and let this be the last time I have occasion to speak to you on this subject."

Reader, did you ever hate? I hope not. I never did but once; and I trust I never shall again. Somebody has called it "the atmosphere of hell;" and I believe it is so. . . .

VII. A PERILOUS PASSAGE IN THE SLAVE
GIRL'S LIFE

AFTER my lover went away, Dr. Flint contrived a new plan. He seemed to have an idea that my fear of my mistress was his greatest obstacle. In the blandest tones, he told me that he was going to build a small house for me, in a secluded place, four miles away from the town. I shuddered; but I was constrained to listen, while he talked of his intention to give me a home of my own, and to make a lady of me. Hitherto, I had escaped my dreaded fate, by being in the midst of people. My grandmother had already had high words with my master about me. She had told him pretty plainly what she thought of his character, and there was considerable gossip in the neighborhood about our affairs, to which the open-mouthed jealousy of Mrs. Flint contributed not a little. When my master said he was going to build a house for me, and that he could do it with little trouble and expense, I was in hopes something would happen to frustrate his scheme; but I soon heard that the house was actually begun. I vowed before my Maker that I would never enter it. I had rather toil on the plantation from dawn till dark; I had rather live and die in jail, than drag on, from day to day, through such a living death. I was determined that the master, whom I so hated and loathed, who had blighted the prospects of my youth, and made my life a desert, should not, after my long struggle with him, succeed at last in trampling his victim under his feet. I would do any thing, every thing, for the sake of defeating him. What *could* I do? I thought and thought, till I became desperate, and made a plunge into the abyss.

And now, reader, I come to a period in my unhappy life, which I would gladly forget if I could. The remembrance fills me with sorrow and shame. It pains me to tell you of it; but I have promised to tell you the truth, and I will do it honestly, let it cost me what it may. I will not try to screen myself behind the plea of compulsion from a master; for it was not so. Neither can I plead ignorance or thoughtlessness. For years, my master had done his utmost to pollute my mind with foul images, and to destroy the pure principles inculcated by my grandmother, and the good mistress of my childhood. The influences of slavery had had the same effect on me that they had on other young girls; they had made me prematurely knowing, concerning the evil ways of the world. I knew what I did, and I did it with deliberate calculation. . .

I have told you that Dr. Flint's persecutions and his wife's jealousy had given rise to some gossip in the neighborhood. Among others, it chanced that a white unmarried gentleman had obtained some knowledge of the circumstances in which I was placed. He knew my grandmother, and often spoke to me in the street. He became interested for me, and asked questions about my master, which I answered in part. He expressed a great deal of sympathy, and a wish to aid me. He constantly sought opportunities to see me, and wrote to me frequently. I was a poor slave girl, only fifteen years old. . . .

When I found that my master had actually begun to build the lonely cottage, other feelings mixed with those I have described. Revenge, and calculations of interest, were added to flattered vanity and sincere gratitude for kindness. I knew nothing would enrage Dr. Flint so much as to know that I favored another; and it was something to triumph over my tyrant even in that small way. I thought he would revenge himself by selling me, and I was sure my friend, Mr. Sands, would buy me. He was a man of more generosity and feeling than my master, and I thought my freedom could be easily obtained from him. The crisis of my fate now came so near that I was desperate. I shuddered to think of being the mother of children that should be owned by my old tyrant. I knew that as soon as a new fancy took him, his victims were sold far off to get rid of them; especially if they had children. I had seen several women sold, with his babies at the breast. He never allowed his offspring by slaves to remain long in sight of himself and his wife. Of a man who was not my master I could ask to have my children well supported; and in this case, I felt confident I should obtain the boon. I also felt quite sure that they would be made free. With all these thoughts revolving in my mind, and seeing no other way of escaping the doom I so much dreaded, I made a headlong plunge. Pity me, and pardon me, O virtuous reader! You never knew what it is to be a slave; to be entirely unprotected by law or custom; to have the laws reduce you to the condition of a chattel, entirely subject to the will of another. You never exhausted your ingenuity in avoiding the snares, and eluding the power of a hated tyrant; you never shuddered at the sound of his footsteps, and trembled within hearing of his voice. I know I did wrong. No one can feel it more sensibly than I do. The painful and humiliating memory will haunt me to my dying day. Still, in looking back, calmly, on the events of my life, I feel that the slave woman ought not to be judged by the same standard as others.

The months passed on. I had many unhappy hours. I secretly mourned over the sorrow I was bringing on my grandmother, who had so tried to shield me from harm. I knew that I was the greatest comfort of her old age, and that it was a source of pride to her that I had not degraded myself, like most of the slaves. I wanted to confess to her that I was no longer worthy of her love; but I could not utter the dreaded words.

As for Dr. Flint, I had a feeling of satisfaction and triumph in the thought of telling *him*. From time to time he told me of his intended arrangements, and I was silent. At last, he came and told me the cottage was completed, and ordered me to go to it. I told him I would never enter it. He said, "I have heard enough of such talk as that. You shall go, if you are carried by force; and you shall remain there."

I replied, "I will never go there. In a few months I shall be a mother."

He stood and looked at me in dumb amazement, and left the house without a word. I thought I should be happy in my triumph over him. But now that the truth was out, and my relatives would hear of it, I felt wretched. Humble as were their circumstances, they had pride in my good character. Now, how could I look them in the face? My self-respect was gone? I had resolved that I would be virtuous, though I was a slave. I had said, "Let the storm beat! I will brave it till I die." And now, how humiliated I felt!

I went to my grandmother. My lips moved to make confession, but the words stuck in my throat. I sat down in the shade of a tree at her door and began to sew. I think she saw something unusual was the matter with me. The mother of slaves is very watchful. She knows there is no security for her children. After they have entered their teens she lives in daily expectation of trouble. This leads to many questions. If the girl is of a sensitive nature, timidity keeps her from answering truthfully, and this well-meant course has a tendency to drive her from maternal counsels. Presently, in came my mistress, like a mad woman, and accused me concerning her husband. My grand-mother, whose suspicions had been previously awakened, believed what she said. She exclaimed, "O Linda! has it come to this? I had rather see you dead that to see you as you now are. You're a disgrace to your dead mother." She tore from my fingers my mother's wedding ring and her silver thimble. "Go away!" she exclaimed, "and never come to my house again." Her reproaches fell so hot and heavy, that they left me no chance to answer. Bitter tears, such as the eyes never shed but once, were my only answer. I rose from my seat, but fell back again, sobbing. She did not speak to me; but the tears were running down her furrowed cheeks, and they scorched me like fire. She had always been so kind to me! So kind! How I longed to throw myself at her feet, and tell her all the truth! But she had ordered me to go, and never to come there again. After a few minutes, I mustered strength, and started to obey her. With what feelings did I now close that little gate, which I used to open with such an eager hand in my childhood! It closed upon me with a sound I never heard before.

Where could I go? I was afraid to return to my master's. I walked on recklessly, not caring where I went, or what would become of me. When I had gone four or five miles, fatigue compelled me to stop. I sat down on the stump of an old tree. The stars were shining through the boughs above me. How they mocked me, with their bright, calm light! The hours passed by, and as I sat there along a chilliness and deadly sickness came over me. I sank on the ground. My mind was full of horrid thoughts. I prayed to die; but the prayer was not answered. At last, with great effort I roused myself, and walked some distance further, to the house of a woman who had been a friend of my mother. When I told her why I was there, she spoke soothingly to me; but I could not be comforted. I thought I could bear my shame if I could only be reconciled to my grandmother. I longed to open my heart to her. I thought if she could know the real state of the case, and all I had been bearing for years, she would perhaps judge me less harshly. My friend advised me to send for her. I did so; but days of agonizing suspense passed before she came. Had she utterly forsaken me? No. She came at last. I knelt before her, and told her the things that had poisoned my life; how long I had been persecuted; that I saw no way of escape; and in an hour of extremity I had become desperate. She listened in silence. I told her I would bear any thing and do any thing, if in time I had hopes of obtaining her forgiveness. I begged of her to pity me, for my dead mother's sake. And she did pity me. She did not say, "I forgive;" but she looked at me lovingly, with her eyes full of tears. she laid her old hand gently on my head, and murmured, "Poor child! Poor child!"

IX. THE NEW TIE TO LIFE

I RETURNED to my good grandmother's house. She had an interview with Mr. Sands. When she asked him why he could not have left her one ewe lamb,—whether there were not plenty of slaves who did not care about character,—he made no answer; but he spoke kind and encouraging words. He promised to care for my child, and to buy me, be the conditions what they might.

I had not seen Dr. Flint for five days. I had never seen him since I made the avowal to him. He talked of the disgrace I had brought on myself; how I had sinned against my master, and mortified my old grandmother. He intimated that if I had accepted his proposals, he, as a physician, could have saved me from exposure. He even condescended to pity me. Could he have offered wormwood more bitter? He, whose persecutions had been the cause of my sin!

"Linda," said he, "though you have been criminal towards me, I feel for you, and I can pardon you if you obey my wishes. Tell me whether the fellow you wanted to marry is the father of your child. If you deceive me, you shall feel the fires of hell."

I did not feel as proud as I had done. My strongest weapon with him was gone. I was lowered in my own estimation, and had resolved to bear his abuse in silence. But when he spoke contemptuously of the lover who had always treated me honorably; when I remembered that but for him I might have been a virtuous, free, and happy wife, I lost my patience. "I have sinned against God and myself," I replied; "but not against you."

He clinched his teeth, and muttered, "Curse you!" He came towards me, with ill-suppressed rage, and exclaimed, "You obstinate girl! I could grind your bones to powder! You have thrown yourself away on some worthless rascal. You are weak-minded, and have been easily persuaded by those who don't care a straw for you. The future will settle accounts between us. You are blinded now; but hereafter you will be convinced that your master was your best friend. My lenity towards you is a proof of it. I might have punished you in many ways. I might have had you whipped till you fell dead under the lash. But I wanted you to live; I would have bettered your condition. Others cannot do it. You are my slave. Your mistress, disgusted by your conduct, forbids you to return to the house; therefore I leave you here for the present; but I shall see you often. I will call tomorrow."

He came with frowning brows, that showed a dissatisfied state of mind. After asking about my health, he inquired whether my board was paid, and who visited me. He then went on to say that he had neglected his duty; that as a physician there were certain things that he ought to have explained to me. Then followed talk such as would have made the most shameless blush. He ordered me to stand up before him. I obeyed. "I command you," said he, "to tell me whether the father of your child is white or black." I hesitated. "Answer me this instant!" he exclaimed. I did answer. He sprang upon me like a wolf, and grabbed my arm as if he would have broken it. "Do you love him?" said he, in a hissing tone.

"I am thankful that I do not despise him," I replied.

He raised his hand to strike me; but it fell again. I don't know what arrested the blow. He sat down, with lips tightly compressed. At last he spoke. "I came here," said he, "to make you a friendly proposition; but your ingratitude chafes me beyond endurance. You turn aside all my good intentions towards you. I don't know what it is that keeps me from killing you." Again he rose, as if he had a mind to strike me.

But he resumed. "On one condition I will forgive your insolence and crime. You must henceforth have no communication of any kind with the father of your child. You must not ask anything from him, or receive any thing from him. I will take care of you and your child. You had better promise this at once, and not wait till you are deserted by him. This is the last act of mercy I shall show towards you."

I said something about being unwilling to have my child supported by a man who had cursed it and me also. He rejoined, that a woman who had sunk to my level had no right to expect any thing else. He asked, for the last time, would I accept his kindness? I answered that I would not.

"Very well," said he; "then take the consequences of your wayward course. Never look to me for help. You are my slave, and shall always be my slave. I will never sell you, that you may depend upon."

Hope died away in my heart as he closed the door after him. I had calculated that in his rage he would sell me to a slave-trader; and I knew the father of my child was on the watch to buy me. . . .

When my babe was born, they said it was premature. It weighed only four pounds; but God let it live. I heard the doctor say I could not survive till morning. I had often prayed for death; but now I did not want to die, unless my child could die too. Many weeks passed before I was able to leave my bed. I was a mere wreck of my former self. For a year there was scarcely a day when I was free from chills and fever. My babe also was sickly. His little limbs were often racked with pain. Dr. Flint continued his visits, to look after my health; and he did not fail to remind me that my child was an addition to his stock of slaves. . . .

X. ANOTHER LINK TO LIFE

I HAD not returned to my master's house since the birth of my child. The old man raved to have me thus removed from his immediate power; but his wife vowed, by all that was good and great, she would kill me if I came back; and he did not doubt her word. Sometimes he would stay away for a season. He labored, most unnecessarily, to convince me that I had lowered myself. The venomous old reprobate had no need of descanting on that theme. I felt humiliated enough. My unconscious babe was the ever-present witness of my shame. I listened with silent contempt when he talked about my having forfeited *his* good opinion; but I shed bitter tears that I was no longer worthy of being respected by the good and pure. Alas! slavery still held me in its poisonous grasp. There was no chance for me to be respectable. There was no prospect of being able to lead a better life. . . .

When Dr. Flint learned that I was again to be a mother, he was exasperated beyond measure. He rushed from the house, and returned with a pair of shears. I had a fine head of hair; and he often railed about my pride of arranging it nicely. He cut every hair close to my head, storming and swearing all the time. I replied to some of his abuse, and he struck me. Some months before, he had pitched me down stairs in a fit of passion; and the injury I received was so serious I was unable to turn myself in bed for many days. He then said, "Linda, I swear by God I will never raise my hand against you again;" but I knew that he would forget his promise. . . .

When they told me my new-born babe was a girl, my heart was heavier than it had ever been before. Slavery is terrible for men; but it is far more terrible for women. Superadded to the burden common to all, *they* have wrongs, and sufferings, and mortifications peculiarly their own. . . .

My grandmother belonged to the church; and she was very desirous of having the children christened. I knew Dr. Flint would forbid it, and I did not venture to attempt it. But chance favored me. He was called to visit a patient out of town, and was obliged to be absent during Sunday. "Now is the time," said my grandmother, "we will take the children to church, and have them christened.". . . .

When my baby was about to be christened, the former mistress of my father stepped up to me, and proposed to give it her Christian name. To this I added the surname of my father, who had himself no legal right to it; for my grandfather, on the paternal side was a white gentleman. What tangled skeins are the genealogies of slavery! I loved my father; but it mortified me to be obliged to bestow his name on my children. . . .

XI. SCENES AT THE PLANTATION

[When Linda continued to refuse Dr. Flint's overtures, he warned her that he intended to sell her children as soon as they were old enough, and then arranged to place her on a plantation as a servant to his son, who was about to be   married.]

Early the next morning I left my grandmother's with my youngest child. My boy was ill, and I left him behind. I had many sad thoughts as the old wagon jolted on. Hitherto, I had suffered alone; now, my little one was to be treated as a slave. As we drew near the great house, I thought of the time when I was formerly sent there out of revenge. I wondered for what purpose I was now sent. I could not tell. I resolved to obey orders so far as duty required; but within myself, I determined to make my stay as short as possible. Mr. Flint was waiting to receive us, and told me to follow him up stairs to receive orders for the day. My little Ellen was left below in the kitchen. It was a change for her, who had always been so carefully tended. My young master said she might amuse herself in the yard. This was kind of him, since the child was hateful to his sight. My task was to fit up the house for the reception of the bride. In the midst of sheets, tablecloths, towels, drapery, and carpeting, my head was as busy planning, as were my fingers with the needle. At noon I was allowed to go to Ellen. She had sobbed herself to sleep. I heard Mr. Flint say to a neighbor, "I've got her down here, and I'll soon take the town notions out of her head. My father is partly to blame for her nonsense. He ought to have broke her in long ago." The remark was made within my hearing, and it would have been quite as manly to have made it to my face. He *had* said things to my face which might, or might not, have surprised his neighbor if he had known of them. He was "a chip of the old block.". . .

The six weeks were nearly completed, when Mr. Flint's bride was expected to take possession of her new home. The arrangements were all completed, and Mr. Flint said I had done well. He expected to leave home on Saturday, and return with his bride the following Wednesday. After receiving various orders from him, I ventured to ask permission to spend Sunday in town. It was granted; for which favor

I was thankful. It was the first I had ever asked of him, and I intended it should be the last. It needed more than one night to accomplish the project I had in view; but the whole of Sunday would give me an opportunity. I spent the Sabbath with my grandmother. . . .

My plan was to conceal myself at the house of a friend, and remain there a few weeks till the search was over. My hope was that the doctor would get discouraged, and, for fear of losing my value, and also of subsequently finding my children among the missing, he would consent to sell us; and I knew somebody would buy us. . . .

On Monday I returned to the plantation, and busied myself with preparations for the important day. Wednesday came. It was a beautiful day, and the faces of the slaves were as bright as the sunshine. The poor creatures were merry. They were expecting little presents from the bride, and hoping for better times under her administration. I had no such hopes for them. I knew that the young wives of slaveholders often thought their authority and importance would be best established and maintained by cruelty; and what I had heard of young Mrs. Flint gave me no reason to expect that her rule over them would be less severe than that of the master and overseer. Truly, the colored race are the most cheerful and forgiving people on the face of the earth. That their masters sleep in safety is owing to their superabundance of heart; and yet they look upon their sufferings with less pity than they would bestow on those of a horse or a dog.

I stood at the door with others to receive the bridegroom and bride. She was a handsome, delicate-looking girl, and her face flushed with emotion at sight of her new home. I thought it likely that visions of a happy future were rising before her. It made me sad; for I knew how soon clouds would come over her sunshine. She examined every part of the house, and told me she was delighted with the arrangements I had made. I was afraid old Mrs. Flint had tried to prejudice her against me, and I did my best to please her. . . .

My mistress and I got along very well together. At the end of a week, old Mrs. Flint made us another visit, and was closeted a long time with her daughter-in-law. I had my suspicions what was the subject of the conference. The old doctor's wife had been informed that I could leave the plantation on one condition, and she was very desirous to keep me there. If she had trusted me, as I deserved to be trusted by her, she would have had no fears of my accepting that condition. When she entered her carriage to return home, she said to young Mrs. Flint, "Don't neglect to send for them as quick as possible." My heart was on the watch all the time, and I at once concluded that she spoke of my children. The doctor came the next day, and as I entered the room to spread the tea table, I heard him say, "Don't wait any longer. Send for them to-morrow." I saw through the plan. They thought my children's being there would fetter me to the spot, and that it was a good place to break us all in to abject submission to our lot as slaves. After the doctor left, a gentleman called, who had always manifested friendly feelings towards my grandmother and her family. Mr. Flint carried him over the plantation to show him the results of labor performed by men and women who were unpaid, miserably clothed, and half famished. The cotton crop was all they thought of. It was duly admired, and the gentleman returned with specimens to show his friends. I was ordered to carry water to wash his hands. As I did so, he said, "Linda, how do you like your new home?" I told him I liked it as well as I expected. He replied, "They don't think you are contented, and to-morrow they are going to bring your children to be with you. I am sorry for you, Linda. I hope they will treat you kindly." I hurried from the room, unable to thank him. My suspicions were correct. My children were to be brought to the plantation to be "broke in."

To this day I feel grateful to the gentleman who gave me this timely information. It nerved me to immediate action.

XII. THE FLIGHT

MR. FLINT was hard pushed for house servants, and rather than lose me he had restrained his malice. I did my work faithfully, though not, of course, with a willing mind. They were evidently afraid I should leave them. Mr. Flint wished that I should sleep in the great house instead of the servants' quarters. . . . Mr. Flint twice called from his chamber door to inquire why the house was not locked up. I replied that I had not done my work. "You have had time enough to do it," said he. "Take care how you answer me!"

I shut all the windows, locked all the doors, and went up to the third story, to wait till midnight. How long those hours seemed, and how fervently I prayed that God would not forsake me in this hour of utmost need! I was about to risk everything on the throw of a die; and if I failed, O what would become of me and my poor children? They would be made to suffer for my fault.

At half past twelve I stole softly down stairs. I stopped on the second floor, thinking I heard a noise. I felt my way down into the parlor, and looked out of the window. The night was so intensely dark that I could see nothing. I raised the window very softly and jumped out. Large drops of rain were falling, and the darkness bewildered me. I dropped on my knees, and breathed a short prayer to God for guidance and protection. I groped my way to the road, and rushed towards the town with almost lightning speed. I arrived at my grandmother's house, but dared not see her. She would say, "Linda, you are killing me;" and I knew that would unnerve me. I tapped softly at the window of a room, occupied by a woman, who had lived in the house several years. I knew she was a faithful friend, and could be trusted with my secret. I tapped several times before she heard me. At last she raised the window, and I whispered, "Sally, I have run away. Let me in, quick." She opened the door softly, and said in low tones, "For God's sake, don't. Your grandmother is trying to buy you and de chillern. Mr. Sands was here last week. He tole her he was going away on business, but he wanted her to go ahead about buying you and de chillern, and he would help her all he could. Don't run away, Linda. Your grandmother is all bowed down wid trouble now."

I replied, "Sally, they are going to carry my children to the plantation to-morrow; and they will never sell them to any body so long as they have me in their power. Now, would you advise me to go back?"

"No, chile, no," answered she. "When dey finds you is gone, dey won't want de plague ob de chillern; but where is you going to hide? Dey knows ebery inch ob dis house."

I told her I had a hiding-place, and that was all it was best for her to know. I asked her to go into my room as soon as it was light, and take all my clothes out of my trunk, and pack them in hers; for I knew Mr. Flint and the constable would be there early to search my room. I feared the sight of my children would be too much for my full heart; but I could not go out into the uncertain future without one last look. I bent over the bed where lay my little Benny and baby Ellen. Poor little ones! Fatherless and motherless! Memories of their father came over me. He wanted to be kind to them; but they were not all to him, as they were to my womanly heart. I knelt and prayed for the innocent little sleepers. I kissed them lightly, and turned away.

As I was about to open the street door, Sally laid her hand on my shoulder, and said, "Linda, is you gwine all alone? Let me call your uncle."

"No, Sally," I replied, "I want no one to be brought into trouble on my account."

I went forth into the darkness and rain. I ran on till I came to the house of the friend who was to conceal me. . . .

The tidings made the old doctor rave and storm at a furious rate. It was a busy day for them. My grandmother's house was searched from top to bottom. As my trunk was empty, they concluded I had taken my clothes with me. Before ten o'clock every vessel northward bound was thoroughly examined, and the law against harboring fugitives was read to all on board. At night a watch was set over the town. Knowing how distressed my grandmother would be, I wanted to send her a message; but it could not be done. Every one who went in or out of her house was closely watched. The doctor said he would take my children, unless she became responsible for them, which of course she willingly did. The next day was spent in searching. Before night, the following advertisement was posted at every corner, and in every public place for miles round:—

"$300 REWARD! Ran away from the subscriber, an intelligent, bright, mulatto girl, named Linda, 21 years of age. Five feet four inches high. Dark eyes, and black hair inclined to curl; but it can be made straight. Has a decayed spot on a front tooth. She can read and write, and in all probability will try to get to the Free States. All persons are forbidden, under penalty of the law, to harbor or employ said slave. $150 will be given to whoever takes her in the state, and $300 if taken out of the state and delivered to me, or lodged in jail.

DR. FLINT". . . .

[The person who concealed Linda was a white woman, herself a slaveowner, who was a friend of Linda's grandmother. After hiding in the woman's house for several days, however, Linda decided that she might be safer elsewhere. In the meantime, Mr. Sands had succeeded in purchasing Linda's two children and her brother William from Dr. Flint by keeping his identity secret and using an intermediary.]

XIII. THE LOOPHOLE OF RETREAT

A SMALL shed had been added to my grandmother's house years ago. Some boards were laid across the joists at the top, and between these boards and the roof was a very small garret, never occupied by any thing but rats and mice. It was a pent roof, covered with nothing but shingles, according to the southern custom for such buildings. The garret was only nine feet long and seven wide. The highest part was three feet high, and sloped down abruptly to the loose board floor.

There was no admission for either light or air. My uncle Philip, who was a carpenter, had very skillfully made a concealed trap-door, which communicated with the storeroom. He had been doing this while I was waiting in the swamp. The storeroom opened upon a piazza. To this hole I was conveyed as soon as I entered the house. The air was stifling; the darkness total. A bed had been spread on the floor. I could sleep quite comfortably on one side; but the slope was so sudden that I could not turn on the other without hitting the roof. The rats and mice ran over my bed; but I was weary, and I slept such sleep as the wretched may, when a tempest has passed over them. Morning came. I knew it only by the noises I heard; for in my small den day and night were all the same. I suffered for air even more than for light. But I was not comfortless. I heard the voices of my children. There was joy and there was sadness in the sound. It made my tears flow. How I longed to speak to them! I was eager to look on their faces; but there was no hole, no crack, through which I could peep. This continued darkness was oppressive. It seemed horrible to sit or lie in a cramped position day after day, without one gleam of light. . . .

My food was passed up to me through the trap-door my uncle had contrived; and my grandmother, my uncle Philip, and aunt Nancy would seize such opportunities as they could, to mount up there and chat with me at the opening. But of course this was not safe in the daytime. It must all be done in darkness. It was impossible for me to move in an erect position, but I crawled about my den for exercise. One day I hit my head against something, and found it was a gimlet. My uncle had left it sticking there when he made the trap-door. I was rejoiced as Robinson Crusoe could have been at finding such a treasure. It put a lucky thought into my head. I said to myself, "Now I will have some light. Now I will see my children." I did not dare to begin my work during the daytime, for fear of attracting attention. But I groped round; and having found the side next the street, where I could frequently see my children, I stuck the gimlet in and waited for evening. I bored three rows of holes, one above another; then I bored out the interstices between. I thus succeeded in making one hole about an inch long and an inch broad. I sat by it till late into the night, to enjoy the little whiff of air that floated in. In the morning I watched for my children. The first person I saw in the street was Dr. Flint. I had a shuddering, superstitious feeling that it was a bad omen. Several familiar faces passed by. At last I heard the merry laugh of children, and presently two sweet little faces were looking up at me, as though they knew I was there, and were conscious of the joy they imparted. How I longed to *tell* them I was there!

My condition was now a little improved. But for weeks I was tormented by hundreds of little red insects, fine as a needle's point, that pierced through my skin, and produced an intolerable burning. The good grandmother gave me herb teas and cooling medicines, and finally I got rid of them. The heat of my den was intense, for nothing but thin shingles protected me from the scorching summer's sun. But I had my consolations. Through my peeping-hole I could watch the children, and when they were near enough, I could hear their talk. Aunt Nancy brought me all the news she could hear at Dr. Flint's. From her I learned that the doctor had written to New York to a colored woman, who had been born and raised in our neighborhood, and had breathed his contaminating atmosphere. He offered her a reward if she could find out any thing about me. I know now what was the nature of her reply; but he soon after started for New York in haste, saying to his family that he had business of importance to transact. I peeped at him as he passed on his way to the steamboat. It was a satisfaction to have miles of land and water between us, even for a little while; and it was a still greater satisfaction to know that he believed me to be in the Free States. My little den seemed less dreary than it had done. He returned, as he did from his former journey to New York, without obtaining any satisfactory information. When he passed our house next morning, Benny was standing at the gate. He had heard them say that he had gone to find me, and he called out, "Dr. Flint, did you bring my mother home? I want to see her." The doctor stamped his foot at him in a rage, and exclaimed, "Get out of the way, you little damned rascal! If you don't, I'll cut off your head."

Benny ran terrified into the house, saying, "You can't put me in jail again. I don't belong to you now." It was well that the wind carried the words away from the doctor's ear. I told my grandmother of it, when we had our next conference at the trap-door; and begged of her not to allow the children to be impertinent to the irascible old man.

Autumn came, with a pleasant abatement of heat. My eyes had become accustomed to the dim light, and by holding my book or work in a certain position near the aperture I contrived to read and sew. That was a great relief to the tedious monotony of my life. But when winter came, the cold penetrated through the thin shingle roof, and I was dreadfully chilled. The winters there are not so long, or so severe, as in northern latitudes; but the houses are not built to shelter from cold, and my little den was peculiarly comfortless. The kind grand-mother brought me bed-clothes and warm drinks. Often I was obliged to lie in bed all day to keep comfortable; but with all my precautions, my shoulders and feet were frostbitten. O, those long, gloomy days, with no object for my eye to rest upon, and no thoughts to occupy my mind, except the dreary past and the uncertain future!

XIV. STILL IN PRISON

WHEN spring returned, and I took in the little patch of green the aperture commanded, I asked myself how many more summers and winters I must be condemned to spend thus. I longed to draw in a plentiful draught of fresh air, to stretch my cramped limbs, to have room to stand erect, to feel the earth under my feet again. My relatives were constantly on the lookout for a chance of escape; but none offered that seemed practicable, and even tolerably safe. The hot summer came again, and made the turpentine drop from the thin roof over my head. . . .

I suffered much more during the second winter than I did during the first. My limbs were benumbed by inaction, and the cold filled them with cramp. I had a very painful sensation of coldness in my head; even my face and tongue stiffened, and I lost the power of speech. Of course it was impossible, under the circumstances, to summon any physician. My brother William came and did all he could for me. Uncle Phillip also watched tenderly over me; and poor grandmother crept up and down to inquire whether there were any signs of returning life. I was restored to consciousness by the dashing of cold water in my face, and found myself leaning against my brother's arm, while he bent over me with streaming eyes. He afterwards told me he thought I was dying, for I had been in an unconscious state sixteen hours. I next became delirious, and was in great danger of betraying myself and my friends. To prevent this, they stupefied me with drugs. I remained in bed six weeks, weary in body and sick at heart. . . .

In the midst of my illness, grandmother broke down under the weight of anxiety and toil. The idea of losing her, who had always been my best friend and a mother to my children, was the sorest trial I had yet had. O, how earnestly I prayed that she might recover! How hard it seemed, that I could not tend upon her, who has so long and so tenderly watched over me!

One day the screams of a child nerved me with strength to crawl to my peeping-hole, and I saw my son covered with blood. A fierce dog, usually kept chained, had seized and bitten him. A doctor was sent for, and I heard the groans and screams of my child while the wounds were being sewed up. O, what torture to a mother's heart, to listen to this and be unable to go to him!

But childhood is like a day in spring, alternately shower and sunshine. Before night Benny was bright and lively, threatening the destruction of the dog; and great was his delight when the doctor told him the next day that the dog had bitten another boy and been shot. Benny recovered from his wounds; but it was long before he could walk. . . .

I heard from uncle Phillip, with feelings of unspeakable joy and gratitude, that the crisis was passed and grandmother would live. I could now say from my heart, "God is merciful. He has spared me the anguish of feeling that I caused her death."

XV. THE CANDIDATE FOR CONGRESS

THE summer had nearly ended, when Dr. Flint made a third visit to New York, in search of me. Two candidates were running for Congress, and he returned in season to vote. The father of my children was the Whig candidate. The doctor had hitherto been a stanch Whig; but now he exerted all his energies for the defeat of Mr. Sands. He invited large parties of men to dine in the shade of his trees, and supplied them with plenty of rum and brandy. If any poor fellow drowned his wits in the bowl, and, in the openness of his convivial heart, proclaimed that he did not mean to vote the Democratic ticket, he was shoved into the street without ceremony.

The doctor expended his liquor in vain. Mr. Sands was elected; an event which occasioned me some anxious thoughts. He had not emancipated my children, and if he should die they would be at the mercy of his heirs. Two little voices, that frequently met my ear, seemed to plead with me not to let their father depart without striving to make their freedom secure. . . I supposed he would call before he left, to say something to my grandmother concerning the children, and I resolved what course to take.

The day before his departure for Washington, I made arrangements, towards evening, to get from my hiding-place into the store-room below. I found myself so stiff and clumsy that it was with great difficulty I could hitch from one resting place to another. When I reached the storeroom my ankles gave way under me, and I sank exhausted on the floor. It seemed as if I could never use my limbs again. But the purpose I had in view roused all the strength I had. I crawled on my hands and knees to the window, and, screened behind a barrel, I waited for his coming. The clock struck nine, and I knew the steamboat would leave between ten and eleven. My hopes were failing. But presently I hear his voice, saying to some one, "Wait for me a moment. I wish to see aunt Martha." When he came out, as he passed the window, I said, "Stop one moment, and let me speak for my children." He started, hesitated, and then passed on, and went out of the gate. I closed the shutter I had partially opened, and sank down behind the barrel. I had suffered much; but seldom had I experienced a keener pang than I then felt. Had my children, then, become of so little consequence to him? And had he so little feeling for their wretched mother that he would not listen a moment while she pleaded for them? Painful memories were so busy within me, that I forgot I had not hooked the shutter, till I heard some one opening it. I looked up. He had come back. "Who called me?" said he, in a low tone. "I did," I replied. "Oh, Linda," said he, "I knew your voice; but I was afraid to answer, lest my friend should hear me. Why do you come here? Is it possible you risk yourself in this house? They are mad to allow it. I shall expect to hear that you are all ruined." I did not wish to implicate him, by letting him know my place of concealment; so I merely said, "I thought you would come to bid grandmother good by, and so I came here to speak a few words to you about emancipating my children. Many changes may take place during the six months you are gone to Washington, and it does not seem right for you to expose them to the risk of such changes. I want nothing for myself; all I ask is, that you will free my children, or authorize some friend to do it, before you go."

He promised he would do it, and also expressed a readiness to make any arrangements whereby I could be purchased. . . .

[At this juncture William, who had accompanied Mr. Sands to Washington as a servant, decided to claim the freedom that had been promised him eventually and disappeared while on a trip to New York. Sands nevertheless agreed to send little Ellen to live with his relatives in Brooklyn, New York, so that she could attend school there while getting far away from possible claims to her by the Flint family. Plans were begun to send Benny to the North as well. These events helped Linda to decide to attempt herself to escape to the North and freedom. Again it was her uncle Phillip and his friend Peter who made arrange-

ments, this time for passage aboard ship. A fellow slave, Fanny, joined her aboard the vessel so as to escape from a new owner. The ship took them uneventfully to Philadelphia, from where Linda went on to New York. There Linda located her daughter Ellen, but learned that Mr. Sands had not yet emancipated her. Fearing that the woman with whom Ellen was living intended to return to the South, Linda began planning to take her away.]

XVI. A HOME FOUND

MY greatest anxiety now was to obtain employment. My health was greatly improved, though my limbs continued to trouble me with swelling whenever I walked much. The greatest difficulty in my way was, that those who employed strangers required a recommendation; and in my peculiar position, I could, of course, obtain no certificates from the families I had so faithfully served.

One day an acquaintance told me of a lady who wanted a nurse for her babe, and I immediately applied for the situation. The lady told me she preferred to have one who had been a mother, and accustomed to the care of infants. I told her I had nursed two babes of my own. She asked me many questions, but, to my great relief, did not require a recommendation from my former employers. She told me she was an English woman, and that was a pleasant circumstance to me, because I had heard they had less prejudice against color than Americans entertained. It was agreed that we should try each other for a week. The trial proved satisfactory to both parties, and I was engaged for a month.

The heavenly Father had been most merciful to me in leading me to this place. Mrs. Bruce was a kind and gentle lady, and proved a true and sympathizing friend. Before the stipulated month expired, the necessity of passing up and down stairs frequently, caused my limbs to swell so painfully, that I became unable to perform my duties. Many ladies would have thoughtlessly discharged me; but Mrs. Bruce made arrangements to save me steps, and employed a physician to attend upon me. I had not yet told her that I was a fugitive slave. She noticed that I was often sad, and kindly inquired the cause. I spoke of being separated from my children, and from relatives who were dear to me; but I did not mention the constant feeling of insecurity which oppressed my spirits. I longed for some one to confide in; but I had been so deceived by white people, that I had lost all confidence in them. If they spoke kind words to me, I thought it was for some selfish purpose. I had entered this family with the distrustful feelings I had brought with me out of slavery; but ere six months had passed, I found that the gentle deportment of Mrs. Bruce and the smiles of her lovely babe were thawing my chilled heart. My narrow mind also began to expand under the influences of her intelligent conversation, and the opportunities for reading, which were gladly allowed me whenever I had leisure from my duties. I gradually became more energetic and more cheerful.

The old feeling of insecurity, especially with regard to my children, often threw its dark shadow across my sunshine. Mrs. Bruce offered me a home for Ellen; but pleasant as it would have been I did not dare to accept it, for fear of offending the Hobbs family. Their knowledge of my precarious situation placed me in their power, and I felt that it was important for me to keep on the right side of them, till, by dint of labor and economy, I could make a home for my children. . . .

I have stated that when Dr. Flint put Ellen in jail, at two years old, she had an inflammation of the eyes, occasioned by measles. This disease still troubled her; and kind Mrs. Bruce proposed that she should come to New York for a while, to be under the care of Dr. Elliott, a well known oculist. It did not occur to me that there was any thing improper in a mother's making such a request; but Mrs. Hobbs was very angry, and refused to let her go. Situated as I was, it was not politic to insist upon it. I made no complaint, but I longed to be entirely free to act a mother's part towards my children. The next time I went over to Brooklyn, Mrs. Hobbs, as if to apologize for her anger, told me she had employed her own physician to attend to Ellen's eyes, and that she had refused my request because she did not consider it safe to trust her in New York. I accepted the explanation in silence; but she had told me that my child *belonged* to her daughter, and I suspected that her real motive was a fear of my conveying her property away from her. Perhaps I did her injustice; but my knowledge of Southerners made it difficult for me to feel otherwise.

Sweet and bitter were mixed in the cup of my life, and I was thankful that it had ceased to be entirely bitter. I loved Mrs. Bruce's babe. When it laughed and crowed in my face, and twined its little tender arms confidingly about my neck, it made me think of the time when Benny and Ellen were babies, and my wounded heart was soothed. One bright morning, as I stood at the window, tossing baby in my arms, my attention was attracted by a young man in sailor's dress, who was closely observing every house as he passed. I looked at him earnestly. Could it be my brother William? It *must* be he and yet, how changed! I placed the baby safely, flew down stairs, opened the front door, beckoned to the sailor, and in less than a minute I was clasped in my brother's arms. How much we had to tell each other! How we laughed, and how we cried, over each other's adventures! I took him to Brooklyn, and again saw him with Ellen, the dear child whom he had loved and tended so carefully, while I was shut up in my miserable den. He stayed in New York a week. His old feelings of affection for me and Ellen were as lively as ever. There are no bonds so strong as those which are formed by suffering together. . . .

XVII. THE OLD ENEMY AGAIN

NOT long afterwards I received a letter from one of my friends at the south, informing me that Dr. Flint was about to visit the north. The letter had been delayed, and I supposed he might be already on the way. Mrs. Bruce did not know I was a fugitive. I told her that important business called me to Boston, where my brother then was, and asked permission to bring a friend to supply my place as nurse, for a fortnight. I started on my journey immediately; and as soon as I arrived, I wrote to my grandmother that if Benny came, he must be sent to Boston. I knew she was only waiting for a good chance to send him north, and, fortunately, she had the legal power to do so, without asking leave of any body. She was a free woman; and when my children were purchased, Mr. Sands preferred to have the bill of sale drawn up in her name. It was conjectured that he advanced the money, but it was not known. At the south, a gentleman may have a shoal of colored children without any disgrace; but if he is known to purchase them, with the view of setting them free, the example is thought to be dangerous to their "peculiar institution," and he becomes unpopular.

There was a good opportunity to send Benny in a vessel coming directly to New York. He was put on board with a letter to a friend, who was requested to see him off to Boston. Early one morning, there was a loud rap at my door, and in rushed Benjamin, all out of breath. "O mother!" he exclaimed, "here I am! I run all the way; and I come all alone. How d'you do?"

O reader, can you imagine my joy? No, you cannot, unless you have been a slave mother. Benjamin rattled away as fast as his tongue could go. "Mother, why don't you bring Ellen here? I went over to

Brooklyn to see her, and she felt very bad when I bid her good by. She said, "O Ben, I wish I was going too.' I thought she'd know ever so much, but she don't know so much as I do; for I can read, and she can't. And, mother, I lost all my clothes coming. What can I do to get some more? I 'spose free boys can get along here at the north as well as white boys."

I did not like to tell the sanguine, happy little fellow how much he was mistaken. I took him to a tailor, and procured a change of clothes. The rest of the day was spent in mutual asking and answering of questions, with the wish constantly repeated that the good old grandmother was with us, and frequent injunctions from Benny to write to her immediately, and be sure to tell her every thing about his voyage, and his journey to Boston.

Dr. Flint made his visit to New York, and made every exertion to call upon me, and invite me to return with him; but not being able to ascertain where I was, his hospitable intentions were frustrated, and the affectionate family, who were waiting for me with "open arms," were doomed to disappointment.

As soon as I knew he was safely at home, I placed Benjamin in the care of my brother William, and returned to Mrs. Bruce. There I remained through the winter and spring, endeavoring to perform my duties faithfully, and finding a good degree of happiness in the attractions of my baby Mary, the considerate kindness of her excellent mother, and occasional interviews with my darling daughter.

But when summer came, the old feeling of insecurity haunted me. It was necessary for me to take little Mary out daily, for exercise and fresh air, and the city was swarming with Southerners, some of whom might recognize me. How weather brings out snakes and slaveholders, and I like one class of the venomous creatures as little as I do the other. What a comfort it is, to be free to *say* so! . . .

XVIII. THE FUGITIVE SLAVE LAW

[Learning that Mrs. Hobbs' brother had betrayed her where-abouts in a letter to Dr. Flint, Linda confessed to Mrs. Bruce, her employer, that she was a fugitive slave. Aided by the Bruces, she journeyed to Boston, taking Ellen with her, and spent the winter there. Then, upon the death of his wife, Mr. Bruce wrote Linda asking if she would accompany him as a nurse for his daughter on a trip to England. She did so, leaving Ellen with a friend to attend school and placing

Benny to learn a trade. Upon her return to Boston ten months later she was reunited with her daughter, but discovered that her son had gone as a sailor on a whaling voyage. After two years, her brother William aided her by sending Ellen to a boarding school in New York State. She then joined William in his venture of opening an antislavery reading room and book store in Rochester, New York. The venture failed, however, and she spent nearly a year in the home of Isaac and Amy Post, active in the antislavery cause in that city. As it happened, the Posts were the only persons who were identified by their own names in her autobiography. It was Amy Post who first encouraged Harriet Jacobs to tell her story as a contribution to antislavery propaganda.]

My brother, being disappointed in his project, concluded to go to California; and it was agreed that Benjamin should go with him. Ellen liked her school, and was a great favorite there. They did not know her history, and she did not tell it, because she had no desire to make capital out of their sympathy. But when it was accidentally discovered that her mother was a fugitive slave, every method was used to increase her advantages and diminish her expenses.

I was alone again. It was necessary for me to be earning money, and I preferred that it should be among those who knew me. On my return from Rochester, I called at the house of Mr. Bruce, to see Mary, the darling little babe that had thawed my heart, when it was freezing into a cheerless distrust of all my fellowbeings. She was growing a tall girl now, but I loved her always. Mr. Bruce had married again, and it was proposed that I should become nurse to a new infant. I had but one hesitation, and that was my feeling of insecurity in New York, now greatly increased by the passage of the Fugitive Slave Law. However, I resolved to try the experiment. I was again fortunate in my employer. The new Mrs. Bruce was an American, brought up under aristocratic influences, and still living in the midst of them; but if she had any prejudice against color, I was never made aware of it; and as for the system of slavery, she had a most hearty dislike of it. No sophistry of Southerners could blind her to its enormity. She was a person of excellent principles and a noble heart. To me, from that hour to the present, she has been a true and sympathizing friend. Blessings be with her and hers! . . .

All that winter I lived in a state of anxiety. When I took the children out to breathe the air, I closely observed the countenances of all I met. I dreaded the approach of summer, when snakes and slaveholders make their appearance. I was, in fact, a slave in New

York, as subject to slave laws as I had been in a Slave State. Strange incongruity in a State called free!

Spring returned, and I received warning from the south that Dr. Flint knew of my return to my old place, and was making preparations to have me caught. I learned afterwards that my dress, and that of Mrs. Bruces's children, had been described to him by some of the Northern tools, which slaveholders employ for their base purposes, and then indulge in sneers at their cupidity and mean servility.

I immediately informed Mrs. Bruce of my danger, and she took prompt measures for my safety. My place as nurse could not be supplied immediately, and this generous, sympathizing lady proposed that I should carry her baby away. It was a comfort to me to have the child with me; for the heart is reluctant to be torn away from every object it loves. But how few mothers would have consented to have one of their own babes become a fugitive, for the sake of a poor, hunted nurse, on whom the legislators of the country had let loose the bloodhounds! When I spoke of the sacrifice she was making, in depriving herself of her dear baby, she replied, "It is better for you to have baby with you, Linda; for if they get on your track, they will be obliged to bring the child to me; and then, if there is a possibility of saving you, you shall be saved." . . .

I was sent into New England, where I was sheltered by the wife of a Senator, whom I shall always hold in grateful remembrance. This honorable gentleman would not have voted for the Fugitive Slave Law, as did the senator in "Uncle Tom's Cabin;" on the contrary, he was strongly opposed to it; but he was enough under its influence to be afraid of having me remain in his house many hours. So I was sent into the country, where I remained a month with the baby. When it was supposed that Dr. Flint's emissaries had lost track of me, and given up the pursuit for the present, I returned to New York.

XIX. FREE AT LAST

MRS. BRUCE, and every member of her family, were exceedingly kind to me. I was thankful for the blessings of my lot, yet I could not always wear a cheerful countenance. I was doing harm to no one; on the contrary, I was doing all the good I could in my small way; yet I could never go out to breathe God's free air without trepidation at my heart. This seemed hard; and I could not think it was a right state of things in any civilized country. . . .

I kept close watch of the newspapers for arrivals; but one Saturday night, being much occupied, I forgot to examine the Evening Express as usual. I went down into the parlor for it, early in the morning, and found the boy about to kindle a fire with it. I took it from him and examined the list of arrivals. Reader, if you have never been a slave, you cannot imagine the acute sensation of suffering at my heart, when I read the names of Mr. and Mrs. Dodge, at a hotel in Cortland Street. It was a third-rate hotel, and that circumstance convinced me of the truth of what I had heard, that they were short of funds and had need of my value, as *they* valued me; and that was by dollars and cents. I hastened with the paper to Mrs. Bruce. Her heart and hand were always open to every one in distress, and she always warmly sympathized with mine. It was impossible to tell how near the enemy was. He might have passed and repassed the house while we were sleeping. He might at that moment be waiting to pounce upon me if I ventured out of doors. I had never seen the husband of my young mistress, and therefore I could not distinguish him from any other stranger. A carriage was hastily ordered; and, closely veiled, I followed Mrs. Bruce, taking the baby again with me into exile. After various turnings and crossings, and returnings, the carriage stopped at the house of one of Mrs. Bruce's friends, where I was kindly received. Mrs. Bruce returned immediately, to instruct the domestics what to say if any one came to inquire for me.

It was lucky for me that the evening paper was not burned up before I had a chance to examine the list of arrivals. It was not long after Mrs. Bruce's return to her house, before several people came to inquire for me. One inquired for me, another asked for my daughter Ellen, and another said he had a letter from my grandmother, which he was requested to deliver in person.

They were told, "She *has* lived here, but she has left."

"How long ago?"

"I don't know, sir."

"Do you know where she went?"

"I do not, sir." And the door was closed. . . .

The next day, baby and I set out in a heavy snow storm, bound for New England again. . . .

Without my knowledge, Mrs. Bruce employed a gentleman in New York to enter into negotiations with Mr. Dodge. He proposed to pay three hundred dollars down, if Mr. Dodge would sell me, and enter into obligations to relinquish all claim to me or my children forever after. He who called himself my master said he scorned so small an offer for such a valuable servant. The gentleman replied, "You can do as you choose, sir. If you reject this offer you will never get any thing; for the woman has friends who will convey her and her children out of the country."

Mr. Dodge concluded that "half a loaf was better than no bread," and he agreed to the proffered terms. By the next mail I received this brief letter from Mrs. Bruce: "I am rejoiced to tell you that the money for your freedom has been paid to Mr. Dodge. Come home to-morrow. I long to see you and my sweet babe." . . .

I had objected to having my freedom bought, yet I must confess that when it was done I felt as if a heavy load had been lifted from my weary shoulders. When I rode home in the cars I was no longer afraid to unveil my face and look at people as they passed. I should have been glad to have met Daniel Dodge himself; to have had him seen me and known me that he might have mourned over the untoward circumstances which compelled him to sell me for three hundred dollars.

When I reached home, the arms of my benefactress were thrown round me, and our tears mingled. As soon as she could speak, she said, "O Linda, I'm *so* glad it's all over! You wrote to me as if you thought you were going to be transferred from one owner to another. But I did not buy you for your services. I should have done just the same, if you had been going to sail for California to-morrow. I should, at least, have the satisfaction of knowing that you left me a free woman. . . .

My grandmother lived to rejoice in my freedom; but not long after, a letter came with a black seal. She had gone "where the wicked cease from troubling, and the weary are at rest."

Time passed on, and a paper came to me from the south, containing an obituary notice of my uncle Phillip. It was the only case I ever knew of such an honor conferred upon a colored person. It was written by one of his friends, and contained these words: "Now that death has laid him low, they call him a good man and a useful citizen; but what are eulogies to the black man, when the world has faded from his vision? It does not require man's praise to obtain rest in God's kingdom." So they called a colored man a *citizen*? Strange words to be uttered in that region!

Reader, my story ends with freedom; not in the usual way, with marriage. I and my children are now free! We are as free from the power of slaveholders as are the white people of the north; and though that, according to my ideas, is not saying a great deal, it is a vast improvement in *my* condition. The dream of my life is not yet realized. I do not sit with my children in a home of my own. I still long for a hearthstone of my own, however humble. I wish it for my children's sake far more than for my own. But God so orders circumstances as to keep me with my friend Mrs. Bruce. Love, duty, gratitude, also bind me to her side. It is a privilege to serve her who pities my oppressed people, and who has bestowed the inestimable boon of freedom on me and my children.

It has been painful to me, in many ways, to recall the dreary years I passed in bondage. I would gladly forget them if I could. Yet the retrospection is not altogether without solace; for with those gloomy recollections come tender memories of my good old grandmother, like light, fleecy clouds floating over a dark and troubled sea.

Mary Antin (1881-1949)

THIS memoir differs from the other autobiographies in this book in that Mary Antin limited it to her childhood. It is also the only one the reveals the deep shock experienced by immigrants who found themselves immersed for the first time in an alien culture, including its language, and who had to come to terms with it. Largely for that reason Antin's story is the richest in its descriptions of the values and ways of life of Americans in their times.

As Jews in Czarist Russia in the late nineteenth century, Antin's family were members of a persecuted minority. They emigrated to escape religious harassment, and also, as other Europeans had done for generations, to evade compulsory military service and to seek economic opportunity. Between 1900 and 1910, for example, nearly 1.6 million people emigrated from Russia to the United States; many of these were Jews. In the case of Pinchus and Hannah Antin and their four children it was mainly their poverty, brought about by severe illnesses, that drove them to seek a better life in America, which was widely reported to be a kind of paradise. Pinchus Antin emigrated in 1891, followed by his family three years later.

The forced acculturation of immigrants began on arrival. Officials often assigned them new, more "American" names. Here Pinchus became Israel, Hannah became Esther, and thirteen-year-old Maryashe became Mary. But Mary, excited by the wonders and promise of her new life, and following the lead of their father, who urged his wife and children to cast off their old ways for new, regretted only that her new name was not more different from the old. Soon the Antins, caught up in earning a living, going to school, and experiencing the variety of life and people in cosmopolitan Boston, fell away from most of the traditional observances of Orthodox Judaism, and adolescent Mary found herself an unbeliever. Only the persistence of her mother preserved some of the ritual, with its deep importance for family solidarity.

Mary, reveling in the free play for her imagination and talents made possible by Boston's schools, cultural institutions, ethnic diversity, and street life, welcomed avidly the processes of Americanization. She learned English quickly, wrote essays and poems that were printed in the newspapers, went for grammar school to the elite Girls' Latin School, participated as a kind of juvenile mascot in the meetings and outings of the Natural History Club, made up of proper Bostonian adults, and within six years of her arrival succeeded in having published an account of her family's emigration, *From Polotzk to Boston* (1899), drawn from her letters to her uncle.

The newcomer's rapid progress and successes depended heavily, however, on sacrifices by others. Her family, never far from poverty despite their efforts, subsidized her education, and as part of that subsidy her older sister entered a workshop for employment instead of sharing Mary's school life. Help came from Mr. Rosenblum, the grocer who extended credit to her family for years without demanding payment and who took almost as much pride as her family in the accomplishments of this little Jewish girl. Help came as well from native Americans like Miss Dillingham, the devoted schoolteacher who befriended and guided Antin, and the venerable author and philanthropist Edward Everett Hale, then pastor of South Congregational Church, both of whom responded warmly to the girl's intellectual curiosity and her celebration of American ideals and opportunities.

Antin followed her star to New York, where she studied at Barnard and Columbia Teacher's Colleges, married a Gentile of Lutheran background, Amadeus William Grabau, whom she had met in her days in the Natural History Club, had a daughter, and became involved in the intellectual and cultural life of her new home. In 1911, when Antin was only thirty, the *Atlantic Monthly* published in serial form her autobiography, in which she followed her life from Russia to America through her school days in Boston. The account appeared the next year as a book, *The Promised Land*; symbolically, the book carried on its cover a drawing of the Statue of Liberty, which had been erected in New York harbor only a few years before her arrival in the

United States. Antin soon published another book, *They Who Knock at Our Gates* (1914), in which she strongly opposed the rising demand for restrictions on immigration.

As Mary Antin came to stand as a model of successful assimilation, rejecting part of her heritage in the process, she continued to write under her maiden name, which was of course also that of her family. She was a New Woman, part of a movement toward feminist self-assertion. But she was also still her parents' child, explaining that ". . . the aspiring immigrant is not content to progress alone. . . . He must take his family with him as he rises."

While Antin's story avoids neither the difficulties of life in Russia nor the hardships of poor immigrants in Boston, it nevertheless reads like the gradual realization of a dream. We can easily believe that there is much truth in that picture, for she was a talented and spirited girl who learned English and adopted American ways readily, made friends easily, and, apparently, found out what she wanted and how to get it. Does the tone of her memoir reflect this reading of assimilation-as-success? Are there darker sides, for her or others in her family, to the abandonment of old ways and the embracing of the new?

Part of the significance of Antin's account lies in its report of the opening up of new roles for females. In her case, did the assumption of a new role as an educated woman, free to participate in new intellectual and cultural activities, involve conflict with dominant male values? Why or why not?

The Promised Land

Mary Antin*

I. WITHIN THE PALE

WHEN I was a little girl, the world was divided into two parts; namely, Polotzk, the place where I lived, and a strange land called Russia. All the little girls I knew lived in Polotzk, with their fathers and mothers and friends. Russia was the place where one's father went on business. It was so far off, and so many bad things happened there, that one's mother and grandmother and grown-up aunts cried at the railroad station, and one was expected to be sad and quiet for the rest of the day, when the father departed for Russia. . . .

Polotzk and Vitebsk were now bound together by the continuity of the earth, but between them and Russia a formidable barrier still interposed. I learned, as I grew older, that much as Polotzk disliked to go to Russia, even more did Russia object to letting Polotzk come. People from Polotzk were sometimes turned back before they had finished their business, and often they were cruelly treated on the way. It seemed there were certain places in Russia—St. Petersburg, and Moscow, and Kiev—where my father or my uncle or my neighbor must never come at all, no matter what important things invited them. The police would seize them and send them back to Polotzk, like

* From *The Promised Land.* Boston, Houghton Mifflin Co., 1912.

wicked criminals, although they had never done any wrong. . . .

I do not know when I became old enough to understand. The truth was borne in on me a dozen times a day, from the time I began to distinguish words from empty noises. . . . There was no time in my life when I did not hear and see and feel the truth—the reason why Polotzk was cut off from the rest of Russia. It was the first lesson a little girl in Polotzk had to learn. But for a long while I did not understand. Then there came a time when I knew that Polotzk and Vitebsk and Vilna and some other places were grouped together as the "Pale of Settlement," and within this area the Czar commanded me to stay, with my father and mother and friends, and all other people like us. We must not be found outside the Pale, because we were Jews.

So there was a fence around Polotzk, after all. The world was divided into Jews and Gentiles. This knowledge came so gradually that it could not shock me. It trickled into my consciousness drop by drop. By the time I fully understood that I was a prisoner, the shackles had grown familiar to my flesh. . . .

The thing that really mattered was the necessity of breaking the Jewish laws of daily life while in the service. A soldier often has to eat trefah* and work on Sabbath. He had to shave his beard and do reverence to Christian things. He could not attend daily services at the synagogue; his private devotions were disturbed by the jeers and insults of his coarse Gentile comrades. He might resort to all sorts of tricks and shams, still he was obliged to violate Jewish law. When he returned home, at the end of his term of service, he could not rid himself of the stigma of those enforced sins. For four years he had led the life of a Gentile.

Piety alone was enough to make the Jews dread military service, but there were other things that made it a serious burden. Most men of twenty-one—the age of conscription—were already married and had children. During their absence their families suffered, their business often was ruined. At the end of their term they were beggars. As beggars, too, they were sent home from their military post. If they happened to have a good uniform at the time of their dismissal, it was stripped from them, and replaced by a shabby one. They received a free ticket for the return journey, and a few kopecks a day for expenses. In this fashion they were hurried back into the Pale, like escaped prisoners. The Czar was done with them. If within a limited time they were found outside the Pale, they would be seized and sent home in chains.

* Food forbidden by Jewish dietary law.

There were certain exceptions to the rule of compulsory service. The only son of a family was exempt, and certain others. In the physical examination preceding conscription, many were rejected on account of various faults. This gave the people the idea of inflicting injuries on themselves, so as to produce temporary deformities on account of which they might be rejected at the examination. Men would submit to operation on their eyes, ears, or limbs, which caused them horrible sufferings, in the hope of escaping service. . . .

Sons of rich fathers could escape service without leaving any marks on their persons. It was always possible to bribe conscription officers. This was a dangerous practice,—it was not the officers who suffered most in case the negotiations leaked out,—but no respectable family would let a son be taken as a recruit till it had made every effort to save him. My grandfather nearly ruined himself to buy his sons out of service; and my mother tells thrilling anecdotes of her younger brother's life, who for years lived in hiding, under assumed names and in various disguises, till he had passed the age of liability for service. . . .

It was bewildering to hear how many kinds of duties and taxes we owed the Czar. We paid taxes on our houses, and taxes on the rents from the houses, taxes on our business, taxes on our profits. I am not sure whether there were taxes on our losses. The town collected taxes, and the county, and the central government; and the chief of police we had always with us. There were taxes for public works, but rotten pavements went on rotting year after year; and when a bridge was to be built, special taxes were levied. . . .

There were things in Polotzk that made you laugh with one eye and weep with the other, like a clown. During an epidemic of cholera, the city officials, suddenly becoming energetic, opened stations for the distribution of disinfectants to the people. A quarter of the population was dead when they began, and most of the dead were buried, while some lay decaying in deserted houses. The survivors, some of them crazy from horror, stole through the empty streets, avoiding one another, till they came to the appointed stations, where they pushed and crowded to get their little bottles of carbolic acid. Many died from fear in those horrible days, but some must have died from laughter. For only the Gentiles were allowed to receive the disinfectant. Poor Jews who had nothing but their new–made graves were driven away from the stations. . . .

Perhaps peaceable conversion of the Jews was not the Czar's only motive when he opened public schools everywhere and compelled parents to send their boys for instruction. Perhaps he just wanted to be good, and really hoped to benefit the country. But to the Jews the public schools appeared as a trap door to the abyss of apostasy. The instructors were always Christians, the teaching was Christian, and the regulations of the schoolroom, as to hours, costume, and manners, were often in opposition to Jewish practices. The public school interrupted the boy's sacred studies in the Hebrew school. Where would you look for pious Jews, after a few generations of boys brought up by Christian teachers? Plainly the Czar was after the souls of the Jewish children. The church door gaped for them at the end of the school course. And all good Jews rose up against the schools, and by every means, fair or foul, kept their boys away. The official appointed to keep the register of boys for school purposes waxed rich on the bribes paid him by anxious parents who kept their sons in hiding.

After a while the wise Czar changed his mind, or he died,— probably he did both,—and the schools were closed. . . .

And then it was the Jews who changed their minds—some of them. They wanted to send their children to school, to learn histories and sciences, because they had discovered that there was good in such things as well as in the Sacred Law. These people were called progressive, but they had no chance to progress. All the czars that came along persisted in the old idea, that for the Jew no door should be opened,—no door out of the Pale, no door out of their medievalism. . . .

II. THE BOUNDARIES STRETCH

THE long chapter of troubles which led to my father's emigration to America began with his own illness. The doctors sent him to Courland to consult expensive specialists, who prescribed tedious courses of treatment. He was far from cured when my mother also fell ill, and my father had to return to Polotzk to look after the business.

Trouble begets trouble. After my mother took to her bed everything continued to go wrong. The business gradually declined, as too much money was withdrawn to pay the doctors' and apothecaries' bills; and my father, himself in poor health, and worried about my mother, was not successful in coping with the growing difficulties. At home, the servants were dismissed, for the sake of economy, and all the housework and the nursing fell on my grandmother and my sister. Fetchke, as a result, was overworked, and fell ill of a fever. The baby, suffering from unavoidable neglect, developed the fractious temper of semi-illness. And by way of a climax, the old cow took it into her head to kick my grandmother, who was laid up for a week with a bruised leg.

Neighbors and cousins pulled us through till grandma got up, and after her, Fetchke. But my mother remained on her bed. Weeks, months, a year she lay there, and half of another year. All the doctors in Polotzk attended her in turn, and one doctor came all the way from Vitebsk. Every country practitioner for miles around was consulted, every quack, every old wife who knew a charm. The apothecaries ransacked their shops for drugs the names of which they had forgotten, and kind neighbors brought in their favorite remedies. There were midnight prayers in the synagogue for my mother, and petitions at the graves of her parents; and one awful night when she was near death, three pious mothers who had never lost a child came to my mother's bedside and bought her, for a few kopecks, for their own, so they might gain the protection of their luck, and so be saved. . . .

Once in a while I was allowed to take a short turn in the sickroom. It was awful to sit beside my mother's bed in the still night and see her helplessness. She had been so strong, so active. She used to lift sacks and barrels that were heavy for a man, and now she did not know me when I gave her the medicine, and when she knew me, she did not care. Would she ever care any more? She looked strange and small in the shadows of the bed. Her hair had been cut off after the first few months; her short curls were almost covered by the ice bag. Her cheeks were red, red, but her hands were so white as they had never been before. In the still night I wondered if she cared to live.

The night lamp burned on. My father grew old. He was always figuring on a piece of paper. We children knew the till was empty when the silver candlesticks were taken away to be pawned. Next, superfluous featherbeds were sold for what they would bring, and then there came a day when grandma, with eyes blinded by tears, groped in the big wardrobe for my mother's satin dress and velvet mantle; and after that it did not matter any more what was taken out of the house.

Then everything took a sudden turn. My mother began to improve, and at the same time my father was offered a good position as superintendent of a gristmill.

As soon as my mother could be moved, he took us all out to the mill, about three versts out of town, on the Polota. We had a pleasant cottage there, with the miller's red-headed, freckled family for our only neighbors. If our rooms were barer than they used to be, the sun shone in at all the windows; and as the leaves on the trees grew denser and darker, my mother grew stronger on her feet, and laughter returned to our house as the song bird to the grove.

We children had a very happy summer. We had never lived in the country before, and we liked the change. It was endless fun to explore the mill; to squeeze into forbidden places, and be pulled out by the angry miller; to tyrannize over the mill hands, and be worshipped by them in return; to go boating on the river, and discover unvisited nooks, and search the woods and fields for kitchen herbs, and get lost, and be found, a hundred times a week. And what an adventure it was to walk the three versts into town, leaving a trail of perfume from the wild-flower posies we carried to our city friends!

But these things did not last. The mill changed hands, and the new owner put a protégé of his own in my father's place. So, after a short breathing spell, we were driven back into the swamp of growing poverty and trouble.

The next year or so my father spent in a restless and fruitless search for a permanent position. My mother had another serious illness, and his own health remained precarious. What he earned did not more than half pay the bills in the end, though we were living very humbly now. Polotzk seemed to reject him, and no other place invited him.

Just at this time occurred one of the periodic anti-Semitic movements whereby government officials were wont to clear the forbidden cities of Jews, whom, in the intervals of slack administration of the law, they allowed to maintain an illegal residence in places outside the Pale, on payment of enormous bribes and at the cost of nameless risks and indignities. . . .

The open cities becoming thus suddenly crowded, every man's chance of making a living was diminished in proportion to the number of additional competitors. Hardship, acute distress, ruin for many; thus spread the disaster, ring beyond ring, from the stone thrown by a despotic official into the ever-full river of Jewish persecution.

Passover was celebrated in tears that year. In the story of the Exodus we would have read a chapter of current history, only for us there was no deliverer and no promised land.

But what said some of us at the end of the long service? Not "May we be next year in Jerusalem," but "Next year—in America!" So there was our promised land, and many faces were turned towards the West. And if the waters of the Atlantic did not part for them, the wanderers rode its bitter flood by a miracle as great as any the rod of Moses ever wrought.

My father was carried away by the westward movement, glad of his own deliverance, but sore at heart for us whom he left behind. It was the last chance for all of us. We were so far reduced in circumstances that he had to travel with borrowed money to a German port, whence he was forwarded to Boston, with a host of others, at the expense of an emigrant aid society.

I was about ten years old when my father emigrated. I was used to his going away from home, and "America" did not mean much more to me than "Kherson," or "Odessa," or any other names of distant places. I understood vaguely, from the gravity with which his plans were discussed, and from references to ships, societies, and other unfamiliar things, that this enterprise was different from previous ones; but my excitement and emotion on the morning of my father's departure were mainly vicarious.

I know the day when "America" as a world entirely unlike Polotzk lodged in my brain, to become the center of all my dreams and speculations. Well I know the day. I was in bed, sharing the measles with some of the other children. Mother brought us a thick letter from father, written just before boarding the ship. The letter was full of excitement. There was something in it besides the description of travel, something besides the pictures of crowds of people, of foreign cities, of a ship ready to put out to sea. My father was traveling at the expense of a charitable organization, without means of his own, without plans, to a strange world where he had no friends; and yet he wrote with the confidence of a well-equipped soldier going into battle. The rhetoric is mine. Father simply wrote that the emigration committee was taking good care of everybody, that the weather was fine, and the ship comfortable. But I heard something, as we read the letter together in the darkened room, that was more than the words seemed to say. There was a elation, a hint of triumph, such as had never been in my father's letters before. I cannot tell how I knew it. I felt a stirring, a straining in my father's letter. It was there, even though my mother stumbled over strange words, even though she cried, as women will when somebody is going away. My father was inspired by a vision. He saw something—he promised us something. It was this "America." And "America" became my dream.

While it was nothing new for my father to go far from home in search of his fortune, the circumstances in which he left us were unlike anything we had experienced before. We had absolutely no reliable source of income, no settled home, no immediate prospects. We hardly knew where we belonged in the simple scheme of our society. My mother, as a bread-winner, had nothing like her former success. Her health was permanently impaired, her place in the business world had long been filled by others, and there was no capital to start her anew. Her brothers did what they could for her. They were well-to-do, but they all had large families, with marriageable daughters and sons to be bought out of military service. The allowance they made her was generous compared to their means,—affection and duty could do no more,—but there were four of us growing children, and my mother was obliged to make every effort within her power to piece out her income. . . .

I am sure I made as serious efforts as anybody to prepare myself for life in America on the lines indicated in my father's letters. In America, he wrote, it was no disgrace to work at a trade. Workmen and capitalists were equal. The employer addressed the employee as *you*, not, familiarly, as *thou*. The cobbler and the teacher had the same title, "Mister." And all the children, boys and girls, Jews and Gentiles, went to school! Education would be ours for the asking, and economic independence also, as soon as we were prepared. He wanted Fetchke and me to be taught some trade; so my sister was apprenticed to a dressmaker and I to a milliner. . . .

Not that my father had grown suddenly rich. He was so far from rich that he was going to borrow every cent of the money for our third-class passage; but he had a business in view which he could carry on all the better for having the family with him; and, besides, we were borrowing right and left anyway, and to no definite purpose. With the children, he argued, every year in Russia was a year lost. They should be spending the precious years in school, in learning English, in becoming Americans. United in America, there were ten chances of our getting to our feet again to one chance in our scattered, aimless state.

So at last I was going to America! Really, really going, at last! The boundaries burst. The arch of heaven soared. A million suns shone out of every star. The winds rushed in from outer space, roaring in my ears, "America! America!". . .

[In 1894 Mrs. Antin and her children, with the tickets for the ocean voyage that her husband had purchased with the earnings of his three years in America, made their way by rail from Polotzk to Hamburg in Germany. After two weeks in quarantine there they embarked on a ship bound for Boston. There Mr. Antin met them to welcome them to a new and different life. All the while, thirteen-year-

old Maryashe was observing intently the details that, to fulfill a promise, she would include in letters to her uncle Moses back in Polotzk.]

III. THE PROMISED LAND

. . .BY the time we joined my father, he had surveyed many avenues of approach toward the coveted citadel of fortune. One of these, heretofore untried, he now proposed to essay, armed with new courage, and cheered on by the presence of his family. In partnership with an energetic little man who had an English chapter in his history, he prepared to set up a refreshment booth on Crescent Beach. But while he was completing arrangements at the beach we remained in town, where we enjoyed the educational advantages of a thickly populated neighborhood; namely, Wall Street, in the West End of Boston.

Anybody who knows Boston knows that the West and North Ends are the wrong ends of that city. They form the tenement district, or, in the newer phrase, the slums of Boston. Anybody who is acquainted with the slums of any American metropolis knows that that is the quarter where poor immigrants foregather, to live, for the most part, as unkempt, half-washed, toiling, unaspiring foreigners; pitiful in the eyes of social missionaries, the despair of boards of health, the hope of ward politicians, the touchstone of American democracy. The well-versed metropolitan knows the slums as a sort of house of detention for poor aliens, where they live on probation till they can show a certificate of good citizenship.

He may know all this and yet not guess how Wall Street, in the West End, appears in the eyes of a little immigrant from Polotzk. What would the sophisticated sight-seer say about Union Place, off Wall Street, where my new home waited for me. He would say that it is no place at all, but a short box of an alley. Two rows of three-story tenements are its sides, a stingy strip of sky is its lid, a lettered pavement is the floor, and a narrow mouth its exit.

But I saw a very different picture on my introduction to Union Place. I saw two imposing rows of brick buildings, loftier than any dwelling I had ever lived in. Brick was even on the ground for me to tread on, instead of common earth or boards. Many friendly windows stood open, filled with uncovered heads of women and children. I thought the people were interested in us, which was very neighborly. I looked up to the topmost row of windows, and my eyes were filled with the May blue of an American sky!

In our days of affluence in Russia we had been accustomed to upholstered parlors, embroidered linen, silver spoons and candle-sticks, goblets of gold, kitchen shelves shining with copper and brass. We had featherbeds heaped halfway to the ceiling; we had clothes presses dusky with velvet and silk and fine woollen. The three small rooms into which my father now ushered us, up one flight of stairs, contained only the necessary beds, with lean mattresses; a few wooden chairs; a table or two; a mysterious iron structure, which later turned out to be a stove; a couple of unornamental kerosene lamps; and a scanty array of cooking—utensils and crockery. And yet we were all impressed with our new home and its furniture. It was not only because we had just passed through our seven lean years, cooking in earthen vessels, eating black bread on holidays and wearing cotton; it was chiefly because these wooden chairs and tin pans were American chairs and pans that they shone glorious in our eyes. And if there was anything lacking for comfort or decoration we expected it to be presently supplied—at least, we children did. Perhaps my mother alone, of us newcomers, appreciated the shabbiness of the little apartment, and realized that for her there was as yet no laying down of the burden of poverty.

Our initiation into American ways began with the first step on the new soil. My father found occasion to instruct or correct us even on the way from the pier to Wall Street, which journey we made crowded together in a rickety cab. He told us not to lean out of the windows, not to point, and explained the word "greenhorn." We did not want to be "greenhorns," and gave the strictest attention to my father's instruc-tions. I do not know when my parents found opportunity to review together the history of Polotzk in the three years past, for we children had no patience with the subject; my mother's narrative was con-stantly interrupted by irrelevant questions, interjections, and expla-nations.

The first meal was an object lesson of much variety. My father produced several kinds of food, ready to eat, without any cooking, from little tin cans that had printing all over them. He attempted to introduce us to a queer, slippery kind of fruit, which he called "banana," but had to give up for the time being. After the meal, he had better luck with a curious piece of furniture on runners, which he called "rocking-chair." There were five of us newcomers, and we found five different ways of getting into the American machine of perpetual motion, and as many ways of getting out of it. One born and bred to the use of a rocking-chair cannot imagine how ludicrous people can make themselves when attempting to use it for the first time. We laughed immoderately over our various experiments with the novelty, which was a wholesome way of letting off steam after the unusual excitement of the day.

In our flat we did not think of such a thing as storing the coal in the bathtub. There was no bathtub. So in the evening of the first day my father conducted us to the public baths. As we moved along in a little procession, I was delighted with the illumination of the streets. So many lamps, and they burned until morning, my father said, and so people did not need to carry lanterns. In America, then, everything was free, as we had heard in Russia. Light was free; the streets were as bright as a synagogue on a holy day. Music was free; we had been serenaded, to our gaping delight, by a brass band of many pieces, soon after our installation on Union Place.

Education was free. That subject my father had written about repeatedly, as comprising his chief hope for us children, the essence of American opportunity, the treasure that no thief could touch, not even misfortune or poverty. It was the one thing that he was able to promise us when he sent for us; surer, safer than bread or shelter. . . .

It was a great disappointment to be told by my father that we were not to enter upon our school career at once. It was too near the end of the term, he said, and we were going to move to Crescent Beach in a week or so. We had to wait until the opening of the schools in September. What a loss of precious time—from May till September!

Not that the time was really lost. Even the interval on Union Place was crowded with lessons and experiences. We had to visit the stores and be dressed from head to foot in American clothing; we had to learn the mysteries of the iron stove, the washboard, and the speaking-tube; we had to learn to trade with the fruit peddler through the window, and not to be afraid of the policeman; and, above all, we had to learn English.

The kind people who assisted us in these important matters form a group by themselves in the gallery of my friends. If I had never seen them from those early days till now, I should still have remembered them with gratitude. When I enumerate the long list of my American teachers, I must begin with those who came to us on Wall Street and taught us our first steps. To my mother, in her perplexity over the cookstove, the woman who showed her how to make the fire was an angel of deliverance. A fairy godmother to us children was she who led us to a wonderful country called "uptown," where, in a dazzlingly beautiful palace called a "department store," we exchanged our hateful homemade European costumes, which pointed us out as "greenhorns" to the children on the street, for real American machine-made garments, and issued forth glorified in each other's eyes.

With our despised immigrant clothing we shed also our impossible Hebrew names. A committee of our friends, several years ahead of us in American experience, put their heads together and concocted American names for us all. Those of our real names that had no pleasing American equivalents they ruthlessly discarded, content if they retained the initials. My mother, possessing a name that was not easily translatable, we punished with the undignified nickname of Annie. Fetchke, Joseph, and Deborah issued as Frieda, Joseph, and Dora, respectively. As for poor me, I was simply cheated. The name they gave me was hardly new. My Hebrew name being Maryashe in full, Mashke for short, Russianized into Marya *(Mary-ya)*, my friends said that it would hold good in English as *Mary*; which was very disappointing, as I longed to possess a strange-sounding American name like the others.

I am forgetting the consolation I had, in this matter of names, from the use of my surname, which I had had no occasion to mention until now. I found on my arrival that my father was "Mr. Antin" on the slightest provocation, and not, as in Polotzk, on state occasions alone. And so I was "Mary Antin," and I felt very important to answer to such a dignified title. It was just like America that even plain people should wear their surnames on week days.

As a family we were so diligent under instruction, so adaptable, and so clever in hiding our deficiencies, that when we made the journey to Crescent Beach, in the wake of our small wagon-load of household goods, my father had very little occasion to admonish us on the way, and I am sure he was not ashamed of us. So much we had achieved toward our Americanization during the two weeks since our landing.

Crescent Beach is a name that is printed in very small type on the maps of environs of Boston, but a life-size strip of sand curves from Winthrop to Lynn; and that is historic ground in the annals of my family. . . .

Into this grand cycle of the seaside day I came to live and learn and play. A few people came with me, as I had already intimated; but the main thing was that I came to live on the edge of the sea—I, who had spent my life inland, believing that the great waters of the world were spread out before me in the Dvina. My idea of the human world had grown enormously during the long journey; my idea of the world outside the earth now budded and swelled during my prolonged experience of the wide and unobstructed heavens. . . .

Let no one suppose that I spent my time entirely, or even chiefly, in inspired solitude. By far the best part of my day was spent in play—frank, hearty, boisterous play, such as comes natural to American children. In Polotzk I had already begun to be considered too old for play, excepting set games or organized frolics. Here I found myself included with children who still played, and I willingly returned to childhood. There were plenty of playfellows. My father's energetic little partner had a little wife and a large family. He kept them in the little cottage next to ours; and that the shanty survived the tumultuous presence of that brood is a wonder to me to-day. The young Wilners included an assortment of boys, girls, and twins, of every possible variety of age, sex, disposition, and sex. They swarmed in and out of the cottage all day long, wearing the door–sill hollow, and trampling the ground to powder. They swung out of windows like monkeys, slid up the roof like flies, and shot out of trees like fowls. Even a small person like me couldn't go anywhere without being run over by a Wilner; and I could never tell which Wilner it was because none of them ever stood still long enough to be identified; and also because I suspected that they were in the habit of interchanging conspicuous articles of clothing, which was very confusing. . . .

I am forgetting the more serious business which had brought us to Crescent Beach. While we children disported ourselves like mermaids and mermen in the surf, our respective fathers dispensed cold lemonade, hot peanuts, and pink popcorn, and piled up our respective fortunes, nickel by nickel, penny by penny. I was very proud of my connection with the public life of the beach. I admired greatly our shining soda fountain, the rows of sparkling glasses, the pyramids of oranges, the sausage chains, the neat white counter, and the bright array of tin spoons. It seemed to me that none of the other refreshment stands on the beach—there were a few—were half so attractive as ours. I thought my father looked very well in a long white apron and shirt sleeves. He dished out ice cream with enthusiasm, so I supposed he was getting rich. It never occurred to me to compare his present occupation with the position for which he had been originally destined; or if I thought about it, I was just as well content, for by this time I had by heart my father's saying, "America is not Polotzk." All occupations were respectable, all men were equal, in America. . . .

And all this splendor and glory and distinction came to a sudden end. There was some trouble about a license—some fee or fine—there was a storm in the night that damaged the soda fountain and other fixtures—there was talk and consultation between the houses of Antin and Wilner—and the promising partnership was dissolved. No more would the merry partner gather the crowd on the beach; no more would the twelve young Wilners gambol like mermen and mermaids in the surf. And the less numerous tribe of Antin must also say farewell to the jolly seaside life; for men in such humble business as my father's carry their families, along with their other earthly goods, wherever they go, after the manner of the gypsies. We had driven a feeble stake into the sand. The jealous Atlantic, in conspiracy with the Sunday law, had torn it out. We must seek our luck elsewhere.

In Polotzk we had supposed that "America" was practically synonymous with "Boston." When we landed in Boston, the horizon was pushed back, and we annexed Crescent Beach. And now, espying other lands of promise, we took possession of the province of Chelsea, in the name of our necessity.

In Chelsea, as in Boston, we made our stand in the wrong end of the town. Arlington Street was inhabited by poor Jews, poor Negroes, and a sprinkling of poor Irish. The side streets leading from it were occupied by more poor Jews and Negroes. It was a proper locality for a man without capital to do business. My father rented a tenement with a store in the basement. He put in a few barrels of flour and of sugar, a few boxes of crackers, a few gallons of kerosene, an assortment of soap of the "save the coupon" brands; in the cellar, a few barrels of potatoes, and a pyramid of kindling-wood; in the showcase, an alluring display of penny candy. He put out his sign, with a gilt-letter warning of "Strictly Cash," and proceeded to give credit indiscriminately. That was the regular way to do business on Arlington Street. My father, in his three years' apprenticeship, had learned the tricks of many trades. He knew when and how to "bluff." The legend of "Strictly Cash" was a protection against notoriously irresponsible customers; while none of the "good" customers, who had a record for paying regularly on Saturday, hesitated to enter the store with empty purses.

If my father knew the tricks of the trade, my mother could be counted on to throw all her talent and tact into the business. Of course she had no English yet, but as she could perform the acts of weighing, measuring and mental computation of fractions mechanically, she was able to give her whole attention to the dark mysteries of the language, as intercourse with her customers gave her opportunity. In this she made such rapid progress that she soon lost all sense of disadvantage, and conducted herself behind the counter very much as if she were back in her old store in Polotzk. It was far more cosey than Polotzk—at least, so it seemed to me; for behind the store was the kitchen, where, in the intervals of slack trade, she did her cooking and washing. Arlington Street customers were used to waiting while the storekeeper salted the soup or rescued a loaf from the oven. . . .

Who were my companions on my first day at school? Whose hand was in mine, as I stood, overcome with awe, by the teacher's desk, and whispered my name as my father prompted? Was it Frieda's steady, capable hand? Was it her loyal heart that throbbed, beat for beat with mine, as it had done through all our childish adventures? Frieda's heart did throb that day, but not with my emotions. My heart pulsed with joy and pride and ambition, in her heart longing fought with abnegation. For I was led to the schoolroom, with its sunshine and its singing and the teacher's cheery smile; while she was led to the workshop, with its foul air, care-lined faces, and the foreman's stern command. Our going to school was the fulfillment of my father's best promises to us, and Frieda's share in it was to fashion and fit the calico frocks in which the baby sister and I made our first appearance in a public schoolroom.

I remember to this day the gray pattern of the calico, so affectionately did I regard it as it hung upon the wall—my consecration robe awaiting the beatific day. And Frieda, I am sure, remembers it, too, so longingly did she regard it as the crisp, starchy breadths of it slid between her fingers. But whatever were her longings, she said nothing of them; she bent over the sewing-machine humming an Old-World melody. In every straight, smooth seam, perhaps, she tucked away some lingering impulse of childhood; but she matched the scrolls and flowers with the utmost care. If a sudden shock of rebellion made her straighten up for an instant, the next instant she was bending to adjust a ruffle to the best advantage. And when the momentous day arrived, and the little sister and I stood up to be arrayed, it was Frieda herself who patted and smoothed my stiff new calico; who made me turn round and round, to see that I was perfect; who stooped to pull out a disfiguring basting-thread. If there was anything in her heart besides sisterly love and pride and good-will, as we parted that morning, it was a sense of loss and a woman's acquiescence in her fate; for we had been close friends, and now our ways would lie apart. Longing she felt, but no envy. She did not grudge me what she was denied. Until that morning we had been children together, but now, at the fiat of her destiny, she became a woman, with all a woman's cares; whilst I, so little younger than she, was bidden to dance at the May festival of untroubled childhood. . . .

The two of us stood a moment in the doorway of the tenement house on Arlington Street, that wonderful September morning when I first went to school. It was I that ran away, on winged feet of joy and expectation; it was she whose feet were bound in the treadmill of daily toil. And I was so blind that I did not see that the glory lay on her, and not on me. . . .

At last the four of us stood around the teacher's desk; and my father, in his impossible English, gave us over in her charge, with some broken word of his hopes for us that his swelling heart could no longer contain. I venture to say that Miss Nixon was struck by something uncommon in the group we made, something outside of Semitic features and the abashed manner of the alien. My littler sister was as pretty as a doll, with her clear pink-and-white face, short golden curls, and eyes like blue violets when you caught them looking up. My brother might have been a girl, too, with his cherubic contours of face, rich red color, glossy black hair, and fine eyebrows. Whatever secret fears were in his heart, remembering his former teachers, who had taught with the rod, he stood up straight and uncringing before the American teacher, his cap respectfully doffed. Next to him stood a starved-looking girl with eyes ready to pop out, and short dark curls that would not have made much of a wig for a Jewish bride.

All three children carried themselves rather better than the common run of "green" pupils that were brought to Miss Nixon. But the figure that challenged attention to the group was the tall, straight father, with his earnest face and fine forehead, nervous hands eloquent in gesture, and a voice full of feeling. This foreigner, who brought his children to school as if it were an act of consecration, who regarded the teacher of the primer class with reverence, who spoke of visions, like a man inspired, in a common schoolroom, was not like other aliens, who brought their children in dull obedience to the law; was not like the native fathers, who brought their unmanageable boys, glad to be relieved of their care. I think Miss Nixon guessed what my father's best English could not convey. I think she divined that by the simple act of delivering our school certificates to her he took possession of America. . . .

IV. "MY COUNTRY"

THE public school has done its best for us foreigners, and for the country, when it has made us into good Americans. I am glad it is mine to tell how the miracle was wrought in one case. You should be glad to hear of it, you born Americans; for it is the story of the growth of your country; of the flocking of your brothers and sisters from the far ends of the earth to the flag you love; of the recruiting of your armies of workers, thinkers, and leaders. And you will be glad to hear of it, my comrades in adoption; for it is a rehearsal of your own—experience, the thrill and wonder of which your own hearts have felt.

How long would you say, wise reader, it takes to make an American? By the middle of my second year in school I had reached the sixth grade. When, after the Christmas holidays, we began to study the life of Washington, running through a summary of the Revolution, and the early days of the Republic, it seemed to me that all my reading and study had been idle until then. The reader, the arithmetic, the song book, that had so fascinated me until now, became suddenly sober exercise books, tools wherewith to hew a way to the source of inspiration. When the teacher read to us out of a big book with many bookmarks in it, I sat rigid with attention in my little chair, my hands tightly clasped on the edge of my desk; and I painfully held my breath, to prevent sighs of disappointment escaping, as I saw the teacher skip the parts between bookmarks. When the class read, and it came my turn, my voice shook and the book trembled in my hands. I could not pronounce the name of George Washington without a pause. Never had I prayed, never had I chanted the songs of David, never had I called upon the Most Holy, in such utter reverence and worship as I repeated the simple sentences of my child's story of the patriot. I gazed with adoration at the portraits of George and Martha Washington, till I could see them with my eyes shut. And whereas formerly my self-consciousness had bordered on conceit, and I thought myself an uncommon person, parading my schoolbooks through the streets, and swelling with pride when a teacher detained me in conversation, now I grew humble all at once, seeing how insignificant I was beside the Great.

As I read about the noble boy who would not tell a lie to save himself from punishment, I was for the first time truly repentant of my sins. Formerly I had fasted and prayed and made sacrifice on the Day of Atonement, but it was more than half play, in mimicry of my elders. I had no real horror of sin, and I knew so many ways of escaping punishment. I am sure my family, my neighbors, my teachers in Polotzk—all my world, in fact—strove together, by example and precept, to teach me goodness. Saintliness had a new incarnation in about every third person I knew. I did respect the saints, but I could not help seeing that most of them were a little bit stupid, and that mischief was much more fun than piety. Goodness, as I had known it, was respectable, but not necessarily admirable. The people I really admired, like my Uncle Solomon, and Cousin Rachel, were those who preached the least and laughed the most. . . . But a human being strictly good, perfectly wise, and unfailingly valiant, all at the same time, I had never heard or dreamed of. This wonderful George Washington was as inimitable as he was irreproachable. Even if I had never, never told a lie, I could not compare myself to George Washington; for I was not brave—I was afraid to go out when snowballs whizzed—and I could never be the First President of the United States. . . .

What more could America give a child? Ah, much more! As I read how the patriots planned the Revolution, and the women gave their sons to die in battle, and the heroes led to victory, and the rejoicing people set up the Republic, it dawned on me gradually what was meant by *my country*. The people all desiring noble things, and striving for them together, defying their oppressors, giving their lives for each other—all this it was that made *my country*. It was not a thing that I *understood*; I could not go home and tell Frieda about it, as I told her other things I learned at school. But I knew one could say "my country" and *feel* it, as one felt "God" or "myself." My teacher, my schoolmates, Miss Dillingham, George Washington himself could not mean more than I when they said "my country," after I had once felt it. For the Country was for all the Citizens, and *I was a Citizen*. And when we stood up to sing "America," I shouted the words with all my might. I was in very earnest proclaiming to the world my love for my new–found country.

> "I love thy rocks and rills.
> Thy woods and templed hills."

Boston Harbor, Crescent Beach, Chelsea Square—all was hallowed ground to me. As the day approached when the school was to hold exercises in honor of Washington's Birthday, the halls resounded at all hours with the strains of patriotic songs; and I, who was a model of the attentive pupil, more than once lost my place in the lesson as I strained to hear, through closed doors, some neighboring class rehearsing "The Star-Spangled Banner." If the doors happened to open, and the chorus broke out unveiled—

"O! say, does that Star-Spangled Banner yet wave
O'er the land of the free, and the home of the brave?"—

delicious tremors ran up and down my spine, and I was faint with
suppressed enthusiasm. . . .

On the day of the Washington celebration I recited a poem that
I had composed in my enthusiasm. But "composed" is not the word.
The process of putting on paper the sentiments that seethed in my soul
was really very discomposing. I dug the words out of my heart,
squeezed the rhymes out of my brain, forced the missing syllables out
of their hiding-places in the dictionary. May I never again know such
travail of the spirit as I endured during the fevered days when I was
engaged on the poem. It was not as if I wanted to say that snow was
white or grass was green. I could do that without a dictionary. It was
a question now of the loftiest sentiments, of the most abstract truths,
the names of which were very new in my vocabulary. It was necessary
to use polysyllables, and plenty of them; and where to find rhymes for
such words as "tyranny, " "freedom," and "justice," when you had less
than two years' acquaintance with English! The name I wished to
celebrate was the most difficult of all. Nothing but "Washington"
rhymed with "Washington." It was a most ambitious undertaking, but
my heart could find no rest till it had proclaimed itself to the world; so
I wrestled with my difficulties, and spared not ink, till inspiration
perched on my penpoint, and my soul gave up its best.

When I had done, I was myself impressed with the length,
gravity, and nobility of my poem. My father was overcome with
emotion as he read it. His hands trembled as he held the paper to the
light, and the mist gathered in his eyes. My teacher, Miss Dwight, was
plainly astonished at my performance, and said many kind things,
and asked many questions; all of which I took very solemnly, like one
who had been in the clouds and returned to earth with a sign upon him.
When Miss Dwight asked me to read my poem to the class on the day
of celebration, I readily consented. It was not in me to refuse a chance
to tell my schoolmates what I thought of George Washington.

I was not a heroic figure when I stood up in front of the class to
pronounce the praises of the Father of his Country. Thin, pale, and
hollow, with a shadow of short black curls on my brow, and the staring
look of prominent eyes, I must have looked more frightened than
imposing. My dress added no grace to my appearance. "Plaids" were
in fashion, and my frock was of a red-and-green "plaid" that had a

ghastly effect on my complexion. I hated it when I thought of it, but on the great day I did not know I had any dress on. Heels clapped together, and hands glued to my sides, I lifted up my voice in praise of George Washington. It was not much of a voice; like my hollow cheeks, it suggested consumption. My pronunciation was faulty, my declamation flat. But I had the courage of my convictions. I was face to face with twoscore Fellow Citizens, in clean blouses and extra frills. I must tell them what George Washington had done for their country—for *our* country—for me.

The boys and girls who had never been turned away from any door because of their father's religion sat as if fascinated in their places. But they woke up and applauded heartily when I was done, following the example of Miss Dwight, who wore the happy face which meant that one of her pupils had done well. . . .

It never occurred to me to send my manuscript by mail. In fact, it has never been my way to send a delegate where I could go myself. Consciously or unconsciously, I have always acted on the motto of a wise man who was one of the dearest friends that Boston kept for me until I came. "Personal presence moves the world," said the great Dr. Hale; and I went in person to beard the editor in his armchair. . . .

[Mary Antin's school composition on Washington was accepted for publication by the Boston Herald.*]*

When the paper with my poem in it arrived, the whole house pounced upon it at once. I was surprised to fine that my verses were not all over the front page. The poem was a little hard to find, if anything, being tucked away in the middle of the voluminous sheet. But when we found it, it looked wonderful, just like real poetry, not at all as if somebody we knew had written it. It occupied a gratifying amount of space, and was introduced by a flattering biographical sketch of the author—the *author*!—the material for which the friendly editor had artfully drawn from me during that happy interview. And my name, as I had prophesied, was at the bottom!

When the excitement in the house had subsided, my father took all the change out of the cash drawer and went to buy up the "Herald." He did not count the pennies. He just bought "Heralds," all he could lay his hands on, and distributed them gratis to all our friends, relatives, and acquaintances; to all who could read, and to some who could not. For weeks he carried a clipping from the "Herald" in his breast pocket, and few were the occasions when he did not manage to introduce it into the conversation. He treasured that clipping as for years he had treasured the letters I wrote him from Polotzk.

Although my father bought up most of the issue containing my poem, a few hundred copies were left to circulate among the general public, enough to spread the flame of my patriotic ardor and to enkindle a thousand sluggish hearts. Really, there was something more solemn than vanity in my satisfaction. Pleased as I was with my notoriety—and nobody but I knew how exceedingly pleased—I had a sober feeling about it all. . . .

V. MIRACLES

IT was not always in admiration that the finger was pointed at me. One day I found myself the centre of an excited group in the middle of the schoolyard, with a dozen girls interrupting each other to express their disapproval of me. For I had coolly told them, in answer to a question, that I did not believe in God.

How had I arrived as such a conviction? How had I come, from praying and fasting and Psalm-singing, to extreme impiety? Alas! my backsliding had cost me no travail of spirit. Always weak in my faith, playing at sanctity as I played at soldiers, just as I was in the mood or not, I had neglected my books of devotion and given myself up to profane literature at the first opportunity, in Vitebsk; and I never took up my prayer book again. On my return to Polotzk, America loomed so near that my imagination was fully occupied, and I did not revive the secret experiments with which I used to test the nature and intention of Deity. It was more to me that I was going to America than that I might not be going to Heaven. And when we joined my father, and I saw that he did not wear the sacred fringes, and did not put on the phylacteries and pray, I was neither surprised nor shocked, re-membering the Sabbath night when he had with his own hand turned out the lamp. When I saw him go out to work on Sabbath exactly as on a weekday, I understood why God had not annihilated me with his lightnings that time when I purposely carried something in my pocket on Sabbath; there was no God, and there was no sin. And I ran out to play, pleased to find that I was free, like other little girls in the street, instead of being hemmed about with prohibitions and obligations at every step. And yet if the golden truth of Judaism had not been handed me in the motley rags of formalism, I might not have been so ready to put away my religion.

It was Rachel Goldstein who provoked my avowal of atheism. She asked if I wasn't going to stay out of school during Passover, and I said no. Wasn't I a Jew? she wanted to know. No, I wasn't; I was a Freethinker. What was that? I didn't believe in God. Rachel was horrified. Why, Kitty Maloney believed in God, and Kitty was only a Catholic! She appealed to Kitty.

"Kitty Maloney! Come over here. Don't you believe in God? There, now, Mary Antin!—Mary Antin says she doesn't believe in God!"

Rachel Goldstein's horror is duplicated. Kitty Maloney, who used to mock Rachel's Jewish accent, instantly becomes her voluble ally, and proceeds to annihilate me by plying me with crucial questions.

"You don't believe in God? Then who made you, Mary Antin?"

"Nature made me."

"*Nature* made you! What's that?"

"It's—everything. It's the trees—no, it's what makes the trees grow. *That's* what it is."

"But *God* made the trees, Mary Antin," from Rachel and Kitty in chorus. "Maggie O'Reilly! Listen to Mary Antin. She says there isn't any God. She says the trees made her!"

Rachel and Kitty and Maggie, Sadie and Annie and Beckie, made a circle around me, and pressed me with questions, and mocked me, and threatened me with hell flames and utter extinction. I held my ground against them all obstinately enough, though my argument was exceedingly lame. I glibly repeated phrases I had heard my father use, but I had no real understanding of his atheistic doctrines. I had been surprised into this dispute. I had no spontaneous interest in the subject; my mind was occupied with other things. But as the number of my opponents grew, and I saw how unanimously they condemned me, my indifference turned into a heat of indignation. The actual point at issue was as little as ever to me, but I perceived that a crowd of Free Americans were disputing the right of a Fellow Citizen to have any kind of God she chose. I knew, from my father's teaching, that this persecution was contrary to the Constitution of the United States, and I held my ground as befitted the defender of a cause. George Washington would not have treated me as Rachel Goldstein and Kitty Maloney were doing! "This is a free country," I reminded them in the middle of the argument.

The excitement in the yard amounted to a toy riot. When the school bell rang and the children began to file in, I stood out there as long as any of my enemies remained, although it was my habit to go to my room very promptly. And as the foes of American Liberty crowded and pushed in the line, whispering to those who had not heard that a heretic had been discovered in their midst, the teacher who kept the line in the corridor was obliged to scold and pull the noisy ones into order; and Sadie Cohen told her, in tones of awe, what the commotion was about.

Miss Bland waited till the children had filed in before she asked me, in a tone encouraging confidence, to give my version of the story. This I did, huskily but fearlessly; and the teacher, who was a woman of tact, did not smile or commit herself in any way. She was sorry that the children had been rude to me, but she thought they would not trouble me any more if I let the subject drop. She made me understand, somewhat as Miss Dillingham had done on the occasion of my whispering during prayer, that it was proper American conduct to avoid religious arguments on school territory. I felt honored by this private initiation into the doctrine of the separation of Church and State, and I went to my seat with a good deal of dignity, my alarm about the safety of the Constitution allayed by the teacher's calmness. . . .

My father, in his ambition to make Americans of us, was rather headlong and strenuous in his methods. To my mother, on the eve of departure for the New World, he wrote boldly that progressive Jews in America did not spend their days in praying; and he urged her to leave her wig in Polotzk, as a first step of progress. My mother, like the majority of women in the Pale, had all her life taken her religion on authority; so she was only fulfilling her duty to her husband when she took his hint, and set out upon her journey in her own hair. Not that it was done without reluctance, the Jewish faith in her was deeply rooted, as in the best of Jews it always is. The law of the Fathers was binding to her, and the outward symbols of obedience inseparable from the spirit. But the breath of revolt against orthodox externals was at this time beginning to reach us in Polotzk from the greater world, notably from America. Sons whose parents had impoverished themselves by paying the fine for non-appearance for military duty, in order to save their darlings from the inevitable sins of violated Judaism while in the service, sent home portraits of themselves with their faces shaved; and the grieved old fathers and mothers, after offering up special prayers for the renegades, and giving charity in their name, exhibited the significant portraits on their parlor tables. My mother's own nephew went no farther than Vilna, ten hours' journey from Polotzk, to learn to cut his beard; and even within our town limits young women of education were beginning to reject the wig after marriage. A notorious example was the beautiful daughter of Lozhe the Rav, who was not restrained by her father's conspicuous relation to Judaism from exhibiting her lovely black curls like a maiden; and it was a further sign of the times that the rav did not disown his daughter. What wonder, then, that my poor mother, shaken by these foreshadowings of revolution in our midst, and by the express authority of her husband, gave up the emblem of matrimonial chastity with but a passing struggle? . . .

My father gave my mother very little time to adjust herself. He was only three years from the Old World with its settled prejudices. Considering his education, he had thought out a good deal for himself, but his line of thinking had not as yet brought him to include woman in the intellectual emancipation for which he himself had been so eager even in Russia. This was still in the day when he was astonished to learn that women had written books—had used their minds, their imaginations, unaided. He still rated the mental capacity of the average woman as only a little above that of the cattle she tended. He held it to be a wife's duty to follow her husband in all things. He could do all the thinking for the family, he believed; and being convinced that to hold to the outward forms of orthodox Judaism was to be hampered in the race for Americanization, he did not hesitate to order our family life on unorthodox lines. There was no conscious despotism in this; it was only making manly haste to realize an ideal the nobility of which there was no one to dispute. . . .

My father did not attempt to touch the fundamentals of her faith. He certainly did not forbid her to honor God by loving her neighbor, which is perhaps not far from being the whole of Judaism. If his loud denials of the existence of God influenced her to reconsider her creed, it was merely an incidental result of the freedom of expression he was so eager to practice, after his life of enforced hypocrisy. As the opinions of a mere woman on matters so abstract as religion did not interest him in the least, he counted it no particular triumph if he observed that my mother weakened in her faith as the years went by. He allowed her to keep a Jewish kitchen as long as she pleased, but he did not want us children to refuse invitations to the table of our Gentile neighbors. He would have no bar to our social intercourse with the world around us, for only by freely sharing the life of our neighbors could we come into our full inheritance of American freedom and opportunity. On the holy days he bought my mother a ticket for the synagogue, but the children he sent to school. On Sabbath eve my mother might light the consecrated candles, but he kept the store open until Sunday morning. My mother might believe and worship as she pleased, up to the point where her orthodoxy began to interfere with the American progress of the family.

The price that all of us paid for this disorganization of our family life has been levied on every immigrant Jewish household where the first generation clings to the traditions of the Old World, while the second generation leads the life of the New. Nothing more pitiful could be written in the annals of the Jews; nothing more inevitable; nothing more hopeful. Hopeful, yes; alike for the Jew and for the country that has given him shelter. For Israel is not the only party that has put up a forfeit in this contest. The nations may well sit by and watch the struggle, for humanity has a stake in it. I say this, whose life has borne witness, whose heart is heavy with revelations it has not made. And I speak for thousands; oh, for thousands! . . .

VI. DOVER STREET

WHAT happened next was Dover Street.

And what was Dover Street?

Ask rather, What was it not? Dover street was my fairest garden of girlhood, a gate of paradise, a window facing a a broad avenue of life. Dover Street was a prison, a school of discipline, a battlefield of sordid strife. The air in Dover Street was heavy with evil odors of degradation, but a breath from the uppermost heavens rippled through, whispering of infinite things. In Dover Street the dragon poverty gripped me for a last fight, but I overthrew the hideous creature, and sat on his neck as on a throne. In Dover Street I was shackled with a hundred chains of disadvantage, but with one free hand I planted little seeds, right there in the mud of shame, that blossomed into the honeyed rose of widest freedom. In Dover Street there was often no loaf on the table, but the hand of some noble friend was ever in mine. The night in Dover Street was rent with cries of wrong, but the thunders of truth crashed through the pitiful clamor and died out in prophetic silences.

Outwardly, Dover Street is a noisy thoroughfare cut through a South End slum, in every essential the same as Wheeler Street. Turn down any street in the slums, at random, and call it by whatever name you please, you will observe there the same fashions of life, death, and endurance. Every one of those streets is a rubbish heap of damaged humanity, and it will take a powerful broom and an ocean of soapsuds to clean it out. . . .

We had no particular reason for coming to Dover Street. It might just as well have been Applepie Alley. For my father had sold, with the goods, fixtures, and good-will of the Wheeler Street store, all his hopes of ever making a living in the grocery trade; and I doubt if he got a silver dollar the more for them. We had to live somewhere, even if we were not making a living, so we came to Dover Street, where tenements were cheap; by which I mean that rent was low. The ultimate cost of life in those tenements, in terms of human happiness, is high enough.

Our new home consisted of five small rooms up two flights of stairs, with the right of way through the dark corridors. In the "parlor" the dingy paper hung in rags and the plaster fell in chunks. One of the bedrooms was absolutely dark and air-tight. The kitchen windows looked out on a dirty court, at the back of which was the rear tenement of the estate. To us belonged, along with the five rooms and the right of way aforesaid, a block of upper space the length of a pulley line across this court, and the width of an arc described by a windy Monday's wash in its remotest wanderings.

The little front bedroom was assigned to me, with only one partner, my sister Dora. A mouse could not have led a cat much of a chase across this room; still we found space for a narrow bed, a crazy bureau, and a small table. From the window there was an unobstructed view of a lumberyard, beyond which frowned the blackened walls of a factory. The fence of the lumberyard was gay with theatre posters and illustrated advertisements of tobacco, whiskey, and patent baby foods. When the window was open, there was a constant clang and whir of electric cars, varied by the screech of machinery, the clatter of empty wagons, or the rumble of heavy trucks. . . .

It must not be supposed that I enjoyed any degree of privacy, because I had half a room to myself. We were six in the five rooms; we were bound to be always in each other's way. And as it was within our flat, so it was in the house as a whole. All doors, beginning with the street door, stood open most of the time; or if they were closed, the tenants did not wear out their knuckles knocking for admittance. I could stand at any time in the unswept entrance hall and tell, from an analysis of the medley of sounds and smells that issued from doors ajar, what was going on in the several flats from below up. That guttural, scolding voice, unremittent as the hissing of a steam pipe, is

Mrs. Rasnosky. I make a guess that she is chastising the infant Isaac for taking a second lump of sugar in his tea. *Span! Bam!* yes, and she is rubbing in her objections with the flat of her hand. That blubbering and moaning, accompanying an elephantine tread, is fat Mrs. Casey, second floor, home drunk from an afternoon out, in fear of the vengeance of Mr. Casey; to propitiate whom she is burning a pan of bacon, as the choking fumes and outrageous sizzling testify. I hear a feeble whining, interrupted by long silences. It is that scabby baby on the third floor, fallen out of bed again, with nobody home to pick him up. . . .

In front of the door I squeeze through a group of children. They are going to play tag, and are counting to see who should be "it":—

> "My-mother-and-your-mother-went-out-to-hang-clothes;
> My-mother-gave-your-mother-a-punch-in-the-nose."

If the children's couplet does not give a vivid picture of the life, manners, and customs of Dover Street, no description of mine can ever do so. . . .

Surely this was the time for me to take my sister's place in the workshop. I had every fair chance until now; school, my time to myself, liberty to run and play and make friends. I had graduated from grammar school; I was of legal age to go to work. What was I doing, sitting at home and dreaming? . . .

A new life began for me when I entered the Latin School in September. Until then I had gone to school with my equals, and as a matter of course. Now it was distinctly a feat for me to keep in school, and my school-mates were socially so far superior to me that my poverty became conspicuous. The pupils of the Latin School, from the nature of the institution, are an aristocratic set. They come from refined homes, dress well, and spend the recess hour talking about parties, beaux, and the matinee. As students they are either very quick or very hard-working; for the course of study, in the lingo of the school world, is considered "stiff." The girl with half her brain asleep, or with too many beaux, drops out by the end of the first year; or a one and only beau may be the fatal element. At the end of the course the weeding process has reduced the once numerous tribe of academic candidates to a cosey little family.

By all these tokens I should have had serious business on my hands as a pupil in the Latin School, but I did not find it hard. To make myself letter-perfect in my lessons required long hours of study, but that was my delight. To make myself at home in an alien world was also within my talents; I had been practicing it day and night for the past four years. To remain unconscious of my shabby and ill-fitting clothes when the rustle of silk petticoats in the schoolroom protested against them was a matter still within my moral reach. . . .

Everything helped, you see. My schoolmates helped. Aristocrats though they were, they did not hold themselves aloof from me. Some of the girls who came to school in carriages were especially cordial. They rated me by my scholarship, and not by my father's occupation. They teased and admired me by turns for learning the footnotes in the Latin grammar by heart; they never reproached me for my ignorance of the latest comic opera. And it was more than good breeding that made them seem unaware of the incongruity of my presence. It was a generous appreciation of what it meant for a girl from the slums to be in the Latin School, on the way to college. If our intimacy ended on the steps of the school-house, it was more my fault than theirs. Most of the girls were democratic enough to have invited me to their homes, although to some, of course, I was "impossible." But I had no time for visiting; school work and reading and family affairs occupied all the daytime, and much of the night time. . . .

Still I had moments of depression, when my whole being protested against the life of the slum. I resented the familiarity of my vulgar neighbors. I felt myself defiled by the indecencies I was compelled to witness. Then it was I took to running away from home. I went out in the twilight and walked for hours, my blind feet leading me. I did not care where I went. If I lost my way, so much the better; I never wanted to see Dover Street again.

But behold, as I left the crowds behind, and the broader avenues were spanned by the open sky, my grievances melted away, and I fell to dreaming of things that neither hurt nor pleased. A fringe of trees against the sunset became suddenly the symbol of the whole world, and I stood and gazed and asked questions of it. The sunset faded; the trees withdrew. The wind went by, but dropped no hint in my ear. The evening star leaped out between the clouds, and sealed the secret with a seal of splendor.

A favorite resort of mine, after dark, was the South Boston Bridge, across South Bay and the Old Colony Railroad. This was so near home that I could go there at any time when the confusion in the house drove me out, or I felt the need of fresh air. I liked to stand leaning on the bridge railing, and look down on the dim tangle of railroad tracks below. I could barely see them branching out, elbowing, winding, and sliding out into the night in pairs. I was fascinated by the dotted lights, the significant red and green of signal lamps. These simple things stood for a complexity that it made me dizzy to think of. Then the blackness below me was split by the fiery eye of a monster engine, his breath enveloped me in blinding clouds, his long body shot by, rattling a hundred claws of steel; and he was gone, with an imperative shriek that shook me where I stood.

So would I be, swift on my rightful business, picking out my proper track from the million that cross it, pausing for no obstacles, sure of my goal. . . .

VII. THE LANDLADY

FROM sunrise to sunset the day was long enough for many things besides school, which occupied five hours. There was time for me to try to earn my living; or at least the rent of our tenement. Rent was a standing trouble. We were always behind, and the landlady was very angry; so I was particularly ambitious to earn the rent. I had had one or two poems published since the celebrated eulogy of George Washington, but nobody had paid for my poems—yet. I was coming to that, of course, but in the mean time I could not pay the rent with my writing. To be sure, my acquaintance with men of letters gave me an opening. A friend of mine introduced me to a slightly literary lady, who introduced me to the editor of the "Boston Searchlight," who offered me a generous commission for subscriptions to his paper.

If our rent was three and one-half dollars per week, payable on strong demand, and the annual subscription to the "Searchlight" was one dollar, and my commission was fifty per cent, how many subscribers did I need? How easy! Seven subscribers a week—one a day! Anybody could do that. Mr. James, the editor, said so. He said I could get two or three any afternoon, between the end of school and supper. If I worked all Saturday—my head went dizzy computing the amount of my commissions. It would be rent and shoes and bonnets and everything for everybody.

Mrs. Hutch seldom succeeded in collecting the full amount of the rents from her tenants. I suppose that made the bookkeeping complicated, which must have been wearing on her nerves; and hence her temper. We lived, on Dover Street, in fear of her temper. Saturday had a distinct quality about it, derived from the imminence of Mrs. Hutch's visit. Of course I awoke on Saturday morning with the no-school feeling; but the grim thing that leaped to its feet and glowered down on me, while the rest of my consciousness was still yawning on its back, was the Mrs.-Hutch-is-coming- and-there's-no-rent feeling. . . .

It did require strength to lift the burden of life, in the gray morning, on Dover Street; especially on Saturday morning. Perhaps my mother's pack was the heaviest to lift. To the man of the house, poverty is a bulky dragon with gripping talons and a poisonous breath; but he bellows in the open, and it is possible to give him knightly battle, with the full swing of the angry arm that cuts to the enemy's vitals. To the housewife, want is an insidious myriapod creature that crawls in the dark, mates with its own offspring, breeds all the year round, persists like leprosy. The woman has an endless, inglorious struggle with the pest; her triumphs are too petty for applause, her failures too mean for notice. Care, to the man, is a hound to be kept in leash and mastered. To the woman, care is a secret parasite that infects the blood.

Mrs. Hutch, of course, was only one symptom of the disease of poverty, but there were times when she seemed to me the sharpest tooth of the gnawing canker. Surely as sorrow trails behind sin, Saturday evening brought Mrs. Hutch. The landlady did not rail. Her movements were anything but impassive. She climbed the stairs with determination and landed at the top with emphasis. Her knock on the door was clear, sharp, unfaltering; it was impossible to pretend not to hear it. Her "Good-evening" announced business; her manner of taking a chair suggested the throwing-down of the gauntlet. Invariably she asked for my father, calling him Mr. Anton, and refusing to be corrected; almost invariably he was not at home—was out looking for work. Had he left her the rent? My mother's gentle "No, ma'am" was the signal for the storm. I do not want to repeat what Mrs. Hutch said. It would be hard on her, and hard on me. She grew red in the face; her voice grew shriller with every word. My poor mother hung her head where she stood; the children stared from the corners; the frightened baby cried. The angry landlady rehearsed our sins like a prophet foretelling doom. We owed so many weeks rent; we were too lazy to work; we never intended to pay; we lived on others; we deserved to be put out without warning. She reproached us all for coming to America. She enumerated her losses through nonpayment of her rents; told us that she did not collect the amount of her taxes; showed us how our irregularities were driving a poor widow to ruin.

My mother did not attempt to excuse herself, but when Mrs. Hutch began to rail against my absent father, she tried to put in a word in his defence. The landlady grew all the shriller at that, and silenced my mother impatiently. Sometimes she addressed herself to me. I always stood by, if I was at home, to give my mother the moral support of my dumb sympathy. I understood that Mrs. Hutch had a special grudge against me, because I did not go to work as a cash girl and earn three dollars a week. I wanted to explain to her how I was preparing myself for a great career, and I was ready to promise her the payment of the arrears as soon as I began to get rich. But the landlady would not let me put in a word. And I was sorry for her, because she seemed to be having such a bad time.

At last Mrs. Hutch got up to leave, marching out as determinedly as she had marched in. At the door she turned, in undiminished wrath, to shoot her parting dart:—

"And if Mr. Anton does not bring me the rent on Monday, I will serve notice of eviction of Tuesday, without fail."

We breathed when she was gone. My mother wiped away a few tears, and went to the baby, crying in the windowless, air-tight room.

I was the first to speak.

"Isn't she queer, mamma!" I said. "She never remembers how to say our name. She insists on saying *Anton-Anton. Celia, say Anton.*" And I made the baby laugh by imitating the landlady, who had made her cry.

But when I went to my little room I did not mock Mrs. Hutch. I thought about her, thought long and hard, and to a purpose. I decided that she must hear me out once. She must understand about my plans, my future, my good intentions. It was too irrational to go on like this, we living in fear of her, she in distrust of us. If Mrs. Hutch would only trust me, and the tax collectors would trust her, we could all live happily forever.

I was the more certain that my argument would prevail with the landlady, if only I could make her listen, because I understood her point of view. I even sympathized with her. What she said about the babies, for instance, was not all unreasonable to me. There was this last baby, my mother's sixth, born on Mrs. Hutch's premises—yes, in the windowless, air-tight bedroom. Was there any need of this baby? When May was born, two years earlier, on Wheeler Street, I had accepted her; after a while I even welcomed her. She was born an American, and it was something to me to have one genuine American relative. I had to sit up with her the whole of her first night on earth, and I questioned her about the place she came from, and so we got acquainted. As my mother was so ill that my sister Frieda, who was nurse, and the doctor from the dispensary had all they could do to take care of her, the baby remained in my charge a good deal, and so I got used to her. But when Celia came I was two years older, and my outlook was broader; I could see around a baby's charms, and discern the disadvantages of possessing the baby. I was supplied with all kinds of relatives now—I had a brother-in-law, and an American-born nephew, who might become a President. Moreover, I knew there was not enough to eat before the baby's advent, and she did not bring any supplies with her that I could see. The baby was one too many. There was no need of her. I resented her existence. I recorded my resentment in my journal. . . .

VIII. A KINGDOM IN THE SLUMS

I DID not always wait for the Natural History Club to guide me to delectable lands. Some of the happiest days of that happy time I spent with my sister in East Boston. We had a merry time at supper, Moses making clever jokes, without cracking a smile himself; and the baby romping in his high chair, eating what wasn't good for him. But the best of the evening came later, when father and baby had gone to bed, and the dishes were put away, and there was not a crumb left on the red-and-white checked tablecloth. Frieda took out her sewing, and I took a book; and the lamp was between us, shining on the table, on the large brown roses on the wall, on the green and brown diamonds of the oil cloth on the floor, on the baby's rattle on a shelf, and on the shining stove in the corner. It was such a pleasant kitchen—such a cosey, friendly room—that when Frieda and I were left alone I was perfectly happy just to sit there. Frieda had a beautiful parlor, with plush chairs and a velvet carpet and gilt picture frames; but we preferred the homely, homelike kitchen.

I read aloud from Longfellow, or Whittier, or Tennyson; and it was as great a treat to me as it was to Frieda. Her attention alone was inspiring. Her delight, her eager questions doubled the meaning of the lines I read. Poor Frieda had little enough time for reading, unless she stole it from the sewing or the baking or the mending. But she was hungry for books, and so grateful when I came to read to her that it made me ashamed to remember all the beautiful things I had and did not share with her.

It is true I shared what could be shared. I brought my friends to her. At her wedding were some of the friends of whom I was most proud. Miss Dillingham came, and Mr. Hurd; and the humbler guests stared in admiration at our school-teachers and editors. But I had so many delightful things that I could not bring to Frieda—my walks, my dreams, my adventures of all sorts. And yet when I told her about them, I found that she partook of everything. For she had her talent for vicarious enjoyment, by means of which she entered as an actor into my adventures, was present as a witness at the frolic of my younger life. Or if I narrated things that were beyond her, on account of her narrower experience, she listened with an eager longing to understand that was better than some people's easy comprehension. . . .

The way she reached out for everything fine was shown by her interest in the incomprehensible Latin and French books that I brought. She like to hear me read my Cicero, pleased by the movement of the sonorous periods. I translated Ovid and Virgil for her; and her pleasure illumined the difficult passages, so that I seldom needed to have recourse to the dictionary. I shall never forget the evening I read to her, from the "Æneid," the passage in the fourth book describing the death of Dido. I read the Latin first, and then my own version in English hexameters, that I had prepared for a recitation at school. Frieda forgot her sewing in her lap, and leaned forward in rapt attention. When I was through, there were tears of delight in her eyes; and I was surprised myself at the beauty of the words I had just pronounced. . . .

Truly my education was not entirely in the hands of persons who had licenses to teach. My sister's fat baby taught me things about the origin and ultimate destiny of dimples that were not in any of my school-books. Mr. Casey, of the second floor, who was drunk whenever his wife was sober, gave me an insight into the psychology of the beer mug that would have added to the mental furniture of my most scholarly teacher. The bold-faced girls who passed the evening on the corner, in promiscuous flirtation with the cock-eyed youths of the neighborhood, unconsciously revealed to me the eternal secrets of adolescence. My neighbor of the third floor, who sat on the curbstone with the scabby baby in her bedraggled lap, had things to say about the fine ladies who came in carriages to inspect the public bathhouse across the street that ought to be repeated in the lecture halls of every school of philanthropy. Instruction poured into my brain at such a rate that I could not digest it all at the time; but in later years, when my destiny had led me far from Dover Street, the emphatic moral of those lessons became clear. The memory of my experience on Dover Street became the strength of my convictions, the illumined index of my purpose, the aureola of my happiness. And if I paid for those lessons with days of privation and dread, with nights of tormenting anxiety, I count the price cheap. Who would not go to a little trouble to find out what life is made of?

Dover Street was never really my residence—at least, not the whole of it. It happened to be the nook where my bed was made, but I inhabited the City of Boston. In the pearl-misty morning, in the ruby-red evening, I was empress of all I surveyed from the roof of the tenement house. I could point in any direction and name a friend who would welcome me there. Off towards the northwest, in the direction of Harvard Bridge, which some day I should cross on my way to Radcliffe College, was one of my favorite palaces, whither I resorted every day after school.

A low, wide-spreading building with a dignified granite front it was, flanked on all sides by noble old churches, museums, and school-houses, harmoniously disposed around a spacious triangle, called Copley Square. Two thoroughfares that came straight from the green suburbs swept by my palace, one on either side, converged at the apex of the triangle, and pointed off, past the Public Garden, across the historic Common, to the domed State House sitting on a height.

It was my habit to go very slowly up the low, broad steps to the palace entrance, pleasing my eyes with the majestic lines of the building, and lingering to read again the carved inscriptions: *Public Library—Built by the People—Free to All.*

Did I not say it was my palace? Mine, because I was a citizen; mine, though I was born an alien; mine, though I lived on Dover Street. My palace—*mine!* . . .

Bates Hall was the place where I spent my longest hours in the library. I chose a seat far at one end, so that looking up from my books I would get the full effect of the vast reading-room. I felt the grand spaces under the soaring arches as a personal attribute of my being. . . .

Here is where I liked to remind myself of Polotzk, the better to bring out the wonder of my life. That I who was born in the prison of the Pale should roam at will in the land of freedom was a marvel that it did me good to realize. That I who was brought up to my teens almost without a book should be set down in the midst of all the books that ever were written was a miracle as great as any on record. That an outcast should become a privileged citizen, that a beggar should dwell in a palace—this was romance more thrilling than poet ever sung.

Surely I was rocked in an enchanted cradle. . . .

It is so simple, in Boston! You are a school girl, and your teacher gives you a ticket for the annual historical lecture in the Old South Church, on Washington's Birthday. You hear a stirring discourse on some subject in your country's history, and you go home with a heart bursting with patriotism. You sit down and write a letter to the speaker who so moved you, telling him how glad you are to be an American, explaining to him, if you happen to be a recently made American, why you love your adopted country so much better than your native land. Perhaps the patriotic lecturer happens to be a Senator, and he reads your letter under the vast dome of the State House; and it occurs to him that he and his eminent colleagues and the stately capitol and the glorious flag that floats above it, all gathered on the hill above the Common, do his country no greater honor than the outspoken admiration of an ardent young alien. The Senator replies to your letter, inviting you to visit him at the State House; and in the renowned chamber where the august business of the State is conducted, you, an obscure child from the slums, and he, a chosen leader of the people, seal a democratic friendship based on the love of a common flag.

Even simpler than to meet a Senator was it to become acquainted with a man like Edward Everett Hale. "The Grand Old Man of Boston," the people called him, from the manner of his life among them. He kept open house in every public building in the city. Wherever two citizens met to devise a measure for the public weal, he was a third. Wherever a worthy cause needed a champion, Dr. Hale lifted his mighty voice. At some time or another his colossal figure towered above an eager multitude from every pulpit in the city, from every lecture platform. And where is the map of Boston that gives the names of the lost alleys and back ways where the great man went in search of the lame in body, who could not join the public assembly, in quest of the maimed in spirit, who feared to show their faces in the open? If all the little children who have sat on Dr. Hale's knee were started in a procession on the State House steps, standing four abreast, there would be a lane of merry faces across the Common, out to the Public Library, over Harvard Bridge, and away beyond to remoter landmarks.

That I met Dr. Hale is no wonder. It was as inevitable as that I should be a year older every twelvemonth. He was a part of Boston, as the salt wave is a part of the sea. I can hardly say whether he came to me or I came to him. We met, and my adopted country took me closer to her breast. . . .

Once I brought Dr. Hale a present, a copy of a story of mine that had been printed in a journal; and from his manner of accepting it you might have thought that I was a princess dispensing gifts from a throne. I wish I had asked him, that last time I talked with him, how it was that he who was so modest made those who walked with him so great.

Modest as the man was the house in which he lived. A gray old house of a style that New England no longer builds, with a pillared porch curtained by vines, set back in the yard behind the old trees. Whatever cherished flowers glowed in the garden behind the house, the common daisy was encouraged to bloom in front. And was there sun or snow on the ground, the most timid hand could open the gate, the most humble visitor was sure of a welcome. Out of that modest house the troubled came comforted, the fallen came uplifted, the noble came inspired. . . .

A busy life I led, on Dover Street; a happy, busy life. When I was not reciting lessons, nor writing midnight poetry, nor selling papers, nor posing, nor studying sociology, nor pickling bugs, nor interviewing statesmen, nor running away from home, I made long entries in my journal, or wrote forty-page letters to my friends. It was a happy thing that poor Mrs. Hutch did not know what sums I spent for stationery and postage stamps. . . .

. . . The grocer on Harrison Avenue who supplied our table could have taught her to take a more liberal view. We were all anxious to teach her, if she only would have listened. Here was this poor grocer, conducting his business on the same perilous credit system which had driven my father out of Chelsea and Wheeler Street, supplying us with tea and sugar and strong butter, milk freely splashed from rusty cans, potent yeast, and bananas done to a turn,—with everything, in short, that keeps a poor man's family hearty in spite of what they eat,—and all this for the consideration of part payment, with the faintest prospect of a future settlement in full. Mr. Rosenblum had an intimate knowledge of the financial situation of every family that traded with him, from the gossip of his customers around his herring barrel. He knew without asking that my father had no regular employment, and that, consequently, it was risky to give us credit. Nevertheless he gave us credit by the week, by the month, accepted partial payment with thanks, and let the balance stand by the year.

We owed him as much as the landlady, I suppose, every time he balanced our amount. But he never complained; nay, he even insisted on my mother's taking almonds and raisins for a cake for the holidays.

He knew, as well as Mrs. Hutch, that my father kept a daughter at school who was of age to be put to work; but so far was he from reproaching him for it that he detained my father by the half-hour, inquiring about my progress and discussing my future. He knew very well, did the poor grocer, who it was that burned so much oil in my family, but when I came in to have my kerosene can filled, he did not fall upon me with harsh words of blame. Instead, he wanted to hear about my latest triumph at school, and about the great people who wrote me letters and even came to see me; and he called his wife from the kitchen behind the store to come and hear of these grand doings. . . .

Mr. Rosenblum gave me my oil. If he had had postage stamps in stock, he would have given me all I needed, and felt proud to think that he was assisting in my important correspondences. And he was a poor man, and had a large family, and many customers who paid as irregularly as we. He ran the risk of ruin, of course, but he did not scold—not us, at any rate. For he *understood*. He was himself an immigrant Jew of the type that values education, and sets a great price on the higher development of the child. He would have done in my father's place just what my father was doing; borrow, beg, go without, run in debt—anything to secure for a promising child the fulfillment of the promise. That is what America was for. The land of opportunity it was, but opportunities must be used, must be grasped, held, squeezed dry. To keep a child of working age in school was to invest the meager present for the sake of the opulent future. If there was but one child in a family of twelve who promised to achieve an intellectual career, the other eleven, and father, and mother, and neighbors must devote themselves to that one child's welfare, and feed and clothe and cheer it on, and be rewarded in the end by hearing its name mentioned with the names of the great.

So the poor grocer helped to keep me in school for I do not know how many years. And this is one of the things that is done on Harrison Avenue, by the people who pitch rubbish through their windows. Let the City Fathers strike the balance. . . . It was good to get out of Dover Street—it was better for the growing children, better for my weary parents, better for all of us, as the clean grass is better than the dusty pavement. But I must never forget that I came away from Dover Street with hands full of riches . . . . My days in the slums were pregnant with possibilities; it only needed the ripeness of events to make them fruit forth in realities. Steadily as I worked to win America, America advanced to lie at my feet. I was an heir, on Dover Street, awaiting maturity. I was a princess waiting to be led to the throne. . . .

IX. THE HERITAGE

BUT lest I be reproached for a sudden affectation of reserve, after having trained my reader to expect the fullest particulars, I am willing to add a few details. I went to college, as I proposed, though not to Radcliffe. Receiving an invitation to live in New York that I did not like to refuse, I went to Barnard College instead. There I took all the honors that I deserved; and if I did not learn to write poetry, as I once supposed I should, I learned at least to think in English without an accent. Did I get rich? you may want to know, remembering my ambition to provide for the family. I can reply that I have earned enough to pay Mrs. Hutch the arrears, and satisfy all my wants. And where have I lived since I left the slums? My favorite abode is a tent in the wilderness, where I shall be happy to serve you a cup of tea out of a tin kettle, and answer further questions.

And is this really to be the last word? Yes, though a long chapter of the romance of Dover Street is left untold. I could fill another book with anecdotes, telling how I took possession of Beacon Street, and learned to distinguish the lord of the manor from the butler in full dress. I might trace my steps from my bare room overlooking the lumber–yard to the satin drawing–rooms of the Back Bay, where I drank afternoon tea with gentle ladies whose hands were as delicate as their porcelain cups. My journal of those days is full of comments on the contrasts of life, that I copied from my busy thoughts in the evening, after a visit to my aristocratic friends. Coming straight from the cushioned refinement of Beacon Street, where the maid who brought my hostess her slippers spoke in softer accents than the finest people on Dover Street, I sometimes stumbled over poor Mr. Casey lying asleep in the corridor; and the shock of the contrast was like a searchlight turned suddenly on my life, and I pondered over the revelation, and wrote touching poems, in which I figured as a heroine of two worlds.

I might quote from my journals and poems, and build up the picture of that double life. I might rehearse the names of the gracious friends who admitted me to their tables, although I came direct from the reeking slums. I might enumerate the priceless gifts they show-ered on me; gifts bought not with gold but with love. It would be a pleasant task to recall the high things that passed in the gilded drawing-rooms over the afternoon tea. It would add a splendor to my simple narrative to weave in the portraits of the distinguished men and women who busied themselves with the humble fortunes of a school-girl. And finally, it would relieve my heart of a burden of gratitude to publish, once for all, the amount of my indebtedness to the devoted friends who took me by the hand when I walked in the paths of obscurity, and led me, by a pleasanter lane than I could have found by myself, to the open fields where obstacles thinned and opportunities crowded to meet me. Outside America I should hardly be believed if I told how simply, in my experience, Dover Street merged into the Back Bay. These are matters to which I long to testify, but I must wait till they recede into the past.

I can conjure up no better symbol of the genuine, practical equality of all our citizens than the Hale House Natural History Club, which played an important part in my final emancipation from the slums. For all I was regarded as a plaything by the serious members of the club, the attention and kindness they lavished on me had a deep significance. Every one of those earnest men and women unconsciously taught me my place in the Commonwealth, as the potential equal of the best of them. Few of my friends in the club, it is true, could have rightly defined their benevolence toward me. Perhaps some of them thought they befriended me for charity's sake, because I was a starved waif from the slums. Some of them imagined they enjoyed my society, because I had much to say for myself, and a gay manner of meeting life. But all these were only secondary motives. I myself, in my unclouded perception of the true relation of things that concerned me, could have told them all why they spent their friendship on me. They made way for me because I was their foster sister. They opened their homes to me that I might learn how good Americans lived. In the least of their attentions to me, they cherished the citizen in the making. The Natural History Club had spent the day at Nahant, studying marine life in the tide pools, scrambling up and down the cliffs with no thought for decorum, bent only on securing the starfish, limpets, seaurchins, and other trophies of the chase. There had been a merry luncheon on the rocks, with talk and laughter between sandwiches, and strange jokes, intelligible only to the practicing naturalist. The tide had rushed in at its proper time, stealing away our seaweed cushions, drowning our transparent pools, spouting in the crevices, booming and hissing, and tossing high the snowing foam.

From the deck of the jolly excursion steamer which was carrying us home, we had watched the rosy sun dip down below the sea. The members of the club, grouped in twos and threes, discussed the day's successes, compared specimens, exchanged field notes, or watched the western horizon in sympathetic silence.

It had been a great day for me. I had seen a dozen new forms of life, had caught a hundred fragments of the song of nature by the sea; and my mind was seething with meanings that crowded in. I do not remember to which of my learned friends I addressed my questions on this occasion, but he surely was one of the most learned. For he took up all my fragments of dawning knowledge in his discourse, and welded them into a solid structure of wisdom, with windows looking far down the past and a tower overlooking the future. I was so absorbed in my private review of creation that I hardly realized when we landed, or how we got into the electric cars, till we were a good way into the city.

At the Public Library I parted from my friends, and stood on the broad stone steps, my jar of specimens in my hand, watching the car that carried them glide out of sight. My heart was full of a stirring wonder. I was hardly conscious of the place where I stood, or of the day, or the hour. I was in a dream, and the familiar world around me was transfigured. My hair was damp with sea spray; the roar of the tide was still in my ears. Mighty thoughts surged through my dreams, and I trembled with understanding.

I sank down on the granite ledge beside the entrance to the Library, and for a mere moment I covered my eyes with my hand. In that moment I had a vision of myself, the human creature, emerging from the dim places where the torch of history has never been, creeping slowly into the light of civilized existence, pushing more steadily forward to the broad plateau of modern life, and leaping, at last, strong and glad, to the intellectual summit of the latest century.

What an awful stretch of years to contemplate! What a weighty past to carry in memory! How shall I number the days of my life, except by the stars of the night, except by the salt drops of the sea?

But hark to the clamor of the city all about! This is my latest home, and it invites me to a glad new life. The endless ages have indeed throbbed though my blood, but a new rhythm dances in my veins. My spirit is not tied to the monumental past, any more than my feet were bound to my grandfather's house below the hill. The past was only my cradle, and now it cannot hold me, because I am grown too big; just as the little house in Polotzk, once my home, has now become a toy of memory, as I move about at will in the wide spaces of this splendid palace, whose shadow covers acres. No! it is not I that belong to the past, but the past that belongs to me. America is the youngest of the nations, and inherits all that went before in history. And I am the youngest of America's children, and into my hands is given all her priceless heritage, to the last white star espied through the telescope, to the last great thought of the philosopher. Mine is the whole majestic past, and mine is the shining future.

Margaret Sanger (1879-1966)

THROUGH the nineteenth century American women's ability to shape their own fates grew in a pattern that was more or less predictable because it was clearly visible and openly defined. Women's articulateness in writing led them into speaking in public, while their energetic organization for social reform led them into demands and action for equality before the law and free entry into occupations. While those goals of equal rights were highly controversial they were debated and pursued openly.

In the new century, however, an even more controversial aspect of women's control of their fates, previously largely hidden because it touched the most intimate aspects of life, emerged unexpectedly when Margaret Sanger, a nurse, initiated an open campaign for birth control. This crusade became Sanger's life's work.

Born in Corning, New York, the sixth of the eleven children of Michael and Anne Higgins, she grew up in an unorthodox home. Her mother was a Catholic who did not practice her faith; her father, the strongest influence on the girl, was a talented stonecarver who in his work produced angels and crosses on funerary monuments for the religious, but who at home was a freethinker and a socialist, challenging his children to think for themselves.

His daughter Margaret, who entered teaching to support herself after receiving a secondary education, soon had to return home to care for her mother, who was gravely ill with tuberculosis. She read medical books to learn about the disease, and, after the death of her mother, envisioned becoming a physician, convinced that she might have been able to save her with fuller knowledge. For the time being she was needed to run the household, but when the opportunity came she entered nursing training in the hope that it might lead to a career in medicine.

Her work in nursing, at hospitals in White Plains, New York, and then in New York City, opened her eyes to the desperate circumstances of the very poor, including the economic burdens brought by a succession of unwanted babies, but she possessed no usable answers. In 1902 she married a young architect, William Sanger, and with him had three children. After ten years of living in a suburb the couple moved to New York City and became caught up in the excitement of discussion and agitation in socialist and union activities. In helping to recruit working women to the Socialist Party, Sanger found herself giving talks, and then writing pamphlets, to educate them about sex and reproduction; one of her pamphlets was barred from the U.S. mails for using the words "syphilis" and "gonorrhea." When she returned to doing occasional nursing in obstetrical cases, she again confronted the ways in which excessive childbearing impaired maternal health and contributed to poverty, but this time turned to research and self-education to seek answers. Her quest led her from New York libraries to Europe, in late 1913, to learn as much as she could about contraceptive techniques and about governmental policies in regard to them. Clearly her restlessness in her marriage played a part in her turning to this new career; she spent time with other men friends, including the radical labor leader William "Big Bill" Haywood, and Havelock Ellis, the British writer on the psychology of sex, and she separated from her husband in 1914.

On her return to the United States she began a career of publication, opening of birth control clinics, and agitation for eliminating legal prohibitions on giving information and advice on contraception. The barriers were formidable and she was for years either being prosecuted or in danger of it. Her work in publicizing, recruiting, and advocacy produced a succession of organizations that eventuated, after public opinion had grown to support birth control, in the Planned Parenthood Association of America of 1942.

In her many books and articles, including her autobiography, Sanger preached birth control and family planning for all women, not only the poor, as necessary to allow them to attain the freedom and power to lead broader, more fulfilling, and more useful lives. In 1922 she was married to J. Noah H. Slee, a wealthy industrialist. She spent her later years in Tucson, Arizona.

To what extent does Sanger see the limitation of births through contraception as opening new and different roles for women in society, rather than simply producing better wives and mothers? Since her own contribution to reform involved so intimate an aspect of women's lives, does her story reveal a self-consciousness that is peculiarly female—or might a man have written it? How do you respond to this autobiographer and her work?

An Autobiography

*Margaret Sanger**

I. FROM WHICH I SPRING

THE streets of Corning, New York, where I was born, climb right up from the Chemung River, which cuts the town in two; the people who live there have floppy knees from going up and down. When I was a little girl the oaks and the pines met the stone walks at the top of the hill, and there in the woods my father built his house, hoping mother's "congestion of the lungs" would be helped if she could breathe the pure, balsam-laden air.

My mother, Anne Purcell, always had a cough, and when she braced herself against the wall the conversation, which was forever echoing from room to room, had to stop until she recovered. She was slender and straight as an arrow, with head well set on sloping shoulders, black, wavy hair, skin white and spotless, and with wide-apart eyes, gray-green, flecked with amber. Her family had been Irish as far back as she could trace; the strain of the Norman conquerors had run true throughout the generations, and may have accounted for her unfaltering courage.

Mother's sensitivity to beauty found some of its expression in

* From *Margaret Sanger: An Autobiography*. New York: W.W. Norton & Co., 1938. By permission of Grant Sanger, M.D.

flowers. We had no money with which to buy them, and she had no time to grow them, but the woods and fields were our garden. I can never remember sitting at a table not brightened with blossoms; from the first spring arbutus to the last goldenrod of autumn we had an abundance.

Although this was the Victorian Age, our home was almost free from Victorianism. Father himself had made our furniture. He had even cut and polished the slab of the big "marble-topped table," as it was always called. Only in the spare room stood a piece bought at a store—a varnished washstand. The things you made yourself were not considered quite good enough for guests. Sometimes father's visitors were doctors, teachers, or perhaps the village priest, but mostly they were the artisans of the community—cabinet makers, masons, carpenters who admired his ideas as well as shared his passion for hunting. In between tramping the woods and talking they had helped to frame and roof the house, working after hours to do this.

Father, Michael Hennessy Higgins, born in Ireland, was a nonconformist through and through. All other men had beards or mustaches—not he. His bright red mane, worn much too long according to the family, swept back from his massive brow; he would not clip it short as most fathers did. Actually it suited his finely–modeled head. He was nearly six feet tall and hard-muscled; his keen blue eyes were set off by pinkish, freckled skin. Homily and humor rippled unceasingly from his generous mouth in a brogue which he never lost. The jokes with which he punctuated every story were picked up, retold, and scattered about. When I was little they were beyond me, but I could hear my elders laughing.

The scar on father's forehead was his badge of war service. When Lincoln had called for volunteers against the rebellious South, he had taken his only possessions, a gold watch inherited from his grandfather and his own father's legacy of three hundred dollars, and had run away from his home in Canada to enlist. But he had been told he was not old enough, and was obliged to wait impatiently a year and a half until, on his fifteenth birthday, he had joined the Twelfth New York Volunteer Cavalry as a drummer boy.

One of father's adventures had been the capture of a Confederate captain on a fine mule, the latter being counted the more valuable acquisition to the regiment. We were brought up in the tradition that he had been one of three men selected by Sherman for bravery. That made us very proud of him. Better not start anything with father; he could beat anybody! But he himself had been appalled by the brutalities of war; never thereafter was he interested in fighting, unless perhaps his Irish sportsmanship cropped out when two well-matched dogs were set against each other.

Immediately upon leaving the Army father had studied anatomy, medicine, and phrenology, but these had been merely for perfecting his skill in modeling. He made his living by chiseling angels and saints out of huge blocks of white marble or gray granite for tombstones in cemeteries. He was a philosopher, a rebel, and an artist, none of which was calculated to produce wealth. Our existence was like that of any artist's family—chickens today and feathers tomorrow.

Christmases were on the poverty line. If any of us needed a new winter overcoat or pair of overshoes, these constituted our presents. I was the youngest of six, but after me others kept coming until we were eleven. Our dolls were babies—living, wriggling bodies to bathe and dress instead of lifeless faces that never cried or slept. A pine beside the door was our Christmas tree. Father liked us to use natural things and we had to rely upon ingenuity rather than the village stores, so we decorated it with white popcorn and red cranberries which we strung ourselves. Our most valuable gift was that of imagination.

We had little time for recreation. School was five miles away and we had to walk back and forth twice a day as well as perform household duties. The boys milked the cow, tended the chickens, and took care of Tom, the old white horse which pulled our sleigh up and down the hill. The girls helped put the younger children to bed, mended clothes, set the table, cleaned the vegetables, and washed the dishes. We accepted all this with no sense of deprivation or aggrievement, being, if anything, proud of sharing responsibility.

And we made the most of our vacations. There were so many of us that we did not have to depend upon outsiders, and Saturday afternoons used to put on plays by ourselves in the barn. Ordinarily we were shy about displaying emotions; we looked upon tears and temper in other homes with shocked amazement as signs of ill-breeding. Playacting, however, was something else again. Here we could find outlet for histrionic talent and win admiration instead of lifted eyebrows. I rather fancied myself as an actress, and often mimicked some of the local characters, to the apparent pleasure of my limited audience of family and neighbors. It was not long before I slipped into declaiming. *The Lady of Lyons* was one of my specialties. . . .

We were all, brothers and sisters alike, healthy and strong, vigorous and active; our appetites were curtailed only though necessity. We played the same games together and shared the same sports—baseball, skating, swimming, hunting. Nevertheless, except that we all had red hair, shading from carrot to bronze, we were sharply distinct physically. The girls were small and feminine, the boys husky and brawny. When I went out into the world and observed men, otherwise admirable, who could not pound a nail or use a saw, pick, shovel, or ax, I was dumfounded. I had always taken for granted that any man could make things with his hands.

I expected this even of women. My oldest sister, Mary, possessed, more than the rest of us, an innate charm and gentleness. She could do anything along domestic lines—embroidery, dress making, tailoring, cooking; she could concoct the most delicious and unusual foods, and mix delicate pastries. But she was also an expert at upholstering, carpentry, painting, roofing with shingles or with thatch. When Mary was in the house, we never had to send for a plumber. She rode gracefully and handled the reins from the carriage seat with equal dexterity; she could milk a cow and deliver a baby; neighbors called her to tend their sick cattle, or, when death came, to lay out the body; she tutored in mathematics and Latin, and was well-read in the classics, yet she liked most the theater, and was a dramatic critic whose judgment was often sought. In all that she did her sweetness and dearness were apparent, though she performed her many kindnesses in secret. She left the home roof while I was still a child, but she never failed to send Christmas boxes in which every member of the family shared, each gift beautifully wrapped and decorated with ribbons and cards.

My brothers were ardent sportsmen, although they might not have been outstanding scholars. They could use their fists and were as good shots as their father. For that matter, we all knew how to shoot; any normal person could manage a gun. Father was a great hunter. Our best times were when friends of his came to spend the night, talking late, starting early the next morning for the heavy woods which were full of foxes, rabbits, partridge, quail, and pheasant. . . .

Father took little or no responsibility for the minute details of the daily tasks. I can see him when he had nothing on hand, laughing and joking or reading poetry. Mother, however, was everlastingly busy sewing, cooking, doing this and that. For so ardent and courageous a woman he must have been trying, and I still wonder at her patience. She loved her children deeply, but no one ever doubted that she idolized her husband, and through the years of her wedded life to her early death never wavered in her constancy. Father's devotion to mother, though equally profound, never evidenced itself in practical ways.

The relation existing between our parents was unusual for its day; they had the idea of comradeship and not merely loved but liked and respected each other. There was no quarreling or bickering; none of us had to take sides, saying, "Father is right," or, "Mother is right." We knew that if we pleased one we pleased the other, and such an atmosphere leaves its mark; we felt secure from emotional uncertainty, and were ourselves guided towards certainty in our future. We were all friends together, though not in the modern sense of familiarity. A little dignity and formality were always maintained and we were invariably addressed by our full names. The century of the child had not yet been ushered in.

In those days young people, unless invited to speak, were seen and not heard. But as soon as father considered us old enough to have ideas or opinions, we were given full scope to express them, no matter how adolescent. He hated the slavery of pattern and following of examples and believed in the equality of the sexes; not only did he come out strongly for woman suffrage in the wake of Susan B. Anthony, but he advocated Mrs. Bloomer's bloomers as attire for women, though his wife and daughters never wore them. He fought for free libraries, free education, free books in the public schools, and freedom of the mind from dogma and cant. Sitting comfortably with his feet on the table he used to say, "You should give something back to your country because you as a child were rocked in the cradle of liberty and nursed at the breast of the goddess of truth." Father always talked like that.

Although the first Socialist in the community, father also took single tax in his stride and became the champion and friend of Henry George. *Progress and Poverty* was one of the latest additions to our meager bookshelf. He laughed and rejoiced when he came upon what to him were meaty sentences, reading them aloud to mother, who accepted them as fine because he said they were fine. The rest of us all had to plow through the book in order, as he said, to "elevate the mind." To me it still remains one of the dullest ever written.

Mother's loyalty to father was tested repeatedly. Hers were the responsibilities of feeding and clothing and managing on his income, combined with the earnings of the oldest children. But father's generosity took no cognizance of fact. Once he was asked to buy a dozen bananas for supper. Instead, he purchased a stalk of fifteen dozen, and on his way home gave every single one to schoolboys and girls playing at recess. On another occasion he showed up with eight of a neighbor's children; the ninth had been quarantined for diphtheria. They lived with us for two months, crowded into our beds, tucked in between us at the table. Mother welcomed them as she did his other guests. The house was always open. She was not so much social-minded as inherently hospitable. But with her frail body and slim pocketbook, it took courage to smile.

Once only that I can remember did mother's patience give way. That was when father invaded her realm too drastically and invited Henry George to lecture at the leading hotel—with banquet thrown in. From the money saved for the winter coal he had taken enough to entertain fifty men whose children were well-fed and well-clothed. This was the sole time I ever knew my parents to be at odds, though even then I heard no quarreling words. Whatever happened between them I was not sure, but father spent several days wooing back the smile and light to her eyes.

After Henry George's visit we had to go without coal most of the winter. . . .

In the predominantly Roman Catholic community of Corning, set crosses in the cemeteries were the rule for the poor and, before they went out of style, angels in various poses for the rich. I used to watch father at work. The rough, penciled sketch indicated little; even less did the first unshaped block of stone. He played with the hard, unyielding marble as though it were clay, making a tiny chip for a mouth, which grew rounder and rounder. A face then emerged, a shoulder, a sweep of drapery, praying hands, until finally the whole stood complete with wings and halo.

Although Catholics were father's best patrons, by nature and upbringing he deplored their dogma. He joined the Knights of Labor, who were agitating against the influx of unskilled immigrants from Catholic countries, and this did not endear him to his clientele. Still less did his espousal of Colonel Robert G. Ingersoll, a man after his own heart, whose works he had eagerly studied and used as texts. Once when the challenger was sounding a ringing defiance in near-by towns, father extended an invitation to speak in Corning and enlighten it. He collected subscriptions to pay for the only hall in town, owned by Father Coghlan. A notice was inserted in the paper that the meeting would be held the following Sunday, but chiefly the news spread by word of mouth. "Better come. Tell all your friends."

Sunday afternoon arrived, and father escorted "Colonel Bob"

from the hotel to the hall, I trotting by his side. We pushed through the waiting crowd, but shut doors stared silently and reprovingly—word had also reached Father Coghlan.

Some were there to hear and learn, others to denounce. Antipathies between the two suddenly exploded in action. Tomatoes, apples, and cabbage stumps began to fly. This was my first experience of rage directed against those holding views which were contrary to accepted ones. It was my first, but by no means my last. I was to encounter it many times, and always with the same bewilderment and disdain. My father apparently felt only the disdain. Resolutely he announced the meeting would take place in the woods near our home an hour later, then led Ingersoll and the "flock" through the streets. I trudged along again, my small hand clasped in his, my head held just as high. . . .

Father never talked about religion without bringing in the ballot box. In fact, he took up Socialism because he believed it Christian philosophy put into practice, and to me its ideals still come nearest to carrying out what Christianity was supposed to do. Unceasingly he tried to inculcate in us the idea that our duty lay not in considering what might happen to us after death, but in doing something here and now to make the lives of other human beings more decent. "You have no right to material comforts without giving back to society the benefit of your honest experience," was one of his maxims, and his parting words to each of his sons and daughters who had grown old enough to fend for themselves were, "Leave the world better because you, my child, have dwelt in it."

This was something to live up to. . . .

II. BLIND GERM OF DAYS TO BE

OFTEN when my brothers and sisters and I meet we remind each other of funny or exciting adventures we used to have, but I never desire to live that early part of my life again. Childhood is supposed to be a happy time. Mine was difficult, though I did not then think of it as a disadvantage nor do I now.

It never occurred to me to ask my parents for pocket money, but the day came during my eighth year when I was desperately in want of ten cents. *Uncle Tom's Cabin* was coming to town. On Saturday afternoon I started out with one of my playmates, she with her dime, I with nothing but faith. We reached the Corning Opera House half an hour early. The throng at the entrance grew thicker and thicker. Curtain time had almost come, and still no miracle. Nevertheless, I simply had to get into that theater. All about me had tickets or money or both. Suddenly I felt something touch my arm—the purse of a woman who was pressed close beside me. It was open, and I could see the coveted coins within. One quick move and I could have my heart's desire. The longing was so deep and hard that it blotted out everything except my imperative need. I had to get into that theater.

I was about to put out my hand towards the bag when the doors were thrown wide and the crowd precipitately surged forward. Being small, I was shoved headlong under the ropes and into the safety of the nearest seat. But I could take no joy in the play.

As I lay sleepless that night, after a prayer of thanks for my many blessings, the crack of Simon Legree's whip and the off-stage hounds baying after Eliza were not occupying my mind. Their places were taken by pictures of the devil which had tempted me and the hand of God which had been stretched out to save me from theft.

Following this experience, which might have been called a spiritual awakening, I began to connect my desires with reasoning about consequences. This was difficult, because my feelings were strong and urgent. I realized I was made up of two Me's—one the thinking Me, the other, willful and emotional, which sometimes exercised too great a power; there was danger in her leadership and I set myself the task of uniting the two by putting myself through ordeals of various sorts to strengthen the head Me. . . .

Corning was not on the whole a pleasant town. Along the river flats lived the factory workers, chiefly Irish; on the heights above the rolling clouds of smoke that belched from the chimneys lived the owners and executives. The tiny yards of the former were a-sprawl with children; in the gardens on the hills only two or three played. This contrast made a track in my mind. Large families were associated with poverty, toil, unemployment, drunkenness, cruelty, fighting, jails; the small ones with cleanliness, leisure, freedom, light, space, sunshine.

The fathers of the small families owned their homes; the young looking mothers had time to play croquet with their husbands in the evenings on the smooth lawns. Their clothes had style and charm, and the fragrance of perfume clung about them. They walked hand in hand on shopping expeditions with their children, who seemed positive in their right to live. To me the distinction between happiness and unhappiness in childhood was one of small families and of large families rather than of wealth and poverty.

In our home, too, we felt the economic pressure directly ascribable to size. I was always apprehensive that we might some day be like the families on the flats, because we always had another baby coming, another baby coming. A new litter of puppies was interesting but not out of the ordinary; so, likewise, the cry of a new infant never seemed unexpected. Neither excited any more curiosity than breakfast or dinner. No one ever told me how they were born. I just knew.

I was little more than eight when I first helped wash the fourteen-and-a-half-pound baby after one of mother's deliveries. She had had a "terrible hard time," but father had pulled her through, and, in a few weeks, tired and coughing, she was going about her work, believing as usual that her latest was the prize of perfect babies. . . .

After this illness mother coughed more than ever and it was evident the pines were not helping her. Father decided to move; the house was so obviously marked and he had to be gone so much he thought it unsafe for us to live alone so far away. . . .

III. BOOKS ARE THE COMPASSES

SO we moved into town, still on the western hills. It marked the beginning of my adolescence, and such breaks are always disturbing. In the house in the woods we had all been children together, but now some of us were growing up.

Nevertheless there were always smaller ones to be put to bed, to be rocked to sleep; there were feet and knees to be scrubbed and hands to be washed. Although we had more space, home study sometimes seemed to me impossible. The living room was usually occupied by the older members of the family, and the bedrooms were cold. I kept up in my lessons, but it was simply because I enjoyed them.

In most schools teachers and pupils then were natural enemies, and the one I had in the eighth grade was particularly adept at arousing antagonism. She apparently disliked her job and the youngsters under her care as much as we hated her. Sarcasm was both her defense and weapon of attack. One day in mid-June I was delayed in getting off for school. Well aware that being tardy was a heinous crime, I hurried, pulling and tugging at my first pair of kid gloves, which Mary had just given me. But the bell had rung two minutes before I walked into the room, flushed and out of breath.

The teacher had already begun the class. She looked up at the interruption. "Well, well, Miss Higgins, so your ladyship has arrived at last! Ah, a new pair of gloves! I wonder that she even deigns to come to school at all."

Giggles rippled around me as I went into the cloakroom and laid down my hat and gloves. I came back, praying the teacher would pay no more attention to me, but as I walked painfully to my seat she continued repeating with variations her mean comments. Even when I sat down she did not stop. I tried to think of something else, tried not to listen, tried to smile with the others. I endured it as long as I could, then took out my books, pyramiding arithmetic, grammar, and speller, strapped them up, rose, and left.

Mother was amazed when I burst in on her. "I will never go back to the school again!" I exclaimed dramatically. "I have finished forever! I'll go to jail, I'll work, I'll starve, I'll die! But back to that school and teacher I will never go!"

As older brothers and sisters drifted home in the evening, they were as horrified as mother. "But you have only two weeks more," the expostulated.

"I don't care if it's only an hour. I will not go back!"

When it became obvious that I would stick to my point, mother seemed glad to have me to help her. I was thorough and strong and could get through a surprising amount of work in no time. But the rest of the family was seriously alarmed. The next few months were filled with questions I could not answer. "What can you ever be without an education?" "Are you equipped to earn a living?" "Is factory life a pleasant prospect? If you don't go back to school, you'll surely end there."

"All right. I'll go to work!" I announced defiantly. Work, even in the factory, meant money, and money meant independence. I had no rebuttal to their arguments; I was acting on an impulse that transcended reason, and must have recognized that any explanation as to my momentous decision would sound foolish.

Then suddenly father, mother, my second older sister Nan, and Mary, who had been summoned to a family council, tried other tactics. I was sent for two weeks to Chautauqua, there to take courses, hear lectures from prominent speakers, listen to music. This was designed to stimulate my interest in education and dispel any idea I might have of getting a job.

My impulse had been misconstrued. I was not rebelling against education as such, but only against that particular school and that particular teacher. When fall drew near and next session was at hand I was still reiterating that I would not go back, although I still had no answer to Nan's repeated, "What are you going to do?"

Nan was perhaps the most inspiring of all my brothers and sisters. The exact contrary to father, she wanted us all to conform and was in tears if we did not. To her, failure in this respect showed a lack of breeding. Yet even more important than conformity was knowledge, which was the basis for all true culture. She herself wanted to write, and had received prizes for stories from *St. Nicholas* and the *Youth's Companion*. But the family was too dependent upon the earnings of the older girls, and she was obliged to postpone college and her equally ardent desire to study sculpture. She became a translator of French and German until these aspirations could be fulfilled.

At the time of my mutiny Nan was especially disturbed. "You won't be able to get anywhere without an education," she stated firmly. She and Mary, joining forces, together looked for a school reasonable enough for their purses, but good enough academically to prepare me for Cornell. Private education was not so expensive as today, and families of moderate means could afford it. My sisters selected Claverack College and Hudson River Institute, about three miles from the town of Hudson in the Catskill Mountains. Here, in one of the oldest coeducational institutions in the country, the Methodist farmers of the Dutch valley enrolled their sons and daughters; unfortunately it is now gone and with it the healthy spirit it typified. One sister paid my tuition and the other bought my books and clothes; for my board and room I was to work.

Going away to school was epochal in my life. The self-contained family group was suddenly multiplied to five hundred strangers, all living and studying under one roof. The girls' dormitory was at one end, the boys; at the other, but we shared the same dining room and sat together in classes; occasionally a boy could call on a girl in the reception hall if a teacher were present. I like best the attitude of the teachers; they were not so much policemen as companions and friends, and their instruction was more individual and stimulating than at Corning.

I did not have money to do things the other girls did—go off for week-ends or house-parties—but waiting on table or washing dishes did not set me apart. The work was far easier than at home, and a girl was pretty well praised for doing her share. At first the students all appeared to me uninteresting and lacking in initiative. I never found the same imaginative quality I was used to in my family, but as certain ones began to stand out I discovered they had personalities of their own. . . .

I spent three happy years at Claverack. The following season I decided to try my hand at teaching, then a lady-like thing to do. A position was open to me in the first grade of a new public school in southern New Jersey. The majority of the pupils—Poles, Hungarians, Swedes—could not speak English. In they came regularly. I was beside myself to know what to do with eighty-four children who could not understand a word I said. I loved those small, black-haired and tow-headed urchins who became bored with sitting and, on their own, began stunts to entertain themselves. But I was so tired at the end of the day that I often lay down before dressing for dinner and awakened the next morning barely in time to start the routine. In very short order I became aware of the fact that teaching was not merely a job, it was a profession, and training was necessary if you were to do it well. I was not suited by temperament, and therefore had no right to this vocation. I had been struggling for only a brief while when father summoned me home to nurse mother.

She was weak and pale and the high red spots on her cheek bones stood out startlingly against her white face. Although she was now spitting blood when she coughed we still expected her to live on forever. She had been ill so long; this was just another attack among many. Father carried her from room to room, and tried desperately to devise little comforts. We shut the doors and windows to keep out any breath of the raw March air, and in the stuffy atmosphere we toiled over her bed.

In an effort to be more efficient in caring for mother I tried to find out something about consumption by borrowing medical books from the library of the local doctor, who was a friend of the family, and in doing this became so interested in medicine that I decided definitely I would study to be an M.D. When I went back for more volumes and announced my decision the doctor gave them to me, but smiled tolerantly, "You'll probably get over it."

I had been closely confined for a long time when I was invited to Buffalo for the Easter holidays to meet again one of the boys by whom I had been beaued at Claverack. Mother insisted that I needed a vacation. Mary and Nan were both there; I could stay with them, and we planned a pleasant trip to Niagara Falls for the day.

With me out of the way mother sent off the little children one by one on some pretext or another. She had more difficulty with father. The fire bricks in the stove had split and she told him he must go to town and get new ones. Much against his will, because he was vaguely unquiet, he started for the foundry. He had left only because mother seemed to want it so much, but when he had walked a few blocks, he found he could not go on. For some Celtic mystic reason of his own he turned abruptly around and came back to the house. Mother was gasping in death. All the family hated scenes, she most of all. She had known she was to die and wanted to be alone.

It was a folk superstition that a consumptive who survived through the month of March would live until November. Mother died on the thirty-first of the month, leaving father desolate and inconsolable. I came flying home. The house was silent and he hardly spoke. Suddenly the stillness of the night was broken by a wailing and Toss was found with his paws on the coffin, mourning and howling—the most poignant and agonizing sound I had ever heard. . . .

IV. DARKNESS THERE AND NOTHING MORE

[After her mother's death, Margaret Sanger decided that instead of teaching she would train to be a nurse. She wanted to be a physician. but felt that she could not afford the time and money for that training. She hoped to help people like her mother, whom she thought might have been saved with better medical care.]

THE old White Plains Hospital, not at all like a modern institution, had been a three-storied manor house, long deserted because two people had once been found mysteriously dead in it and thereafter nobody would rent or buy. The hospital board, scoffing at superstition, had gladly purchased it at the low price to which it had been reduced. However, in spite of rearrangements and redecorating, many people in White Plains went all the way to the Tarrytown Hospital rather than enter the haunted portals.

Once set in spacious grounds the building was still far back from the road; a high wall immediately behind it shut off the view of the next street and nothing could be seen beyond except the roof of what had been the stable. The surrounding tall trees made it shadowy even in the daytime. To reach the office you had to cross a broad pillared veranda. Parlor and sitting room had been thrown together for the male ward, and an operating room had been tacked on to the rear. The great wide stairway of fumed oak, lighted at night by lowturned gas jets, swept up through the lofty ceiling. On the second floor were the female ward and a few private rooms. The dozen or so nurses slept in the made-over servants' quarters under the gambrel roof.

Student nurses in large modern hospitals have little idea what our life was like in a small one thirty-five years ago. The single bathroom on each floor was way at the back. We did not have a resident interne, and, consequently, had to depend mainly upon our own judgment. Since we had no electricity, we could not ring a bell and have our needs supplied, and had to use our legs for elevators. A probationer had to learn to make dressings, bandages, mix solutions, and toil over sterilizing. She put two inches of water in the washboiler, laid a board across the bricks placed in the bottom, and balanced the laundered linen and gauze on top. Then, clapping on the lid, she set the water to boiling briskly, watched the clock, and when the prescribed number of minutes had elapsed the sterilizing was over.

The great self-confidence with which I entered upon my duties soon received a slight shock. One of our cases was an old man from the County Home. He complained chiefly of pains in his leg and, since his condition was not very serious, the superintendent of nurses left him one afternoon in my care. This was my first patient. When I heard the clapper of his little nickeled bell, I hurried with a professional air to his bedside.

"Missy, will you please bandage up my sore leg? It does me so much good."

Having just had my initial lesson in bandaging, I was elated at this opportunity to try my skill. I set to work with great precision, and, when I had finished, congratulated myself on a neat job, admiring the smooth white leg. My first entry went on his record sheet.

A little later the superintendent, in making her rounds, regarded the old man perplexedly.

"Why have you got your leg bandaged?"

"I asked the nurse to do it for me?"

"Why that leg? It's the other one that hurts."

"Oh, she was so kind I didn't want to stop her.". . .

People then seldom went to hospitals with minor ailments; our patients were commonly the very sick, requiring a maximum of attention. There was no orderly and I could use only my left hand because my right shoulder was still bandaged. I took care of admissions, entered case histories, and, when sharp bells punctuated the waiting stillness, sometimes one coming before I had time to answer the first, I pattered hurriedly up and down the three flights, through the shadows relieved only by the faint red glow from the gas jets. I suppose adventures were inevitable. . . .

A young man of about twenty-five, of well-to-do parents, was admitted as an alcoholic. I remember that I was impressed by the softness of his handshake when I greeted him. He had the first symptoms of delirium tremens but he was not perfectly conscious and needed no more than routine attention.

Sometime in the night the new arrival asked me to get him a drink of water. When I came back into the room and offered it to him he knocked me into the corner ten feet away. As my head banged against the wall, he leaped out of bed after me and reached down for my throat. Though half-stunned and off my feet, I yet had more strength than the man whose flabby muscles refused to obey his will. The patient in the adjoining bed rang and in a few moments the orderly came to my assistance. Between us we got the poor crazed youth into a strait jacket. The doctor who was summoned could do nothing and in the morning the young man mercifully died. . . .

To see a baby born is one of the greatest experiences that a human being can have. Birth to me has always been more awe-inspiring than death. As often as I have witnessed the miracle, held the perfect creature with its tiny hands and tiny feet, each time I have felt as though I were entering a cathedral with prayer in my heart.

There is so little knowledge in the world compared with what there is to know. Always I was deeply affected by the trust patients, rich or poor, male or female, old or young, placed in their nurses. When we appeared they seemed to say, "Ah, here is someone who can tell us." Mothers asked me pathetically, plaintively, hopefully, "Miss Higgins, what should I do not to have another baby right away?" I was at a loss to answer their intimate questions, and passed them along to the doctor, who more often than not snorted, "She ought to be ashamed of herself to talk to a young girl about things like that."

All such problems were thus summarily shoved aside. We had one woman in our hospital who had had several miscarriages and six babies, each by a different father. Doctors and nurses knew every time she went out that she would soon be back again, but it was not their business or anybody's business; it was just "natural."

To be polished off neatly, the nurses in training were assigned to one of the larger city hospitals in which to work during the last three or six months of our course. Mine was the Manhattan Eye and Ear at Forty-first Street and Park Avenue, across the street from the Murray Hill Hotel, and I welcomed the chance to see up-to-date equipment and clockwork discipline. My new environment was considerably less harsh and intense, more comfortable and leisurely.

At one of the frequent informal dances held there my doctor partner received a message—not a call, but a caller. His architect wanted to go over blueprints with him. "Come along," he invited. "See whether you think my new house is going to be as fine as I do."

The architect was introduced. "This is William Sanger."

The three of us bent over the plans. The doctor was the only one unaware of the sudden electric quality of the atmosphere.

At seven-thirty the next morning when I went out for my usual "constitutional," Bill Sanger was on the doorstep. He had that type of romantic nature which appealed to me, and had been waiting there all night. We took our walk together that day and regularly for many days thereafter, learning about each other, exploring each other's minds, and discovering a community of ideas and ideals. His fineness fitted in with my whole destiny, if I can call it such, just as definitely as my hospital training. . . . I returned to White Plains, where Bill came up frequently to see me. On one of our rambles he idly pulled at some vines on a stone wall, and then, with his hands, tilted my face for a kiss. The next morning, to my mortification, four telltale finger marks were outlined on my cheek by poison ivy blisters. The day after that, my face was swollen so that my eyes were tight shut, and I was sick for two months; since my training was finished, I was sent home to convalesce. . . .

V. CORALS TO CUT LIFE UPON

FOR a while I stayed at Corning, and then went back to New York to start nursing in earnest. On one of my free afternoons in August, Bill and I went for a drive, and he suggested we stop in at the house of a friend of his who was a minister. All had been prepared. License and rice were waiting. And so we were married.

The first year is half taken up with love and half with planning a future together which is to endure forever. These dreams feed youthful ambitions, but they seldom can come true in their entirety. In our case the obstacles arose with undue speed.

I was not well. I was paying the cost of long hours in mother's closely confined room and of continuous overwork in the hospital. Medical advice was to go West to live, but I would not go without Bill, and he had a commission which kept him in New York. Accordingly, I was packed off to a small semi-sanitarium near Saranac where the great Dr. Trudeau, specialist in pulmonary tuberculosis, was consulted.

Existence there was depressing. A man might be talking to me one day, full of life and spirit and hope, and the next morning not appear. The dead were ordinarily removed in the quiet of the night, and the doctors made no comment. In this gloomy environment I rested, preparing myself for motherhood. The flood of treatises on child psychology had not yet started, and even the books on the care and feeding of infants were few. But I read whatever I could.

Just before it was time for the baby to be born I returned to the little apartment on St. Nicholas Avenue at 149th Street, then practically suburban. Taking every precaution, we had engaged four doctors in a row. Dr. Schmid had said he would perform the ceremony unless it came at night, in which case his assistant would have to take charge. The assistant had provided that, if he were not available, his assistant would be on call, and this assistant had another assistant to assist him.

When towards three o'clock one morning I felt the first thin, fine pains of warning, Bill tried one after the other of our obstetricians— not one could be located. He had to run around the corner to the nearest general practitioner. Due almost as much to this young doctor's inexperience as to my physical state, the ordeal was unusually hard, but the baby Stuart, given Amelia's family name, was perfectly healthy, strong, and sturdy. I looked upon this as a victory, although it was only partial, because I had to go right back to the mountains. It was a wrench to leave again so soon and at such a time, but I could not believe it would be for long.

With Stuart and a nurse I took rooms in a friendly farmhouse near a small Adirondack village; I did not want the baby in the midst of sick people, and, moreover, I was not welcome at Saranac itself, since Dr. Trudeau did not like to have in residence patients whose illness had progressed beyond a certain stage. One of the most important parts of the treatment was stuffing with food. I was being filled with the then recognized remedy, creosote, and gulped capsule after capsule, which broke my appetite utterly. Still I had to pour down milk and swallow eggs, and always I had to rest and rest and rest.

At the end of eight months I was worse instead of better, and had no interest in living. Nan and Bill's mother were summoned, and two of Dr. Trudeau's associates came to see me. They advised that I should go nearer Saranac and be separated from all personal responsibilities.

"What would you yourself like to do?" they asked.

"Nothing."

"Where would you like to go?"

"Nowhere."

"Would you like to have the baby sent to your brother, or would you rather have your mother-in-law take it?"

"I don't care."

To every suggestion I was negative. I was not even interested in my baby.

The two doctors left. The younger, however, apparently not satisfied with the professional attitude, returned almost immediately, not so much in a medical capacity as one of anxious friendliness. I was still sitting in the same state of listlessness. He laid his hand on my shoulder quietly, but I had all the feeling of being violently shaken. "Don't be like this!" he exclaimed. "Don't let yourself get into such a mental condition. Do something! Want something! You'll never get well if you keep on this way."

I could not sleep that night. I had been rudely jolted from my stupor by the understanding doctor. Obviously preparations were being made for a lingering illness which would terminate in death. But if I had to die I would rather be with those I loved than disappear in the night as a part of the cold routine.

As the first glimmer of dawn appeared through the curtains I got up and stared at the steadily ticking clock. It was not yet five. I dressed quickly, then tiptoed into the bedroom where the nurse and baby were slumbering soundly. I roused her and told her to pack up; we were going back to New York. She looked up in drowsy dismay, but obeyed meekly. The farmer hitched up his horse and we jogged along all the way to the station in the early summer morning, bright with sunshine and cheery with birds.

Bill was waiting at the Grand Central Terminal, quite naturally perplexed. He had that morning received two telegrams, one saying I was to be removed to Saranac at once, pending his approval as to the care of the baby by relatives, and the other from me asking him to meet me because I was coming home. I told him as best I could the reasons for my sudden decision. Though I probably sounded –incoherent he understood and, instead of scolding, soothed me tenderly and exclaimed, "You did just the right thing. I won't let you die."

"And don't make me eat! Don't even mention food to me!" He promised to let me have my own way. . . .

Grant, my second son, was born almost immediately. I loved having a baby to tend again, and wanted at least four more as quickly as my health would permit. I could not wait another five years. I yearned especially for a daughter, and twenty months later my wish came true. . . .

VI. THE TURBID EBB AND FLOW OF MISERY

DURING these years in New York trained nurses were in great demand. Few people wanted to enter hospitals; they were afraid they might be "practiced" upon, and consented to go only in desperate emergencies. Sentiment was especially vehement in the matter of having babies. A woman's own bedroom, no matter how inconveniently arranged, was the usual place for her lying-in. I was not sufficiently free from domestic duties to be a general nurse, but I could ordinarily manage obstetrical cases because I was notified far enough ahead to plan my schedule. And after serving my two weeks I could get home again.

Sometimes I was summoned to small apartments occupied by young clerks, insurance salesmen, or lawyers, just starting out, most of them under thirty and whose wives were having their first or second baby. They were always eager to know the best and latest method in infant care and feeding. In particular, Jewish patients, whose lives centered around the family, welcomed advice and followed it implicitly.

But more and more my calls began to come from the Lower East Side, as though I were being magnetically drawn there by some force outside my control. I hated the wretchedness and hopelessness of the poor, and never experienced that satisfaction in working among them that so many noble women have found. My concern for my patients was now quite different from my earlier hospital attitude. I could see that much was wrong with them which did not appear in the physiological or medical diagnosis. A woman in childbirth was not merely a woman in childbirth. My expanded outlook included a view of her background, her potentialities as a human being, the kind of children she was bearing, and what was going to happen to them.

The wives of small shopkeepers were my most frequent cases, but I had carpenters, truck drivers, dishwashers, and pushcart vendors. I admired intensely the consideration most of these people had for their own. Money to pay doctor and nurse had been carefully saved months in advance—parents-in-law, grandfathers, grandmothers, all contributing.

As soon as the neighbors learned that a nurse was in the building they came in a friendly way to visit, often carrying fruit, jellies, or gefüllte fish made after a cherished recipe. It was infinitely pathetic to me that they, so poor themselves, should bring me food. Later they drifted in again with the excuse of getting the plate, and sat down for a nice talk; there was no hurry. Always back of the little gift was the question, "I am pregnant (or my daughter, or my sister is). Tell me something to keep from having another baby. We cannot afford another yet."

I tried to explain the only two methods I had ever heard of among the middle classes, both of which were invariably brushed aside as unacceptable. They were of no certain avail to the wife because they placed the burden of responsibility solely upon the husband—a burden which he seldom assumed. What she was seeking was self-protection she could herself use, and there was none.

Below this stratum of society was one in truly desperate circumstances. The men were sullen and unskilled, picking up odd jobs now and then, but more often unemployed, lounging in and out of the house at all hours of the day and night. The women seemed to slink on their way to market and were without neighborliness. . . .

Many families took in "boarders," as they were termed, whose small contributions paid the rent. These derelicts, wanderers, alternately working and drinking, were crowded in with the children; a single room sometimes held as many as six sleepers. Little girls were accustomed to dressing and undressing in front of the men, and were often violated occasionally by their own fathers or brothers, before they reached the age of puberty.

Pregnancy was a chronic condition among the women of this class. Suggestions as to what to do for a girl who was "in trouble" or a married woman who was "caught" passed from mouth to mouth—herb teas, turpentine, steaming, rolling downstairs, inserting slippery elm, knitting needles, shoe-hooks. When they had word of a new remedy they hurried to the drugstore, and if the clerk were inclined to be friendly he might say, "Oh, that won't help you, but here's something that may." The younger druggists usually refused to give advice because, it if were to be known, they would come under the law; midwives were even more fearful. The doomed women implored me to reveal the "secret" rich people had, offering to pay me extra to tell them; many really believed I was holding back information for money. They asked everybody and tried anything, but nothing did them any good. On Saturday nights I have seen groups of from fifty to one hundred with their shawls over their heads waiting outside the office of a five-dollar abortionist.

Each time I returned to this district, which was becoming a recurrent nightmare, I used to hear that Mrs. Cohn "had been carried to a hospital, but had never come back," or that Mrs. Kelly "had sent the children to a neighbor and had put her head into the gas oven." Day after day such tales were poured into my ears—a baby born dead, great relief—the death of an older child, sorrow but again relief of a sort—the story told a thousand times of death from abortion and children going into institutions. I shuddered with horror as I listened to the details and studied the reasons back of them—destitution linked with excessive childbearing. The waste of life seemed utterly senseless. One by one worried, sad, pensive, and aging faces marshaled themselves before me in my dreams, sometimes appealingly, sometimes accusingly. . . .

Then one stifling mid-July day of 1912 I was summoned to a Grand Street tenement. My patient was a small, slight Russian Jewess, about twenty-eight years old, of the special cast of features to which suffering lends a madonna-like expression. The cramped three-room apartment was in a sorry state of turmoil. Jake Sachs, a truck driver scarcely older than his wife, had come home to find the three children crying and her unconscious from the effects of a self-induced abortion. He had called the nearest doctor, who in turn had sent for me. Jake's earnings were trifling, and most of them had gone to keep the none-too-strong children clean and properly fed. But his wife's ingenuity had helped them to save a little, and this he was glad to spend on a nurse rather than have her go to a hospital.

The doctor and I settled ourselves to the task of fighting the septicemia. Never had I worked so fast, never so concentratedly. The sultry days and nights were melted into a torpid inferno. It did not seem possible there could be such heat, and every bit of food, ice, and drugs had to be carried up three flights of stairs.

Jake was more kind and thoughtful than many of the husbands I had encountered. He loved his children, and had always helped his wife wash and dress them. He had brought water up and carried garbage down before he left in the morning, and did as much as he could for me while he anxiously watched her progress.

After a fortnight Mrs. Sachs' recovery was in sight. Neighbors, ordinarily fatalistic as to the results of abortion, were genuinely pleased that she had survived. She smiled wanly at all who came to see her and thanked them gently, but she could not respond to their hearty congratulations. She appeared to be more despondent and anxious than she should have been, and spent too much time in meditation.

At the end of three weeks, as I was preparing to leave the fragile patient to take up her difficult life once more, she finally voiced her fears, "Another baby will finish me, I suppose?"

"It's too early to talk about that," I temporized.

But when the doctor came to make his last call, I drew him aside. "Mrs. Sachs is terribly worried about having another baby."

"She well may be," replied the doctor, and then he stood before her and said, "Any more such capers, young woman, and there'll be no need to send for me."

"I know, doctor," she replied timidly, "but," and she hesitated as though it took all her courage to say it, "what can I do to prevent it?"

The doctor was a kindly man, and he had worked hard to save her, but such incidents had become so familiar to him that he had long since lost whatever delicacy he might once have had. He laughed good-naturedly. "You want to have your cake and eat it too, do you? Well, it can't be done."

Then picking up his hat and bag to depart he said, "Tell Jake to sleep on the roof."

I glanced quickly at Mrs. Sachs. Even through my sudden tears I could see stamped on her face an expression of absolute despair. We simply looked at each other, saying no word until the door had closed behind the doctor. Then she lifted her thin, blue-veined hands and clasped them beseechingly. "He can't understand. He's only a man. But you do, don't you? Please tell me the secret, and I'll never breathe it to a soul. *Please!*"

What was I to do? I could not speak the conventionally comforting phrases which would be of no comfort. Instead, I made her as physically easy as I could and promised to come back in a few days to talk with her again. A little later, when she slept, I tiptoed away.

Night after night the wistful image of Mrs. Sachs appeared before me. I made all sorts of excuses to myself for not going back. I was busy on other cases; I really did not know what to say to her or how to convince her of my own ignorance; I was helpless to avert such monstrous atrocities. Time rolled by and I did nothing.

The telephone rang one evening three months later, and Jake Sachs' agitated voice begged me to come at once; his wife was sick again and from the same cause. For a wild moment I thought of sending someone else, but actually, of course, I hurried into my uniform, caught up my bag, and started out. All the way I longed for a subway wreck, and explosion, anything to keep me from having to enter that home again. But nothing happened, even to delay me. I turned into the dingy doorway and climbed the familiar stairs once more. The children were there, young little things.

Mrs. Sach was in a coma and died within ten minutes. I folded her still hands across her heart, remembering how they had pleaded with me, begging so humbly for the knowledge which was her right. I drew a sheet over her pallid face. Jake was sobbing, running hands through his hair and pulling it out like an insane person. Over and over again he wailed, "My God! My God! My God!"

I left him pacing desperately back and forth, and for hours I myself walked and walked and walked through the hushed streets. When I finally arrived home and let myself quietly in, all the household was sleeping. I looked out my window and down upon the dimly lighted city. Its pains and griefs crowded in upon me, a moving picture rolled before my eyes with photographic clearness: women writhing in travail to bring forth little babies; the babies themselves naked and hungry, wrapped in newspapers to keep them from the cold; six-year-old children with pinched, pale, wrinkled faces, old in concentrated wretchedness, pushed into gray and fetid cellars, crouching on stone floors, their small scrawny hands scuttling through rags, making lamp shades, artificial flowers; white coffins, black coffins, coffins, coffins interminably passing in never-ending succession. The scenes piled one upon another on another. I could bear it no longer.

As I stood there the darkness faded. The sun came up and threw its reflection over the house tops. It was the dawn of a new day in my life also. The doubt and questioning, the experimenting and trying, were now to be put behind me. I knew I could not go back merely to keeping people alive.

I went to bed, knowing that no matter what it might cost, I was finished with palliatives and superficial cures; I was resolved to seek out the root of evil, to do something to change the destiny of mothers whose miseries were vast as the sky. . . .

VII. I HAVE PROMISES TO KEEP

HOW were mothers to be saved? I went through many revolving doors, looked around, and, not finding what I was seeking, came out again. I talked incessantly to everybody who seemed to have social welfare at heart. Progressive women whom I consulted were thoroughly discouraging. "Wait until we get the vote. Then we'll take care of that, " they assured me. I tried the Socialists. Here, there, and everywhere the reply came, "Wait until women have more education. Wait until we secure equal distribution of wealth." Wait for this and wait for that. Wait! Wait! Wait!

Having no idea how powerful were the laws which laid a blanket of ignorance over the medical profession as well as the laity, I asked various doctors of my acquaintance, "Why aren't physicians doing something?"

"The people you're worrying about wouldn't use contraception if they had it; they breed like rabbits. And, besides, there's a law against it."

"Information does exist, doesn't it?"

"Perhaps, but I doubt whether you can find it. Even if you do, you can't pass it on. Comstock'll get you if you don't watch out."

In order to ascertain something about this subject which was so mysterious and so unaccountably forbidden, I spent almost a year in the libraries—the Astor, the Lenox, the Academy of Medicine, the Library of Congress, and dozens of others. Hoping that psychological treatises might inform me, I read Auguste Forel and Iwan Block. At one gulp I swallowed Havelock Ellis' *Psychology of Sex*, and had psychic indigestion for months thereafter. I was not shocked, but this mountainous array of abnormalities made me spiritually ill. So many volumes were devoted to the exceptional, and so few to the maladjustments of normal married people, which were infinitely more numerous and urgent.

I read translations from the German in which women were advised to have more children because it could be proved statistically that their condition was improved by childbearing. The only article on the question I could discover in American literature was in the *Atlantic Monthly* by Edward Alsworth Ross of the University of Wisconsin, who brought to the attention of his readers the decline of the birth rate among the upper and educated classes and the increase among the unfit, the consequences of which were sure to be race suicide.

The Englishman, Thomas Robert Malthus, remained little more than a name to me, something like Plato or Henry George. Father talked about him, but he meant mostly agriculture—wheat and food supplies in the national sense. Possibly he had a philosophy but not, to me, a live one. He had been put away on a shelf and, in my mind, had nothing to do with the everyday human problem. I was not looking for theories. What I desired was merely a simple method of contraception for the poor.

The pursuit of my quest took me away from home a good deal. The children used to come in after school and at once hunt for me. "Where's mother?" was the usual question. If they found me at my mending basket they all leaped about for joy, took hands and danced, shouting, "Mother's home, mother's home, mother's sewing." Sewing seemed to imply a measure of permanence.

I, too, wanted to drive away the foreboding barrier of separation by closer contact with them. I wanted to have them solely to myself, to feed, to bathe, to clothe them myself. I had heard of the clean, wind–swept Cape Cod dunes, which appeared to be as far from the ugliness of civilization as I could get. Socialism, anarchism, syndicalism, progressivism—I was tired of them all. At the end of the spring, thoroughly depressed and dissatisfied, I tucked the children under my arms, boarded a Fall River boat, and sailed off, a pioneer to Provincetown. . . .

I spent the entire season at Provincetown, groping for knowledge, classifying all my past activities in their proper categories, weighing the pros and cons of what good there was in them and also what they lacked. It was a period of gestation. Just as you give birth to a child, so you can give birth to an idea. . . .

Big Bill was one of the few who saw what I was aiming at, although fearful that my future might involve the happiness of my children.* Even he did not feel that the small-family question was significant enough to be injected into the labor platform. Nevertheless, as we rambled up and down the beach he came to my aid with that cheering encouragement of which I was so sorely in need. He never wasted words in advising me to "wait." Instead, he suggested that I go to France and see for myself the conditions resulting from generations of family limitation in that country. This struck me as a splendid idea, because it would also give Bill Sanger a chance to paint instead of continuing to build suburban houses.

The trip to Europe seemed so urgent that no matter what sacrifices had to be made, we decided to make them when we came to them. In the fall we sold the house at Hastings, gave away some of our furniture and put the rest in storage. Although we did not realize it at the time, our gestures indicated a clean sweep of the past. . . .

In October the Sangers sailed from Boston on a cabin boat, little and crowded, and one black night two weeks later steamed up the Clyde. The naval program of 1913 was causing every shipyard to run double shifts, and the flare and glare against the somber dark was like fairyland—giant, sparkling starlight reaching from the

* She had met William "Big Bill" Haywood, the radical labor leader, through her work on behalf of unions in New York.

horizon into the sky, a beautiful introduction to Utopia. . . .

Religiously I made the rounds of all the social institutions, and at first everything appeared as I had been led to expect—except the weather. It had always just rained, and, when the sun did show itself, it was seldom for long enough to dry up the walks. Though the streets were clean, they were invariably wet and damp, and nobody wore rubbers. Everywhere could be seen little girls down on their knees, scrubbing the doorsteps in front of the houses, or, again, carrying huge bundles or baskets of groceries to be delivered at the homes of the buyers. The people themselves seemed cold and rigid, as dismal as their climate. Only the policemen had a sense of humor.

As I proceeded, flaws in the vaunted civic enterprises began to display themselves. Glasgow had its show beauty spots, but even the model tenements were not so good as our simplest, lower-middle-class apartment buildings. One had been constructed for the accommodation of "deserving and respectable widows and widowers belonging to the working class" having one or more children with no one to care for them while the parents were away. But the building had been turned over to the exclusive use of widowers. Widows and their children had to shift for themselves.

All tenements were planned scientifically on the basis of so many cubic feet of air and so much light per so many human beings, ranging from quarters for two to those for five. No overcrowding was allowed.

"Well," I asked, "what happens when there are five or six children?"

"Oh, they can't live here," replied the superintendent. "They must go elsewhere."

"But where?"

Conversation ceased.

With particular attention I traced the adventures of one family which had expanded beyond the three-child limit. The parents had first moved over to the fringes of the city, and thereafter as more children were born had traveled from place to place, progressively more dingy, more decrepit. They now had nine and were inhabiting a hovel in the shipbuilding slums, unimaginably filthy and too far from the splendid utilities ever to enjoy them.

The further I looked, the greater grew the inconsistency. The model markets carried chiefly wholesale produce, and the really poor, who were obliged to huddle on the far side of the city, contented themselves with bread and tea and were thankful to have it. Another disappointment was the washhouses, dating from 1878 when they had been deemed a public necessity because men had protested they were being driven from their homes by washing which, on account of the incessant rain, seemed to hang there forever. A stall cost only twopence an hour, less expensive than heating water at home, and there were always women waiting in line. But the tram system, which was on the point of being liquidated in spite of its low fares, forbade laundry baskets, and, consequently, those who were not within walking distance—and they were the ones who needed it most—were deprived of its use.

Throughout the slum section I saw drunken, sodden women whose remaining, snag-like teeth stuck down like fangs and protruded from their sunken mouths. When I asked one of the executive officers of the corporation why they were so much more degraded than the men, he replied, "Oh, the women of Glasgow are all dirty and low. They're hopeless."

"But why should this be?" I persisted.

His only answer was, "It's their own fault."

Bill and I walked about late at night, overwhelmed by the unspeakable poverty. The streets were filled with fighting, shiftless beggars. Hundreds of women were abroad, the big shawls over their heads serving two purposes: one, to keep their shoulders warm; the other, to wrap around the baby which each one carried. It was apparent that their clothing consisted only of a shawl, a petticoat, a wrapper, and shoes. Older children were begging, "A ha'penny for bread, Missus, a ha'penny for bread."

It was infinitely cold, dreary, and disappointing—so much talk about more wages and better subsistence, and here the workers had it and what were they getting?—a little more light, perhaps, a few more pennies a day, the opportunity to buy food a little more cheaply, a few parks in which they could wander, a bank where their money earned a fraction more interest. But as soon as they passed beyond the border of another baby, they were in exactly the same condition as the people beyond the realm of municipal control. . . .

[Margaret Sanger and her husband returned to France from Scotland, he to paint, she to learn more about French methods of birth control.]

The last day of the year, December 31, 1913, Bill and I said goodby, unaware the parting was to be final. With the children I embarked at Cherbourg for home. . . .

VIII. THE WOMAN REBEL

THE *New York* was a nice ship and it was not too wintry to walk about on deck. After the children were safely in bed I paced round and round and absorbed into my being that quiet which comes to you at sea. That it was New Year's Eve added to the poignancy of my emotions but did not obscure the faith within.

I knew something must be done to rescue those women who were voiceless; someone had to express with white hot intensity the conviction that they must be empowered to decide for themselves when they should fulfill the supreme function of motherhood. They had to be made aware of how they were being shackled, and roused to mutiny. To this end I conceived the idea of a magazine to be called the *Woman Rebel*, dedicated to the interests of working women. . . .

With as crystal a view as that which had come to me after the death of Mrs. Sachs when I had renounced nursing forever, I saw the path ahead in its civic, national, and even international direction—a panorama of things to be. Fired with this vision, I went into the lounge and wrote and wrote page after page until the hours of daylight.

Having settled the principles, I left the details to work themselves out. I realized that a price must be paid for honest thinking— a price for everything. Though I did not know exactly how I was to prepare myself, what turn events might take, or what I might be called upon to do, the future in its larger aspects has actually developed as I saw it that night.

The same thoughts kept repeating themselves over and over during the remainder of the otherwise uneventful voyage. As soon as possible after reaching New York, I rented an inexpensive little flat on Post Avenue near Dyckman Street, so far out on the upper end of Manhattan that even the Broadway subway trains managed to burrow their way into sunlight and fresh air. My dining room was my office, the table my desk.

A new movement was starting, and the baby had to have a name. It did not belong to Socialism nor was it in the labor field, and it had much more to it than just the prevention of conception. As a few companions were sitting with me one evening we debated in turn voluntary parenthood, voluntary motherhood, the new motherhood, constructive generation, and new generation. The terms already in use—Neo-Malthusianism, Family Limitation, and Conscious Generation seemed stuffy and lacked popular appeal.

The word control was good, but I did not like limitation—that was too limiting. I was not advocating a one-child or two-child system as in France, nor did I wholeheartedly agree with the English Neo-Malthusians whose concern was almost entirely with limitation for economic reasons. My idea of control was bigger and freer. I wanted family in it, yet family control did not sound right. We tried population control, race control, and birth rate control. Then someone suggested, "Drop the rate." Birth control was the answer; we knew we had it. Our work for that day was done and everybody picked up his hat and went home. The baby was named.

When I first announced that I was going to publish a magazine, "Where are you going to get the money?" was volleyed at me from all sides. I did not know, but I was certain of its coming somehow. Equally important was moral support. Those same young friends and I founded a little society, grandly titled the National Birth Control League, sought aid from enthusiasts for other causes, turning first to the Feminists because they seemed our natural allies. Armed with leaflets we went to Cooper Union to tell them that in the *Woman Rebel* they would have an opportunity to express their sentiments. . . .

Who cared whether a woman kept her Christian name—Mary Smith instead of Mrs. John Jones? Who cared whether she wore her wedding ring? Who cared about her demand for the right to work? Hundreds of thousands of laundresses, cloakmakers, scrub women, servants, telephone girls, shop workers would gladly have changed places with the Feminists in return for the right to have leisure, to be lazy a little now and then. When I suggested that the basis of Feminism might be the right to be a mother regardless of church or state, their inherited prejudices were instantly aroused. They were still subject to the age-old, masculine atmosphere compounded of protection and dominance. . . .

IX. HIGH HANGS THE GAUNTLET

[Margaret Sanger, in the next two years, traveled from Canada to England, Holland, Spain and other countries to learn the techniques of birth control. Her purpose was to bring information back to the U.S., where such information, though not morally sanctioned, was in demand. In England, she met Havelock Ellis, famous author of books on sexual practices. She returned home to face prosecution for circulating a pamphlet on birth control.]

The end of September, 1915, I set sail from Bordeaux. I remember how interminable that voyage was across the dangerous, foggy Atlantic. The shadow of the *Lusitania* hung over us. The ship was absolutely dark, and tension crackled in the very air. My own thoughts were black as the night and the old nervousness, the nervousness that came with a queer gripping at the pit of the stomach, was upon me; a dread presentiment and a foreboding were with me almost incessantly.

When I succeeded in snatching a few hours' sleep I was startled out of unpleasant dreams. One of them was of attempting to struggle through a crowded street against traffic; I was pushed to the curb and had to make my way cautiously. The mechanical, automaton-like crowds were walking, walking, walking, always in the opposite direction. Then suddenly in my dream the people turned into mice—thousands and thousands of them; they even smelled like mice. I awakened and had to open the porthole to rid the room of that musty smell of mice.

At last the lights of Staten Island, winking like specters in the dim dawn, signaled our safe arrival at quarantine. As the ship sidled along the wharf at West Fourteenth Street on that gray October morning, a new exhilaration, a new hope arose in my heart.

To see American faces again after the unutterable despair of Europe, to sense the rough democracy of the porters and of the good-hearted, hard-boiled taxi-drivers; to breathe in the crisp, electric autumn air of home—all these brought with them an irresistible gladness. Because I wanted the feeling to linger, I refused a taxi, picked up my small bag, and walked away from the pier, looking about.

At the first news stand I passed I caught sight of the words. "What Shall We Do About Birth Control?" on the cover of the *Pictorial Review*. It seemed strange to be greeted, not by friends or relatives, but by a phrase of your own carried on a magazine. I purchased it and, singing to myself, went on to a hotel where the children were brought to me. I cannot describe the joy of being reunited with them.

That evening I sat down at my desk and wrote several letters. I notified Judge Hazel and Assistant District Attorney Content that I was now back and ready for trial, and inquired whether the indictments of the previous year were still pending; I was politely informed that they were.

A note more difficult to compose went to the National Birth Control League, which had been re-organized in my absence under the leadership of Mary Ware Dennett, Clara Stillman, and Anita Block. To it had been turned over all my files, including the list of subscribers to the *Woman Rebel*. I asked them what moral support I could expect from the League, saying this would help to determine the length of my stay. . . .

But these problems were suddenly swept aside by a crisis of a more intimate nature, a tragedy about which I find myself still unable to write, though so many years have passed.

A few days after my arrival Peggy was taken ill with pneumonia. When Mr. Content telephoned to say I had better come down and talk it over, I could not go. He was extremely kind, assuring my there was no hurry and he would postpone the trial until I was free. This allowed me to devote my whole attention and time to her.

Peggy died the morning of November 6, 1915.

The joy in the fullness of life went out of it then and has never quite returned. Deep in the hidden realm of my consciousness my little girl has continued to live, and in that strange, mysterious place where reality and imagination meet, she has grown up to womanhood. There she leads an ideal existence untouched by harsh actuality and disillusion.

Men and women from all classes, from nearly every city in America, poured upon my their sympathy. Money for my trial came beyond my understanding—not large amounts, but large for the senders—from miners of West Virginia and lumbermen of the North Woods. Some had walked five miles to read *Family Limitation*; others had had it copied for them. Women wrote of children dead a quarter of a century for whom they were still secretly mourning, and sent me pictures and locks of hair of their own dead babies. I had never fully realized until then that the loss of a child remains unforgotten to every mother during her lifetime.

Public opinion had been focused on Comstock's activities by Bill's sentence, and the liberals had been aroused. Committees of two and three came to request me to take up the purely legislative task of changing the Federal law. Aid would be forthcoming—special trains to Congress, investigations, commissions, and victory in sight before the year was over! It was tempting. It seemed so feasible on the surface, so much easier than agonizing delays through the courts. Many others advised me just as before that in pleading guilty I was choosing the best field in which to make my fight. . . .

"I'm not concerned with going to jail. Going in or staying out has nothing to do with it. The question at stake is whether I have or have not done something obscene. If I have done nothing obscene I cannot plead guilty.". . .

I would not plead guilty on any count. They could not make me.

I felt deep within me that I was right and they were wrong. I still had the naive trust that when the facts were known, the Government would not willfully condemn millions of women to death, misery, or abortion which left them physically damaged and spiritually crippled. . . .

The law specified obscenity, and I had done nothing obscene. I even had the best of the Government as regarded the precise charge. I had not given contraceptive information in the *Woman Rebel*, and therefore had not violated the law either in spirit or principle. But I had done so in circulating *Family Limitation*, and that would inevitably be brought up. I really wanted this, so that birth control would be defined once and for all as either obscene or not obscene. . . .

As the New York *Sun* commented, "The Sanger case presents the anomaly of a prosecutor loath to prosecute and a defendant anxious to be tried," The newspapers were taking ever-increasing notice. A photograph of myself and my two young sons circulated widely and seemed to alter the attitude of a heretofore cynical public. At that time I thought the papers were against me, but looking over these old clippings today I realize this was merely the impersonality of the news columns. Their editorial hesitancy made them appear, like all other conservative and reactionary forces, my opponents. But the rank and file of American newspaperdom, though they must always have their little jokes, have always been sympathetic.

They printed the letter to Woodrow Wilson, initiated by Marie Stopes. It "begged to call the attention" of the President to the fact that I was in danger of criminal prosecution for circulating a pamphlet on birth control, which was allowed in every civilized country except the United States; that England had passed through the phase of prohibiting this subject a generation before; and that to suppress serious and disinterested opinion on anything so important was detrimental to human progress. It respectfully urged the President to exert his powerful influence in behalf of free speech and the betterment of the race. This letter was invaluable by reason of its signatories—Lena Ashwell, William Archer, Percy Ames, Aylmer Maude, M.C. Stopes, Arnold Bennett, Edward Carpenter, Gilbert Murray, and H.G. Wells, whose name was news. If a group of such eminence in England could afford to stand by me, then the same kind of people here might be less timorous. . . .

My radical allies were, according to their habit, collecting money for my defense, but this had no effect on my private financial status. My sister, Ethel, who was living with me, thought I ought to be considering the matter. One day she said, "I've a good case for you. Wouldn't you like to take it?"

"What kind?"

"Maternity. She expects to be delivered in a day or two—probably a Caesarian. She asked for me, but I'd rather you had it."

"I'm not interested, thank you. I've given up nursing."

"Well, Mrs. Sanger," she remarked ironically, "would you mind telling me what you're going to do to earn your living?"

"I'm not interested in earning my living. I've cast myself upon the universe and it will take care of me."

She looked at me sadly and with worried apprehension.

Three days later Ethel received the anticipated summons. On her way out she picked up the mail at the door. In it was a letter from a California acquaintance of hers who did not know where I was but had her address. "Will you please give the enclosed forty-five dollars to Margaret Sanger from her sympathizers?"

Ethel handed it to me with the resigned comment, "Well, here's your check from God."

The editor of the *Woman Rebel* had struck her single match of defiance, but she could be of slight significance in the forward march towards "women's rights." In Feminist circles I was little known. With my personal sorrow, my manifold domestic duties, my social shyness, I avoided meeting new people. My attitude thus created some reluctance among those who might otherwise have hastened to my aid. Indeed, I wanted a certain type of support, but I could not take the initiative in asking for it. . . .

February 18th the Government finally entered a nolle prosequi. Content explained there had been many assertions that the defendant was the victim of persecution, and that had never been the intent of the Federal authorities. "The case had been laid before the grand jurors as impartially as possible and since they had voted an indictment there was nothing that the District Attorney could do but prosecute. Now, however, as it was realized that the indictment was two years old, and that Mrs. Sanger was not a disorderly person and did not make a practice of publishing such articles, the Government had considered there was reason for considerable doubt.". . . .

But I was not content to have a Liberty Dinner and jubilate. I could not consider anything more than a moral victory had been attained. The law had not been tested. I agreed with the loyal *Globe*, which staunchly maintained, "If the matter Mrs. Sanger sent through the mails was obscene two years ago, it is still obscene." I knew and felt instinctively the danger of having a privilege under a law rather than a right. I could not yet afford to breathe a sigh of relief.

The Federal law concerned only printed literature. My own pamphlet had given the impression that the printed word was the best way to inform women, but the practical course of contraceptive technique I had taken in the Netherlands had shown me that one woman was so different from another in structure that each needed particular information applied to herself as an individual. Books and leaflets, therefore, should be of secondary importance. The public health way was through personal instruction in clinics.

A light had been kindled; so many invitations to address meetings in various cities and towns were sent me that I was not able to accept them all but agreed to as many as I could. It was no longer to be only a free speech movement, and I wanted also if possible to present this new idea of clinics to the country. If I could start them, other organizations and even hospitals might do the same. I had a vision of a "chain"—thousands of them in every center of America, staffed with specialists putting the subject on a modern scientific basis through research.

Many states in the West had already granted woman suffrage. Having achieved this type of freedom, I was sure they would receive clinics more readily, especially California which had no law against birth control. The same thing would follow in the East. As I told the *Tribune*, "I have the word of four prominent physicians that they will support me in the work. . . . There will be nurses in attendance at the clinic, and doctors who will instruct women in the things they need to know. All married women or women about to be married will be assisted free and without question."

A splendid promise—but difficult to fulfill, as events were to prove.

X. FAITH I HAVE BEEN A TRUANT IN THE LAW

THE legislative approach seemed to me a slow and tortuous method of making clinics legal; we stood a better and quicker chance by securing a favorable judicial interpretation through challenging the law directly. I decided to open a clinic in New York City, a far more difficult proceeding than in Boston. Section 1142 of the New York statutes was definite: *No one* could give contraceptive information to *anyone* for *any* reason. On the other hand, Section 1145 distinctly stated that physicians could give prescriptions to prevent conception for the cure or prevention of disease. Two attorneys and several doctors assured me this exception referred only to venereal disease. In that case, the intent was to protect the man, which could incidentally promote immorality and permit promiscuity. I was dealing with marriage. I wanted the interpretation to be broadened into the intent to protect women from ill health as the result of excessive childbearing and, equally important, to have the right to control their own destinies.

To change this interpretation it was necessary to have a test case. This, in turn, required my keeping strictly to the letter of the law; that is, having physicians who would give only verbal information for the prevention of disease. But the women doctors who had previously promised to do this now refused. I wrote, telephoned, asked friends to ask other friends to help find someone. None was willing to enter the cause, fearful of jeopardizing her private practice and of running the risk of being censured by her profession: she might even lose her license. . . .

I did not wish to complicate the question of testing the law by having a nurse give information, because a nurse did not come under the Section 1145 exception. But since I could find no doctor I had to do without. Ethel, a registered nurse, had a readiness to share in helping the movement, though she did not belong to it in the same sense as I. Then, as long as I had to violate the law anyhow, I concluded I might as well violate it on a grand scale by including poverty as a reason for giving contraceptive information. I did not see why the hardships and worries of a working man's wife might not be just as detrimental as any disease. I wanted a legal opinion on this if possible.

My next problems were where the money was to come from and where the clinic was to be. Ever since I had announced that I was going to open one within a few months I had been buried under an avalanche of queries as to the place, which for a time I could not answer. The selection of a suitable locality was of the greatest importance. I tramped through the streets of the Bronx, Brooklyn, the lower sides of Manhattan, East and West. I scrutinized the Board of Health vital statistics of all the boroughs—births and infant and maternal mortality in relation to low wages, and also the number of philanthropic institutions in the vicinity.

The two questions—where and how—were settled on one and the same day.

That afternoon five women from the Brownsville Section of Brooklyn crowded into my room seeking the "secret" of birth control. Each had four children or more, who had been left with neighbors. One had just recovered from an abortion which had nearly killed her. "Another will take me off. Then what will become of my family?"

The rocked back and forth as they related their afflictions, told so simply, each scarcely able to let her friend finish before she took up the narration of her own sufferings —the high cost of food, her husband's meager income when he worked at all, her helplessness in the struggle to make ends meet, whining, sickly children, the constant worry of another baby—and always hanging over her night and day, year after year, was fear.

All cried what a blessing and godsend a clinic would be in their neighborhood.

They talked an hour and when they had finished, it seemed as though I myself had been through their tragedies. I was reminded of the story of a Spaniard who had become so desperate over the injustice meted out to innocent prisoners that he had taken a revolver into the street and fired it at the first person he met; killing was his only way of expressing indignation. I felt like doing the same thing.

I decided then and there that the clinic should open at Brownsville, and I would look for a site the next day. How to finance it I did not know, but that did not matter. . . .

I sent a letter to the District Attorney of Brooklyn, saying I expected to dispense contraceptive information from this address. Without waiting for the reply, which never came, we began the fun of fixing up our little clinic. We had to keep furnishing expenses inside the budget, but Fania knew Yiddish and also how to bargain. We bought chairs, desks, floor coverings, curtains, a stove. If I were to leave no loophole in testing the law, we could only give the principles of contraception, show a cervical pessary to the women, explain that if they had had two children they should have one size and if more a larger one. This was not at all ideal, but I had no other recourse at the time. However, we might be able to get a doctor any day and, consequently, we added an examination table to our equipment.

Mr. Rabinowitz spent hours adding touches here and there to make the two shiny and spotless rooms even more snow-white. "More hospital looking," he said.

Meanwhile we had printed about five thousand notices in English, Italian, and Yiddish:

MOTHERS!

Can you afford to have a large family?

Do you want any more children?

If not, why do you have them?

DO NOT KILL, DO NOT TAKE LIFE, BUT PREVENT

Safe, Harmless Information can be obtained of trained Nurses at

46 AMBOY STREET

NEAR PITKIN AVE.—BROOKLYN.

Tell Your Friends and Neighbors.   All Mothers Welcome

A registration fee of 10 cents entitles any mother to this information.

These we poked into letter boxes, house after house, day after day, upstairs, downstairs, all over the place, viewing sadly the unkempt children who swarmed in the alleyways and over the fire escapes of the condemned tenements and played on the rubbish heaps in the vacant lots. Seldom did we see a woman who was not carrying or wheeling a baby. We stopped to talk to each and gave her a supply of leaflets to hand on to her neighbors. When we passed by a drugstore we arranged with the proprietor to prepare himself for supplying the pessaries we were going to recommend.

The morning of October 16, 1916—crisp but sunny and bright after days of rain—Ethel, Fania, and I opened the doors of the first birth control clinic in America, the first anywhere in the world except the Netherlands. I still believe this was an event of social significance.

Would the women come? Did they come? Nothing, not even the ghost of Anthony Comstock, could have kept them away. We had arrived early, but before we could get the place dusted and ourselves ready for the official reception, Fania called, "do come outside and look." Halfway to the corner they were standing in line, at least one hundred and fifty, some shawled, some hatless, their red hands clasping the cold, chapped, smaller ones of their children.

Fania began taking names, addresses, object in coming to the clinic, histories—married or single, any miscarriages or abortions, how many children, were born, what ages. Remembering how the Netherlands clinics in recording nothing had made it almost hopeless to measure what they had accomplished from the human point of view, I had resolved that our files should be as complete as it was possible to make them. Fania had a copy of *What Every Girl Should Know* on her desk, and, if she had a free moment, read from it. When asked, she told where it could be bought, and later kept a few copies for the convenience of those who wanted them.

Children were left with her and mothers ushered in to Ethel or me in the rear room, from seven to ten at once. To each group we explained simply what contraception was ; that abortion was the wrong way—no matter how early it was performed it was taking life; that contraception was the better way, the safer way—it took a little time, a little trouble, but was well worth while in the long run, because life had not yet begun.

Some women were alone, some were in pairs, some with their neighbors, women with their married daughters. Some did not dare talk this over with their husbands, and some had been urged on by them. At seven in the evening they were still coming, and men also, occasionally bringing their timid, embarrassed wives, or once in a while by themselves to say they would stay home to take care of the children if their wives could come. A hundred women and forty men passed through the doors, but we could not begin to finish the line; the rest were told to return "tomorrow."

In the course of the next few days women appeared clutching minute scraps of paper, seldom more than an inch wide, which had crept into print. The Yiddish and Italian papers had picked up the story from the handbills which bore the clinic address, and the husbands had read them on their way from work and clipped them out for their wives. Women who had seen the brief, inconspicuous newspaper accounts came even from Massachusetts, Pennsylvania, New Jersey, and the far end of Long Island.

Newly married couples with little but love, faith, and hope to save them from charity, told of the tiny flats they had chosen, and of their determination to make a go of it together if only the children were not born too soon. A gaunt skeleton suddenly stood up one morning and made an impassioned speech. "They offer us charity when we have more babies than we can feed, and when we get sick with more babies for trying not to have them they just give us more charity talks!"

Women who were themselves already past childbearing age came just to urge us to preserve others from the sorrows of ruined health, overworked husbands, and broods of defective and wayward children growing up in the streets, filling dispensaries and hospitals, filing through the juvenile courts.

We made records of every applicant and, though the details might vary, the stories were basically identical. All were confused, groping among the ignorant sex–teachings of the poor, fumbling without guidance after truth, misled and bewildered in a tangled jungle of popular superstitions and old wives' remedies. Unconsciously they dramatized the terrible need of intelligent and scientific instruction in these matters of life—and death.

As was inevitable many were kept away by the report that the police were to raid us for performing abortions. "Clinic" was a word which to the uneducated usually signified such a place. We would not have minded particularly being raided on this charge, because we could easily disprove it. But these rumors also brought the most pitiful of all, the reluctantly expectant mothers who hoped to find some means of getting out of their dilemmas. Their desperate threats of suicide haunted you at night.

One Jewish wife, after bringing eight children to birth, had had two abortions and heaven knows how many miscarriages. Worn out, beaten down, not only by toiling in her own kitchen, but by taking in extra work from a sweatshop making hats, she was now at the end of her strength, nervous beyond words, and in a state of morbid excitement. "If you don't help me, I'm going to chop up a glass and swallow it tonight."

A woman wrought to the pitch of killing herself was sick—a community responsibility. She, most of all, required concentrated attention and devotion, and I could not let any such go out of the clinic until her mood had been altered. Building up hope for the future seemed the best deterrent. "Your husband and your children need you. One more won't make so much difference." I had to make each promise to go ahead and have this baby and myself promised in return, "You won't ever have to again. We're going to take care of you."

Day after day the waiting room was crowded with members of every race and creed; Jews and Christians, Protestants and Roman Catholics alike made their confessions to us, whatever they may have professed at home or in church. I asked one bright little Catholic what excuse she could make to the priest when he learned she had been to the clinic. She answered indignantly, "It's none of his business. My husband has a weak heart and works only four days a week. He gets twelve dollars, and we can barely live on it now. We have enough children."

Her friend, sitting by, nodded approval. "When I was married," she broke in, "the priest told us to have lots of children and we listened to him. I had fifteen. Six are living. I'm thirty-seven years old now. Look at me! I might be fifty!"

That evening I made a mental calculation of fifteen baptismal fees, nine baby funerals, masses and candles for the repose of nine baby souls, the physical agonies of the mother and the emotional torment of both parents, and I asked myself, "Is this the price of Christianity?"

But it was not altogether sad; we were often cheered by gayer visitors. The grocer's wife on the corner and the widow with six children who kept the lunch room up the street dropped in to wish us luck, and the fat old German baker whose wife gave out handbills to everybody passing the door sent regular donations of doughnuts. Whenever the pressure became so overwhelming that we could not go out for a meal we were sure to hear Mrs. Rabinowitz call downstairs, "If I bring some hot tea now, will you stop the people coming?" Two jovial policemen paused at the doorway each morning to discuss the weather. Reporters looked in speculating on how long we were going to last. The postman delivering his customary fifty to a hundred letters had his little pleasantry, "Farewell, ladies; hope I find you here tomorrow."

Although the line outside was enough to arouse police attention, nine days went by without interference. Then one afternoon when I, still undiscouraged, was out interviewing a doctor, a woman, large of build and hard of countenance, entered and said to Fania she was the mother of two children and that she had no money to support more. She did not appear overburdened or anxious and, because she was so well fed as to body and prosperous as to clothes, did not seem to belong to the community. She bought a copy of *What Every Girl Should Know* and insisted on paying two dollars instead of the usual ten-cent fee.

Fania, who had an intuition about such matters, called Ethel aside and said warningly she was certain this must be a policewoman. But Ethel, who was not of the cautious type, replied, "We have nothing to hide. Bring her in anyhow." She talked with the woman in private, gave her our literature and, when asked about our future plans, related them frankly. The skeptical Fania pinned the two-dollar bill on the wall and wrote underneath, "Received from Mrs.——— of the Police Department, as her contribution." Hourly after that we expected trouble. We had known it must occur sooner or later, but would have preferred it to come about in a different way.

The next day Ethel and Fania were both absent from the clinic. The waiting room was filled almost to suffocation when the door opened and the woman who had been described to me came in.

"Are you Mrs. Sanger?"

"Yes."

"I'm a police officer. You're under arrest."

The doors were locked and this Mrs. Margaret Whitehurst and other plain-clothes members of the vice squad—used to raiding gambling dens and houses of assignation—began to demand names and addresses of the women, seeing them with babies, broken, old, worried, harrowed, yet treating them as though they were inmates of a brothel. Always fearful in the presence of the police, some began to cry aloud and the children on their laps screamed too. For a few moments it was like a panic, until I was able to assure them that only I was under arrest; nothing was going to happen to them, and they could return home if they were quiet. After half an hour I finally persuaded the policemen to let these frightened women go.

All of our four hundred and sixty-four case histories were confiscated, and the table and demonstration supplies were carried off through the patient line outside. The more timid had left, but many had stayed. This was a region where a crowd could be collected by no more urgent gesture than a tilt of the head skyward. Newspaper men with their cameras had joined the throng and the street was packed. Masses of people spilled out over the sidewalk on to the pavement, milling excitedly.

The patrol wagon came rattling up to our door. I had a certain respect for uniformed policemen—you knew what they were about— but none whatsoever for the vice squad. I was white hot with indignation over their unspeakable attitude towards the clinic mothers and stated I preferred to walk the mile to the court rather than sit with them. Their feelings were quite hurt. "Why, we didn't do anything to you, Mrs. Sanger," they protested. Nevertheless I marched ahead, they following behind.

A reporter from the *Brooklyn Eagle* fell into step beside me and before we had gone far suggested, "Now I'll fix it up with the police that you make a getaway, and when we reach that corner you run. I'll stop and talk to them while you skip around the block and get to the station first." It was fantastic for anyone so to misconstrue what I was doing as to imagine I would run around the block for a publicity stunt.

I stayed overnight at the Raymond Street Jail, and I shall never forget it. The mattresses were spotted and smelly, the blankets stiff with dirt and grime. The stench nauseated me. It was not a comforting thought to go without bedclothing when it was so cold, but, having in mind the diseased occupants who might have preceded me, I could not bring myself to creep under the covers. Instead I lay down on top and wrapped my coat around me. The only clean object was my towel, and this I draped over my face and head. For endless hours I struggled with roaches and horrible-looking bugs that came crawling out of the walls and across the floor. When a rat jumped up on the bed I cried out involuntarily and sent it scuttling out.

My cell was at the end of a center row, all opening front and back upon two corridors. The prisoners gathered in one of the aisles the next morning and I joined them. Most had been accused of minor offenses such as shoplifting and petty thievery. Many had weatherbeaten faces, were a class by themselves, laughing and unconcerned. But I heard no coarse language. Underneath the chatter I sensed a deep and bitter resentment; some of them had been there for three or four months without having been brought to trial. The more fortunate had a little money to engage lawyers; others had to wait for the court to assign them legal defenders.

While I was talking to the girls, the matron bustled up with, "The ladies are coming!" and shooed us into our cells. The Ladies, a committee from a society for prison reform, peered at us as though we were animals in cages. A gentle voice cooed at me, Did you come in during the night?"

"Yes," I returned, overlooking the assumption that I was a street walker.

"Can we do anything for you?"

The other inmates were sitting in their corners looking as innocent and sweet as they could, but I startled her by saying, "Yes, you can. Come in and clean up this place. It's filthy and verminous."

The Committee departed hurriedly down the corridor. One more alert member, however, came back to ask, "Is it really very dirty?"

Although I told her in some detail about the blankets, the odors, the roaches, she obviously could not picture the situation. "I'm terribly sorry, but we can't change it."

I was still exasperated over this reply when I was called to the reception room to give an interview to reporters. In addition to answering questions about the raid I said I had a message to the taxpayers of Brooklyn; they were paying money to keep their prisons run in an orderly fashion as in any civilized community and should know it was being wasted, because the conditions at Raymond Street were intolerable.

My bail was arranged by afternoon and when I emerged I saw waiting in front the woman who was going to swallow the glass; she had been there all that time.

I went straight back to the clinic, reopened it, and more mothers came in. I had hoped a court decision might allow us to continue, but now Mr. Rabinowitz came downstairs apologetically. He said he was sorry, and he really was, but the police had made him sign ejection papers, on the ground that I was "maintaining a public nuisance."

In the Netherlands a clinic had been cited as a public benefaction; in the United States it was classed as a public nuisance.

Two uniformed policemen came for me, and with them I was willing to ride in the patrol wagon to the station. As we started I heard a scream from a woman who had just come around the corner on her way to the clinic. She abandoned her baby carriage, rushed through the crowd, and cried, "Come back! Come back and save me!" For a dozen yards she ran after the van before someone caught her and led her to the sidewalk. But the last thing I heard was this poor distracted mother, shrieking and calling, "Come back! Come back!" . . .

[During several years after 1918 Margaret Sanger toured the world in order to see how women fared and what more she could learn about birth control methods.]

XI. WHILE THE DOCTORS CONSULT

AFTER coming back from around the world I found nothing had been done about the Tenth Street clinic, which I had expected to be in operation. No members of the Academy of Medicine had come forth to back Dr. de Vilbiss, and I had paid the rent for the last twelve months while vainly waiting.

I remembered Clinton Chance, a young manufacturer of Birmingham, who had prospered exceedingly both before and during the War. He and his wife, Janet, had become good friends of mine during my 1920 visit to England. Having felt the need of a more sound and fundamental outlet for his riches than that provided by charity, he had come to see that birth control information was far better for his employees than a dole at the birth of every new baby. He was not in any sense a professional philanthropist, but only wanted to help them be self-sufficient.

Clinton had once offered me money to set the birth control movement going in England, but I had refused then because England had enough co-workers, who were handling the situation well, and, furthermore, my place was in the United States. He had then said to me, "I won't give you a contribution for regular current expenses, but if ever you see the necessity for some new project which will advance the general good, call on me."

Now I cabled Clinton at length, explaining my need. He promptly answered, "Yes, go ahead." and soon arrived an anonymous thousand pounds to cover Dr. Bocker's salary for the first year. I made out a contract for two. She was to come in January, 1923, and we were to shoulder the risks and responsibilities together.

Even to choose a name for the venture was not easy. I had been steadily advertising the term "clinic" to America for so long that it had become familiar and, moreover, to poor people it meant that little or no payment was required. But the use of the word itself was legally impossible, and I was not certain that the same might not be true of "center" or "bureau." I wanted it at least to imply the things that clinic meant as I had publicized it, and also to include the idea of research.

Finally, one of the doors of the two rooms adjoining the League offices, readily accessible to me and to the women who came for advice, was lettered, Clinical Research.

It was still a clinic in my mind, though frankly an experiment because I was not even sure women would accept the methods we had to offer them. We started immediately keeping the records, Dr. Bocker wrote down the history of the case on a large card, numbering it to correspond with a smaller one containing the patient's name and address. Each applicant she suspected of a bad heart, tuberculosis, kidney trouble, or any ailment which made pregnancy dangerous, she informed regarding contraception and advised medical care at once.

In our first annual report, which attracted much attention, all our cases were analyzed. We said, "Here is the proof—nine hundred women with definite statistics concerning their ages, physical and mental conditions, and economic status."

As time went on I became less and less pleased with Dr. Bocker's system. She had no follow-up on patients, and I wished the clinic to be like a business in the thoroughness of its routine. I refused to approve methods as a hundred percent reliable until there had been not merely one but three checks on each woman who had been to the clinic. To begin with, she was to return two or three days after her initial visit; she usually did that. But if she did not come back inside three months, then a social worker in our own employ should be sent to call on her. Finally, she was to be examined once a year. Dr. Bocker did not see eye to eye with me that this was the only way to put the work on a sound scientific basis of facts, and we agreed to part company in December of the second year.

Dr. Hannah M. Stone, a fine young woman from the Lying-In Hospital, volunteered to take Dr. Bocker's place without salary. Her gaze was clear and straight, her hair was black, her mouth gentle and sweet. She had a sympathetic response to mothers in distress, and a broad attitude towards life's many problems. When the Lying-In Hospital later found she had connected herself with our clinic, it gave her a choice between remaining with us and resigning from the staff. She resigned. Her courageous stand indicated staunch friendship and the disinterested selflessness essential for the successful operation of the clinic. These qualities have kept her with us all this time, one of the most beloved and loyal workers that one could ever hope for. . . .

Meanwhile, between 1921 and 1926, I received over a million letters from mothers requesting information. From 1923 on a staff of three to seven was constantly busy just opening and answering them. Despite the limitations of the writers and their lack of education, they revealed themselves strangely conscious of the responsibilities of the maternal function.

Childbearing is hazardous, even when carried out with the advantages of modern hygiene and parental care. The upper middle classes are likely to assume all confinements are surrounded by the same attention given the births of their own babies. They do not comprehend it is still possible in the United States for a woman to milk six cows at five o'clock in the morning and bring a baby into the world at nine. The terrific hardships of the farm mother are not in the least degree lessened by maternity. If she and her infant survive, it is only to face these hardships anew, and with additional complications.

In the midst of an era of science and fabulous wealth reaching out for enlightenment to advance our civilization, with millionaires tossing their fortunes into libraries and hospitals and laboratories to discover the secrets and causes of life, here at the doorstep of everyone was this tragic, scarcely recognized condition.

It was an easy and even a pleasant task to reduce human problems to numerical figures in black and white on charts and graphs, but infinitely more difficult to suggest concrete solutions. The reasoning of learned theologians and indefatigable statisticians seemed academic and anemically intellectual if brought face to face with the actuality of suffering. When they confronted me with arguments, this dim, far-off chorus of pain began to resound anew in my ears.

Sensitive women of our clerical staff were constantly breaking down in health under the nervous depression caused by the fact we had so little knowledge to give. One who went to Chicago to help rehabilitate soldiers wrote me, "I'm feeling much better. These men who have lost a leg or arm come in, apparently disqualified forever, but something is being done about them, and it is happy work, not forlorn like yours."

To prove that the story could be told by the mothers themselves, ten thousand letters, with the assistance of Mary Boyd, were selected and these again cut to five hundred. Eventually this historical record appeared in book form as *Motherhood in Bondage*.

Whenever I am discouraged I go to those letters as to a wellspring which sends me on reheartened. They make me realize with increasing intensity that whoever kindles a spark of hope in the breast of another cannot shirk the duty of keeping it alive.

Woman and the New Race, which sold at first for two dollars, had a distribution of two hundred and fifty thousand copies, and it made my heart ache to know that poor women who could ill afford it were buying the book and not finding there what they sought. To the best of my ability I tried to supply general information, but the only way of extending genuine aid was to persuade doctors to give it professionally.

By a happy chance I met Dr. James F. Cooper, tall, blond, distinguished, a fine combination of missionary and physician, who left no stone unturned when a patient came to him, but devoted his whole attention to her—everything in her life was important to him. He was recently back from Fuchow, China, and was establishing himself in Boston as a gynecologist. Since he was thoroughly convinced of the vital necessity for birth control and could talk technically to his profession and interpret to the layman as well, my husband pledged his salary and expenses for two years, and I induced him to associate himself with us as medical director to go forth and try to convince the doctors throughout the country that contraceptive advice would save a large proportion of their women patients.

In January, 1925, Dr. Cooper started on a tour which covered nearly all the states in the Union. In the course of the two years he delivered more than seven hundred lectures. Occasionally he was suspected of ulterior motives, of attempting to advertise the products he recommended, but this did not sway him from his persistence. Where he found laxity on the part of medical organizations he spoke to lay associations, which applied pressure on their own physicians, demanding information. As a result of this trip, doctors really began to awake to the problem of contraception, and when it was ended we had the names of some twenty thousand from Maine to California who had consented to instruct patients referred to them.

At this point began the huge and difficult process of decentralization, so that the New York office need no longer be a clearing house. Each request which lay outside the pale of the Cooper influence required voluminous correspondence. One letter, enclosing a stamped, return-addressed envelope, was mailed to the woman, asking her to furnish us the name of her doctor. We then wrote him to inquire whether he would give her information, and offered to send supplies if she could not afford them. If he said yes, we notified her to that effect; if he said no, we gave some other doctor in her vicinity an opportunity to co-operate.

We were immediately confronted with the situation that even willing doctors had little to recommend. Literally thousands of women reported that such ineffective methods had been tendered them they had refused to pay. We ourselves did not have a great deal, and this put us in a weak position; the acceptance of the theory was ahead of the means of practicing it.

The jelly I had found in Friedrichshaven had turned out to be too expensive, because it was made with a chinosol and Irish moss base, and the price of the former was prohibitive in preparing it for poor women. Dr. Stone and Dr. Cooper, therefore, devised a formula for a jelly with a lactic acid and glycerine base, which was within our means. Most of their cases, however, were sufficiently grave for them not to feel justified in using it alone experimentally. Consequently, they took the precaution of having a double safeguard by combining the chemical contraceptive with the mechanical—jelly with pessary— which proved ninety-eight percent efficacious.

At this time we could not import diaphragms directly. Although I had given various friends going to Germany and England the mission of bringing them in, this could not be done in sufficient quantity. Furthermore, since bootlegging supplies could not continue indefinitely I had to find out how they could legally be made here. . . .

Meanwhile, Julius Schmid, an old established manufacturer, had been importing from his own concern in Germany a few diaphragms, but only on a modest scale because he did not want to run afoul of the Comstock law. As soon as he saw a potential market in the medical profession he fetched from the Fatherland several families who had been making molds there, gave them places to live in, and set up a little center, expanding gradually until eventually he sold more contraceptive supplies than any firm in the world.

But this was all in the future. . . .

XII. CHANGE IS HOPEFULLY BEGUN

AS a cause becomes more and more successful, the ideas of the people engaged in it are bound to change. While still at St. Moritz I had been getting messages and letters about the disturbing situation in the American Birth Control League. I cabled Frances Ackermann to take it in hand, but she replied she was unable to bring about a friendly solution.

I found on my return after eighteen months that the tone of the movement had altered. The machinery I had built up to be ready for an emergency was marking time. An incident which occurred almost immediately was highly indicative. During my absence the League had been invited to participate in the Parents' Exhibition in the Grand Central Palace, and had signed a contract for a certain space. The day before the opening came a letter from Robert E. Simon, who was in charge, stating that William O'Shea, Superintendent of Public Schools, threatened to remove the Board of Education exhibit if ours were there, and he therefore requested our withdrawal.

With time so short I asked an attorney to secure a court injunction to prevent our exclusion. But one member of the Board said no step should be taken without the approval of all; a meeting should be called to discuss what course was to be adopted. I tried to reach various Directors by telephone, but before I could gather a quorum it was too late; the check which paid for our space had been sent back and the Exhibition had opened. We were left out.

Obviously, the old aggressive spirit had been superseded by a doctrinaire program of social activity; the League had settled down. I had always believed that offerings should be voluntarily measured by the individual's desire. In this way you could appeal whenever a special occasion warranted and receive anywhere from one dollar to two or three hundred. Contributors were giving to something that concerned them vitally, and they did it, not because they had signed a pledge for a limited sum, but because they wanted to help forward the movement. I could not share the League's enthusiasm over the fact that our bank account had grown to sizeable proportions—thousands of dollars drawing interest, though I admit it must have been a great relief to a Board whose previous experience had been to hear wails from the President and Treasurer as to our needs for some new project. I knew the apathy which came from a fat bank balance. I knew also the tacit disapproval which would meet every suggestion to touch that precious fund. But my policy had been to spend, not to save, when work ought to be done. I discovered that subscribers to the *Review* had not been informed it was time for them to renew their subscriptions, and that, consequently, they had diminished from thirteen thousand to twenty-five hundred. Accordingly I told the bookkeeper to give fifteen or twenty dollars to the clerk to pay for circularizing. She said she could not do it; a bylaw had been made that nobody could direct the outlay of more than five dollars without a resolution passed by the Board.

There is doubtless a place for organizations that restrict their scope to the status quo. Most charities are like that—they live on securities, install as officers those who keep pace with but are never in advance of general opinion. Two members of the Board, with League-of-Women-Voters training, saw the movement in the light of routine, annual membership dues and a budget, going through the same ritual year after year and remaining that way, performing a quiet service in the community. I looked upon it as something temporary, something to sweep through, to be done with and finished; it was merely an instrument for accomplishment. I wanted us to avail ourselves of every psychological event, to push ahead until hospitals and public health agencies took over birth control as part of their regular program, which would end our function.

Regretfully I found the League was to side-step the greatest and most far-reaching opportunity yet offered it. It was logically equipped to enter the legislative field. But it wanted to progress state by state. I was convinced action in the Federal sphere would be quicker and much broader educationally, and that, furthermore, success there would provide a precedent for the states.

When you build an organization, you try to combine harmonious elements, but you cannot tell what they will turn out to be until a certain interval has elapsed. Some of these women were in the movement for reasons they themselves did not always understand. A few liked the sensation of being important and having personal attention; they were at their best in following an individual, yet I never felt they were doing it for me. The liberals who had started with me had never demanded a reward. What they gave was for the cause; they refused to work *for* people; they worked *with* them or not at all.

Most movements go through the phase of being brought into the drawing room. Those who disagreed with me believed the emphasis should be on social register membership, and argued that my associations had been radical. The answer was "Yes," because the radicals alone had had the vision and the courage to support me in the early days. The women who were raising objections now had only joined up after it had been safe to do so. Moreover, they were, for the most part, New Yorkers, not all of whom had even gone into neighboring states. Their attitude tended to be, "Never you mind the West; let the Empire State make the decisions."

The conflict of views which reigned in various matters was based on lives and environments which had been vastly separated. The time of some of the members of the Board had to depend on what was left from other duties—husbands, children, servants, charities, church entertainments, shopping. To me the cause was not a hobby, not a mere filler in a whirl of many engagements, not something that could wait on this or that mood, but a living inspiration. It came first in my waking consciousness and was my last thought as I fell asleep at night.

I was always willing to present my facts to experts and abide by their superior knowledge, and I gave every consideration to the suggestions of the Board. But I was no paper president. Experience had given me a judgement which entitled me to a certain amount of freedom of action, and I could not well observe the dictates of people who did not know my subject as well as I did.

June 12, 1928, I resigned the presidency of the League. Because the majority of the Directors were against this, and because I wanted to make it easier for Mrs. Robertson–Jones to take over, I stayed on the Board and continued to edit the *Review*.

But the divergence of opinions rapidly crystallized in the next few months. This had to be pondered upon and wisely dealt with. The situation was going to mean constant friction, and the League might easily disintegrate into a dying, static thing. In any event, internal discord was abhorrent. I began to ask myself whether I could pass over the *Review*, which for eleven years had been a vital part of my own being.

Then came a meeting at which the question of the editorship arose. For the first time friend opposed friend. Three voted against me; the other nine were for me. But my mind was now made up. I could fight outside enemies but not those who had been my fellow-workers; I would give complete freedom to others in order to obtain a new freedom for myself. Therefore, I surrendered the *Review* to the League as its private property. I have been sorry that this step was necessary, because the magazine changed from being a national and international medium for the expression of ideas and became merely a house organ. However, I trust that some day it will be possible to broaden its scope of usefulness once more.

The clinic, which had recently been treated rather like an orphan, still remained intact. No one in the League had ever paid any attention to it, and the doctors on the committee had been too busy with their own practices. I felt I was my responsibility, and belonged to me personally. It was an interesting angle on my own psychology. I did not regret the theoretical part of the movement going into other hands, but I would have been traitor to all that had been entrusted to me had I yielded the clinic to women who had shown themselves incapable of the understanding and sympathy required in its operation. . . .

I felt very decidedly that the future of the movement was like that of a growing child. You might guide its first faltering steps, but unless you let it run and fall it never could develop its own strength. The younger generation might need a little pushing and prodding now and then, but I was confident that eventually they were going to build toward a sound civilization.

As things recede in time they become of less and less importance. One of my absolute theories is that any movement which has been based on freedom, as this had been, is like a live cell; there is a biology of ideas as there is a biology of cells, and each goes through a process of evolution. The parent cell splits and the new entities in their turn divide and divide again. Instead of indicating breakdown, it is a sign of health; endless energy is spent trying to keep together forces which should be distinct. Each cell is fulfilling its mission in this separation, which in point of fact is no separation at all. Cohesion is maintained until in the end the whole is a vast mosaic cleaving together in union and strength.

Merely judging by the letters that had come to me I was prepared to find many psychological problems presented. I often thought of the high cost of small families for women who had more or less restricted their procreative powers through other means than contraception. Although the size was limited, it was frequently accompanied by marital unhappiness and hidden psychic disturbances. But the kindness of Dr. Stone aided immeasurably in our informal "court of domestic relations."

One hot July day when I was coming out of the clinic I saw a woman, obviously pregnant, carrying a year-and-a-half-old baby, dragging another one, only a trifle bigger, crying behind her. The little girl's shoes were too short and were pinching her toes. I squirmed myself, remembering my own squeezed feet as a child. I caught up with her. "Can't I carry one of the babies? This one seems tired. Which way are you going?"

"Can you tell me where the jail is?"

"The nearest one is on Spring Street, I think."

"No, there's a jail somewheres around here."

"Didn't you get the address?"

"Yes, but I left it on the table."

"What do you want a jail for?"

"My man's there."

"What for?"

"Leaving me. He always does when I get like this."

"How many children have you?"

"Nine."

"How often has he left you?"

"This is the fourth time now."

"Do you want any more children?"

"No!" emphatically.

"Did you ever know there was a way to stop having so many?"

She almost dropped the infant, took hold of me, and said, "They won't give it to me. I'm asking everybody. They'll give it to the rich. He wants it. He'll even have an operation. But nobody'll tell us."

I wrote down our street and number and said, "You go back to that place where I met you, and the doctor there will tell you about it."

The next day I was called up unofficially by a social worker, one of those who used to send us cases on their own initiative. She wished to explain to me: the husband would be let off if he promised to live with his family and support them; otherwise he had to serve a sentence. His wife had seen him and shown him my note; he had said he would rather go the Island for three years than come out, unless we could not only guarantee his getting the information, but, furthermore, that it would work. He was fed up with having a new baby every year.

We suggested he talk it over with us and bring his wife. She was silent, glum, did not appear to know what it was all about. He was discouraged and doubtful. We gave him the information and he departed. "I'm the one to do this. She won't," glaring at his wife, who tagged on behind him.

We hoped for the best.

About half a year later both returned for the check-up, she with her hand on his arm. This vague, dumb, immobile woman was now in spruce jacket and skirt, head up, stepping lightly. You would never have known her for the same person. The two were off to the movies together. . . .

For four years we went along in the clinic, working steadily, straightening mental tangles and relieving physical distress when we could. Then, early in the morning of April 15, 1929, the telephone in my apartment rang, startling me. I was pretty nervous, having been up all night with Stuart, who had mastoiditis. His temperature was running high, and he was suffering with terrible, indescribable pain.

I took off the receiver. "Hello. This is Anna. The police are here at the clinic." Briefly she related how they had descended without warning, stamped into the basement, and were at that moment tearing things to pieces.

With this meager information pounding through my brain I hastened to the street, hailed a taxi, and urged the driver to go as fast as he could to West Fifteenth Street.

The shade to the glass door was pulled down; the door itself was locked. I knocked and a plain-clothes man of the Vice Squad opened it. "Well, who are you?"

"I'm Mrs. Sanger and want to come in."

My request was passed on to a superior and I heard someone answer, "Let her in."

Inside, in a room more than ordinarily small because partitions had sliced it up to make minute consultation booths, the patients were sitting quietly, some of them weeping. Detectives were hurrying aimlessly here and there like chickens fluttering about a raided roost, calling to each other and, amid the confusion, demanding names and addresses. The three nurses were standing around; Dr. Elizabeth Pissoort was practically in hysterics.

Dr. Stone was aloof, utterly unmoved by the tumult and the noise. I have always admired her attitude. This was the first time in her life she had been arrested, yet she treated it so lightly. "Isn't this fantastic?" she remarked. "Only a few moments ago a visiting physician from the Middle West asked one of he nurses whether we ever had any police interference. 'Oh, no,' the nurse cheerfully replied. 'Those days are over.'"

Stocky Mrs. Mary Sullivan, head of the City Policewomen's Bureau, was superintending the raid in person. Her round, thickset face might have been genial when smiling, but was very terrifying when flushed with anger. She was giving orders to her minions in such rapid succession that it seemed impossible to keep pace with them. I tried to talk to her, asking why she had come and what it was all about.

"You'll see," said Mrs. Sullivan, and went on directing the patrolmen who were removing books from shelves, pictures and diagrams from walls, and sweeping out the contents of medical cabinets. In their zeal I noticed they were seizing articles from the sterilizers, such as gloves and medicine droppers, having no sinister significance whatsoever. They were also gathering up the various strange, weird devices patients had brought us to inquire as to their efficacy, and which we exhibited as curios.

Patrolwoman Anna McNamara, far less assured than her chief, was consulting a list in her hand and turning over the case histories in the files as swiftly as her fingers could move. Many of these contained the personal confessions of women, some of whom had entrusted us with the knowledge that their husbands had venereal disease or insanity. It ran through my mind that dire misfortune could follow in the way of being blackmailed by anyone obtaining the records.

I requested Mrs. Sullivan to show me her search warrant, and saw it had been signed by Chief Magistrate McAdoo. Nevertheless, I cautioned her, "You have no right to touch those files. Not even the nurses ever see them. They are the private property of the doctors, and if you take them you will get into trouble."

"Trouble," she snapped back. "I get into trouble? What about the trouble you're in?"

"I wouldn't change mine for yours."

"Well, this is *my* party. You keep out."

One of the policemen scooped up all the name cards and stuffed them into a waste basket to be carried off as "evidence." This was a prime violation of medical ethics; nothing was more sacred to a doctor than the confidences of his patients. Immediately Anna telephoned Dr. Robert L. Dickinson at the Academy of Medicine that the police were confiscating the case histories of patients and asked him to recommend a lawyer. He suggested Morris L. Ernst, whom Anna then called.

Doctors, nurses, and evidence were being hustled into the street. The patrol wagon had arrived, but I summoned taxicabs in which we rode to the West Twentieth Street station. On the way I heard part of the story, which accounted for my non-arrest. About three weeks earlier a woman who had registered under the name of Mrs. Tierney had come for contraceptive advice and, on examination, was found by both doctors to have rectocele, cystocele, prolapsus of the uterus, erosions, and retroversion. Although not informed of her exact condition, she was instructed, because another pregnancy would be dangerous, and told to return for a check-up. She had now done so under her rightful name of McNamara, including in her entourage Mrs. Sullivan and a police squad. . . .

One hundred and fifty cards, our sole memoranda of names and addresses, were never restored. Catholic patients, whose records had thus been purloined, received mysterious and anonymous telephone calls warning them if they continued to go to the clinic their private lives would be exposed. They came to us asking fearfully, "Will I get in the papers?"

Immediately after the raid various doctors volunteered to go on the stand and testify as to the medical principles involved. The New York County Medical Society was aroused and passed a resolution protesting against the seizure. Through Dr. Dickinson's foresightedness and energetic interest the Academy of Medicine held a special meeting which resolved:

> We view with grave concern any action on the part of the authorities which contravenes the inviolability of the confidential relations which always have and should obtain between physicians and their patients. . . .

Morris Ernst, who had accepted our case, had already won a reputation for his espousal of liberal causes. It was most encouraging to discover a lawyer who was as convinced as we that the principle of the law was the important issue. Although he seemed very young, the moment I talked with him I recognized here was the person for us. He was a good psychologist as well as a good lawyer. He tried to bring everything out, but wanted the evidence correct and the minds of the witnesses straight as to what had happened.

On April 21st, when Magistrate Rosenbluth called the case, the attitude in the courtroom was far different from anything exhibited at previous birth control hearings. Only one witness was heard that day, Mrs. McNamara. In spite of the hostility of Assistant District Attorney Hogan, which was to be expected, and in spite of the Magistrate's prompting that she was a policewoman and not required to tell all, Mrs. McNamara was made to confess she had set out deliberately to deceive the clinic doctors. As she testified under Mr. Ernst's cross-examination what she had done, her stolid face turned from pink to purple. On her first visit she had learned the routine and on her second, being left alone, had copied down the number of every name card lying on Dr. Stone's desk.

Murmurs rose among the spectators, a melodious sound to ears still echoing with the harsh and suspicious accents of a mere twelve years before.

After forty minutes Magistrate Rosenbluth adjourned the hearing over our protests; if the object had been to secure a quieter and less sympathetic audience the ensuing day it failed. Now physicians took the stand: Dr. Dickinson, Dr. Frederick C. Holden, Dr. Foster Kennedy, the neurologist. The climax came when Mr. Hogan asked Dr. Louis T. Harris, former Commissioner of Health of New York City, whether he had ever given any information to a patient regardless of a marriage certificate. Dr. Harris answered, "The birth control clinic is a public health work. Every woman desiring treatment is asked whether she is married."

"Don't they have to bring their marriage certificates with them?"

"No."

The Magistrate leaned forward ponderously and heavily. "Does not the clinic send out social workers to discover the truth of patients' statements?"

Mr. Ernst interpolated, "Did you ever know of a situation where a doctor dispatched a detective to find out whether his patient were married?"

Loud laughter came from the listeners. Judge Rosenbluth pounded his gavel. "Unless there is absolute silence I shall clear the court room." Then, seeming to grow more angry, he added, "On second thought I shall clear it anyhow. Out you go."

The joke was on him. It was the doctors who had laughed the loudest and their presence as witnesses could not be dispensed with. Following a fifteen-minute recess the audience was once again in the room, more partisan than ever. . . .

The raid had been one of the worst errors committed by the opposition, because it had touched the doctors in a most sensitive spot, the sanctity of records, and they were obliged to stand by us, whether they wanted to or not. Even so we were not yet certain that the question had been settled for all time. At any moment our Irish landlord might receive orders from his bishop to eject us. To avoid any such contingency and to take care of the increasing numbers, in 1930 we bought a house of our own at Seventeen West Sixteenth Street.

Our new building gave us not only more room for patients but better opportunities for research. It was a sad commentary that though medicine had evolved into the preventive state where it was causing a revolution in sanitation and health education, contraceptive technique had been little advanced since the days of Mensinga. . . .

[Margaret Sanger again went on tour. She wrote about conditions of the poor in all parts of India and about what she saw in Russia's stand about birth control after the Bolshevik revolution.]

XIII. SLOW GROWS THE SPLENDID PATTERN

LOOKING back at the past is like peering from some promontory upon a varied landscape. The years run through it like a road winding through a valley. With the passage of time you get a far-sweeping view, and the small details become blurred and difficult to recall. I wonder whether there should not be a school course to emphasize the importance of keeping diaries, so that you would know the really momentous happenings to put down. Mostly you scribble notes intended to call up a picture rather than an actual account of what has happened—memoranda of dates, engagements and events, leaving the results to recollection. Some inequality in this chronicle as to what is significant and what is not—some gaps in my remembrance of events—may have been the result.

It is strange what tricks the mind can play. My father, the person who had done most in shaping my growth, died in 1926 at the age of eighty. The day he was buried in Corning I was passing the bank on the corner of the town square with my brothers Dick and Bob, and we chanced to glance simultaneously at the clock tower. Faintly startled, we gazed at each other and Dick exclaimed, "Look at that little tiny thing! I've always thought it was as big as the Eiffel Tower!"

In all of our travels each of us had been convinced that nothing ever was so tall as that tower. That can happen to so many youthful memories. Months and miles that seemed so long then are so short later.

The same year that took my father summoned also my sister Mary, whose cruel immolation at the shrine of family duty had obliged her to forego marriage; even though I had seen her but seldom, she, too, had had an important influence over me and remained a dear presence whose loss I felt deeply. Out of eleven children seven are still living. Families have a separate and distinct role in your existence. They are closer yet more apart than friends, but often you discover that you have nothing save the ties of childhood to keep you together.

What I have been able to contribute to the birth control movement has been the result of forces which set a clear design almost from infancy, each succeeding circumstance tracing the lines more sharply: my being born into a family so large as to be in part responsible for my mother's premature death; my preparation as a nurse, which awoke me to the sorrows of women; the inspiration of having come into contact with great minds and having claimed many as friends. It may have been destiny as some have said—I do not know.

To have helped carry the cause thus far has been at times strenuous, but I have never considered it a sacrifice. Every conscious hour, night and day, in any city, in any country, has brought its compensations. My life has been joyous and exulting and full because it has touched profoundly millions of other lives. It is ever a privilege to be a part of something unquestionably proved of value, something so fundamentally right.

From time to time wonder is expressed that so much has been accomplished in so short a period. The fact remains that in an era when huge fortunes have been spent in alleviating human misery progress has been painfully slow. Countless women still die before their time because the bit of knowledge essential to very life is still not theirs. Birth control must seep down until it reaches the strata where the need is greatest; until it has been democratized there can be no rest.

It is true that great advances have been made in the realm of theory. You can almost tell people's age now by their attitude towards birth control. To the young it is merely one of the accepted facts; if questioned, they assume the whole matter must have been settled long ago.

Over and over again in the past a new epoch has adopted a concept censured by the preceding one, and has wondered derisively how its forefathers could have been so blind to anything so obvious. The use of anesthetics for mothers in childbirth was once condemned as an unholy attempt to escape the Biblical curse pronounced against all women, and, similarly, evolution as striking at the roots of Christianity. Battles over impiety, heresy, blasphemy, obscenity have been fought, temporarily lost, and finally won. Science whittles away such obstructions little by little. "The Moving Finger writes; and having writ moves on." In January, 1937, in that same Town Hall where fifteen years before I had been forbidden to speak, and whence I had been haled into court, I was honored with a medal. Pearl Buck said on one occasion, "The cause conquers because youth is for you. I have lived in China so long, and know what it is to wait until the old ones die and the young can do what is necessary to be done." I am glad both my sons are doctors with a background of human interest to which has been added a scientific quality of mind that can aid in pushing the horizon of service further into the future.

I am often asked, "Aren't you happy now that the struggle is over?" But I cannot agree that it is. Though many disputed barricades have been leaped, you can never sit back, smugly content, believing that victory is forever yours; there is always the threat of its being snatched from you. All freedom must be safeguarded and held. Jubilation is unwarranted while the world is in warring turmoil, each political unit trying to hold on to what it has—some threatening to take it away and others looking covetously towards outlets in countries not yet completely filled. The application of the movement to nations which should, in the interests of peace, control their populations, must endure. . . .

Index

American Birth Control League, 256-57, 258. *See also* National Birth Control League

American Woman Suffrage Association, 44

Anthony, Susan B., 105-06; relationship to Elizabeth Cady Stanton, xxi, 44, 78-79, 106-07; *History of Woman Suffrage*, work on, 94-95, 100-01; woman's rights movement, involvement in, 77-79, 87, 89, 90-92; later influence of, 213

Antin, Dora (Deborah). *See* Antin, Mary: sisters of

Antin, Frieda ("Fetchke"). *See* Antin, Mary: sisters of

Antin, Esther (Hannah) (Mrs. Israel), 159. *See also* Antin, Mary: mother of

Antin, Joseph. *See* Antin, Mary: brother of

Antin, Mary (Maryashe), xix, 159-61

— acculturation/assimilation of Antin family: changing of given names, 159, 174; giving up of Orthodox Jewish observances, 185-87; learning new ways of life, 159, 163-66, 172-74

— Americanization of: 160, 174, 179-83, 187, 196, 199, 201-203

— amusements and recreation: as child, 168, 175; as adolescent, 190-91, 194-95; in slums, 195-96

— birth of, in Polotzk, Russia, 163

— brother of (Joseph): 174, 178

— children born: to her, 60; to mother, 159, 166, 193

— cousin of (Rachel), 180

— economic and social status of family: from wealth to poverty in Russia, 160, 167, 168, 169-70, 171-72; business ventures and poverty in America, 175-77, 188, 191-93, 194

— education: compulsory Christian education for Jewish boys in Russia, 166; her first public schools in America, 173, 177-82, 183-85; Boston Latin School, 189-90; at Boston Public Library, 196-97; by Edward Everett Hale, 197, 198; at Hale House Natural History Society, 201-02; interest in her, by grocer (Mr. Rosenblum), 198-99

— emigration to America: by father, 169-70; by mother with children, 170